THE FEDERAL IMPEACHMENT PROCESS

THE FEDERAL
IMPEACHMENT PROCESS

A CONSTITUTIONAL AND
HISTORICAL ANALYSIS

MICHAEL J. GERHARDT

PRINCETON UNIVERSITY PRESS

PRINCETON, NEW JERSEY

Library of Congress Cataloging-in-Publication Data

Gerhardt, Michael J., 1956–
The Federal impeachment process :
a constitutional and historical analysis / Michael J. Gerhardt.
   p. cm.
Includes bibliographical references and index.
ISBN 0-691-03295-5 (cl. : alk. paper)
1. Impeachments—United States. I. Title.
KF4958.G47 1995
342.73′068—dc20
[347.30268]   95-9213 CIP

This book has been composed in Sabon

Princeton University Press books are printed
on acid-free paper and meet the guidelines for
permanence and durability of the Committee on
Production Guidelines for Book Longevity
of the Council on Library Resources

Printed in the United States of America by
Princeton Academic Press

10 9 8 7 6 5 4 3 2 1

CONTENTS

INTRODUCTION

IMPEACHMENT may well be the undiscovered country of constitutional law. As a matter of academic if not popular concern, it has often been ignored or taken for granted except during national crises such as the nineteenth-century impeachments of President Andrew Johnson and Associate Justice Samuel Chase and the attempted impeachment and forced resignation of President Richard Nixon in 1974. Otherwise, even the members of Congress responsible for exercising federal impeachment power are often viewed as lacking the interest or expertise to use it effectively, as reflected by an almost fifty-year gap in judicial impeachments in this century and the Senate's decision in the 1980s to permit trial committees rather than the full Senate to develop records for the removal proceedings of three federal district judges.

Moreover, the last comprehensive treatise on federal impeachment, Raoul Berger's *Impeachment: The Constitutional Problems*, was published in 1974. Subsequently, the major academic focus has been on judicial discipline and removal,[1] because as their numbers have been increasing, federal judges have become the only targets of impeachment attempts. Serious questions have also been raised about Congress's ability to deal adequately with the rise in judicial impeachments. Many judges and scholars are concerned that the existing mechanism for judicial removal runs the risk of sacrificing the ideals of judicial independence and integrity guaranteed by Article III.

But, if the judicial impeachment process requires revision or reconsideration, then a question arises as to whether the same holds true for other kinds of impeachments. The latter proceedings have been, however, largely ignored in academic writing since the end of the Nixon administration. This oversight—and the corresponding increase of attention on judicial impeachments—may have resulted from a common obsession among constitutional scholars with judicial decision making. This preoccupation may derive in part from the fact that through clerkships and other activities many constitutional law scholars are more familiar with the operations of the judiciary than with those of the other branches. Such scholars often idealize the federal judiciary, particularly Supreme Court justices, as being uniquely capable of making constitutional law. This idealization is based on the apparent belief that the guarantees of life tenure and undiminished compensation set forth in Article III enable federal judges to rise above partisan concerns to make principled judgments about important legal matters, including constitutional interpretation. At the same time, many academicians tend to treat Congress with less respect than they give to the federal judiciary; they seem to view law-making as an inefficient process that is not governed by the same concerns about due process and reasoned elaboration guiding model judicial decision making.

Perhaps nothing more clearly illustrates the nature of the academic attitude about impeachment than the reaction of the constitutional law community to the Supreme Court's 1993 decision in *Walter Nixon v. United States*.[2] When the Court granted certiorari to consider the merits of Nixon's challenge to the constitutionality of the process by which the Senate had removed him from a federal district judgeship, the case received widespread attention. In the months immediately preceding the Court's decision, commentators generally urged the Court to find Nixon's claims justiciable.[3] They were interested in the case because it posed a potentially serious conflict between the judicial and legislative branches, with the judiciary expected to claim the power to define the constitutional limitations of each branch, including even the permissible procedures for judicial impeachments, and the Congress expected to resist such an outcome as redefining to its disadvantage the delicate balance of power between it and the judiciary. Moreover, the prospect of judicial review of the federal impeachment process linked that mechanism for the first time in this century to the Supreme Court and therefore placed impeachment in the forum most familiar to constitutional law scholars. Yet, in the aftermath of the Court's dismissal of Nixon's lawsuit as nonjusticiable, the reaction has been condemnation[4] or silence. The Court left federal impeachment in the hands of Congress, thereby enhancing the prospects that in the area of impeachment Congress may make nonreviewable decisions involving judicial misconduct and the Constitution and that these judgments become as much a part of constitutional law as those made by the Court itself.

This book comprehensively examines *Nixon*'s implications and other significant post-Watergate developments relating to judicial and presidential impeachments. It seeks to clarify the federal impeachment process as a unique political check on judicial and high-level executive misconduct, particularly the special constitutional issues or problems raised by impeachment.

In bringing out the special qualities of the federal impeachment process, this book does not, however, replicate material already thoroughly covered in other impeachment studies, including the details of impeachment proceedings actually conducted or the technicalities and histories of the mechanisms for judicial discipline and removal. Nor does the book try to resolve general separation of powers disputes, which, admittedly, provide a backdrop to the study of impeachment.

Rather, the book emphasizes the original understanding and current potential of the impeachment process as a unique congressional power. Impeachment is a political process designed to investigate, expose, and remedy political crimes committed by a special class of politicians subject to unique political punishments. As such, the impeachment process involves tasks incompatible with judicial decision making, including the formulation of impeachable offenses and the balancing of competing political interests. Moreover, the normal influences operating on Congress in conducting its legislative business, including concerns about reelection and interbranch relationships, interest groups, lobbyists, and the media, tend to operate, but perhaps in a special configuration, in the context of impeachment. The higher the profile of the subject of an attempted impeachment (such as Presidents Johnson and Nixon and Justices Chase and Douglas), the greater the public scrutiny and media attention and the more heightened the concerns among the members of Congress (particularly senators) about the historical, political, and constitutional consequences. Such reactions are consistent with the Constitution's structural design and the framers' expectations. Lower-level judicial impeachments tend to attract less public, interest-group, and media attention, leaving the members of Congress free either to focus strictly on the merits of each case or to ignore those proceedings altogether (for the sake of pursuing what they regard as more pressing business).

Consequently, impeachment differs from other congressional actions, such as lawmaking, in that the former is not subject to checks through the formal actions of the other branches, such as judicial review or presidential veto. Impeachments are unusual legislative judgments that may be curbed primarily if not exclusively by the American people in the electoral process and through compliance with special constitutional constraints, such as the division of impeachment authority between the House of Representatives and the Senate and the requirement that there be concurrence of at least two-thirds of the Senate for a conviction. Thus, none of the existing models for explaining legislative action fit the impeachment process precisely. We need to know how the Congress works and how we should evaluate it in this area. The answers demonstrate some important things about Congress's capabilities and the nature of the Constitution, especially about Congress's unappreciated capacity to make principled judgments about the Constitution and the punishment of impeachable officials and about the kind of charter that established such a mechanism.

The quest for clarifying the federal impeachment process is made more difficult, however, by the fact that the final arguments in an impeachment trial are conducted in private and, hence, make precise detailing of the relative influences on the Senate's final judgment on whether to remove an impeached official virtually impossible. In an effort to provide sound legal analysis of the impeachment process, this book relies instead on the final Senate votes in impeachment trials, anecdotal evidence, survey responses from several United States representatives and senators, the Senate trial committee reports and transcripts from each of three judicial impeachments in the 1980s, senators' public statements and articles on impeachment trials, and testimony before the National Commission on Judicial Discipline and Removal. To the extent that political scientists or others interested in the impeachment process want to construct a more comprehensive model of the impeachment process, they would have to interview every representative and senator involved in each impeachment—a task that is practically impossible in light of this author's own experience as a special consultant to the National Commission on Judicial Discipline and Removal: even though Senators Arlen Specter and Howell Heflin had encouraged their colleagues to respond to a survey on judicial impeachment, only twenty-one senators agreed to do so, and none consented to discuss the subject in person. It is plausible that the refusals of most senators to participate in a congressionally authorized study of judicial impeachment could reflect indifference, other priorities, or a desire to preserve the confidentiality of the impeachment process.

This book further suggests that legal scholars and political scientists should begin to rethink their conceptions of political institutions and the political matters Congress is singularly entrusted by the Constitution to decide. In other words, commentators should try to illuminate the contours of the various nonjusticiable political questions the Constitution entrusts to the Congress through the impeachment process. Moreover, they should try to acknowledge the partisan influences on their approaches to constitutional interpretation and to avoid transforming the political issues entrusted by the Constitution strictly to the discretion of the political branches, particularly Congress, into mandates reflecting their own personal preferences regarding lawmaking and constitutional interpretation. Legal scholars must also be prepared to consult political science to aid their understanding of nonjusticiable political questions, whereas political scientists should work with legal scholars to devise an appropriate model for clarifying how and even whether a political body should make the mixed legal and political judgments unique to the federal impeachment process.

Part I provides a comprehensive historical analysis of the impeachment process. It depicts the debates about the federal impeachment power in both the constitutional convention and the ratification process.

Part II traces the practical problems and most troubling issues raised in actual impeachment proceedings conducted by the House of Representatives and the Senate. It also briefly outlines the appropriate methodology for making sense out of the federal impeachment process, proposing in particular that we integrate what we know about the history, practice, and structure of the federal impeachment process in order to clarify it.

Part III analyzes the most significant constitutional issues, as opposed to the practical problems, recurring in the federal impeachment process. It examines the scope of the officials subject to and the sanctions applicable in impeachment proceedings; whether the impeachment process is the exclusive means by which officers of the United States, including federal judges, may be disciplined and removed from office; the scope of impeachable offenses; and the proper procedure for impeachment proceedings, including whether any presidential privilege applies, what burden of proof or rules of evidence should apply in an impeachment trial, and whether the Senate may appoint special trial committees to receive evidence for removal proceedings (such as the one whose constitutionality was recently at issue in *Walter Nixon v. United States*). Finally, part III examines the implications of *Nixon*, which addressed perhaps the most troublesome issue involving federal impeachment, that is, the degree to which the Constitution authorizes judicial review of challenges to impeachment procedures or decisions.

Part IV examines proposed constitutional amendments to and statutory proposals for reforming the federal impeachment process. These include suggested procedural changes to make impeachment proceedings, particularly Senate impeachment trials, more closely resemble judicial proceedings, and various statutory proposals and proposed constitutional amendments to substitute a different mechanism or forum, in place of the Senate, for trying impeachments. Part IV also considers some of the less grandiose but still significant recommendations made in 1993 by the National Commission on Judicial Discipline and Removal. The book concludes that the future efficacy of the federal impeachment process depends on the willingness of the members of Congress to accept as one of their most important constitutional duties the checking of significant judicial and executive misconduct and abuse of power.

ACKNOWLEDGMENTS

I HAVE THOUGHT about and talked to a lot of people about this book for a long time. I am especially grateful to Jill Fisch, Mike Remington, and Ron Wright for letting me use them as sounding boards for all sorts of issues involving the book. I also want to thank Stephen Carter, Erwin Chemerinsky, Roger Cramton, Walter Dellinger, Neal Devins, Dan Farber, Cynthia Farina, Warren Grimes, Robert Kastenmeier, Tracey Maclin, Jeff Powell, Russell Osgood, Peter Shane, Steve Shiffrin, and Steve Thel for their comments and suggestions regarding various parts of this project. In addition, I greatly appreciate the excellent research assistance provided by Chris Johnson, Stephen King, Patrick Lee, Manly Parks, and Tim Singhel, all of whom worked tirelessly for me on this project when they were students at the Marshall-Wythe School of Law at The College of William & Mary, and by Michael Parker and Tom Redburn, both of whom are members of the Class of 1995 at the Cornell Law School. Last but not least, I am grateful to Jenny Smith for her assistance in organizing the manuscript for publication and Anne Carson for her help in completing the bibliography.

Portions of chapter 11 have been reprinted with permission of the *Duke Law Journal*. Concepts and material from my article "The Constitutional Limits to Impeachment and Its Alternative," published originally in *Texas Law Review* 68 (1989), have been utilized and expanded throughout the book. My thanks to the Texas Law Review Association for permission to reprint and adapt this work.

PART I

THE HISTORICAL ORIGINS OF

THE FEDERAL IMPEACHMENT PROCESS

THIS part examines the most important debates about the federal impeachment process in the federal constitutional and state ratification conventions. This inquiry sheds significant light on the inherently political nature and unique structure of the federal impeachment power. In particular, the framers and ratifiers settled on Congress as the federal impeachment authority because they believed that the special power to punish executive and judicial misconduct should be exercised by an electorally accountable body that was not subject to the control of those whom it was attempting to discipline. Moreover, the framers and ratifiers hoped that in making impeachment decisions, the House of Representatives and especially the Senate would be concerned not so much with achieving short-term political advantage but with the need to punish or vindicate the official involved *and* the long-term ramifications for the Constitution, the balance of power, and the public good.

Chapter One

THE IMPEACHMENT DEBATES IN THE

CONSTITUTIONAL CONVENTION

DEBATES about impeachment in the United States are older than the Constitution itself. Prior to the drafting and ratification of the federal Constitution, there were vast differences in state constitutional provisions regarding the officals subject to, the timing of, the grounds for, and the bodies empowered to conduct or try impeachments.[1] These state procedures were in turn influenced by the English experience with impeachment from the thirteenth through the eighteenth centuries.[2]

A number of scholars have related thoroughly the history of impeachment prior to 1787.[3] Although these studies are not without problems,[4] they are of marginal interest to contemporary students of impeachment, because the framers set forth a special impeachment mechanism in the Constitution that reflected their intention to differentiate the newly proposed federal impeachment process from the English and state experiences with impeachment prior to 1787. Consequently, this chapter focuses on the major discussions of impeachment in the constitutional convention, while the next chapter examines the ratification debates about impeachment. These chapters aim to show the basic concerns of the framers' generation regarding impeachment. Subsequent chapters use additional historical material to illuminate the fundamental aspects of the federal impeachment process, particularly with respect to impeachment issues of contemporary concern.

To be sure, the debates over impeachment at the constitutional convention must be put into perspective. The convention delegates themselves recognized that their views on the meaning of the Constitution mattered less than the opinions of the ratifiers.[5] The delegates took this position because they believed that the Constitution would take effect only if the American people accepted it and that the public's only chance to review and debate the proposed Constitution occurred during ratification. To prevent their own views from dominating ratification, the delegates decided shortly after the beginning of the constitutional convention to conduct all deliberations in secret.[6] The delegates also decided not to call the "yeas" and "nays" by delegate name in order to encourage each other to speak candidly and to avoid playing to the press.[7] Instead, the votes were recorded only by states. To make news leaks more difficult, delegates were allowed to inspect the journal of the proceedings but were not permitted to make a copy of any of its entries. The delegates also agreed that "nothing spoken in the House be printed, or otherwise published or communicated without leave."[8] Moreover, to prevent any unauthorized entry, the convention placed sentries both inside and outside its meeting place.[9]

These precautions ensured that the people who publicly discussed and ratified the new Constitution had no access to any of the notes on the constitutional convention. Indeed, the official reporter of the convention, James Madison, did not publish his notes of the convention until many years after the conclusions of both the constitutional convention and the ratification campaign.[10] Even so, Madison objected for several reasons to relying on the convention debates to guide constitutional interpretation: his awareness of the framers' desire to keep the convention's proceedings secret from the ratifiers; various defects in the historical record, including his having given only an abbreviated account of the proceedings (and possibly having even rewritten or revised portions of his notes after the convention); and the status of the ratifiers as the true sources of the Constitution's authority.[11] Accordingly, he urged subsequent generations to look "for the meaning of [the Constitution] not in the General Convention which proposed, but in the State Conventions which accepted and ratified it."[12]

Nevertheless, it is worth examining in some detail the constitutional convention debates on impeachment because they not only are inherently interesting but also reflect the understanding of reasonable readers of the document at or around the time of its drafting and ratification. The debates may also inform modern students of the Constitution about what certain words may have meant to the framers and ratifiers and about how far constitutional language may be stretched or restricted. If nothing else, the convention debates provide a unique glimpse into the context from which the impeachment clauses sprang.[13]

There are, however, only a handful of matters of current interest on which the historical record on federal impeachment is relatively clear. For one thing, all of the delegates principally involved in the impeachment debates in the constitutional convention were familiar with state impeachment procedures of the period, and the most influential spokespersons—Edmund Randolph, James Madison, George Mason, William Paterson, Hugh Williamson, James Wilson, Benjamin Franklin, Elbridge Gerry, Rufus King, Gouverneur Morris, Alexander Hamilton, and Charles Pinckney—had each had significant experiences with impeachment in their respective states.[14] Moreover, the convention opted to use as its model the basic features of the most popular state impeachment systems—particularly the common provision that only officers could be impeached for criminal acts in office, with removal and disqualification as the only punishments[15]—rather than the English practice under which the Parliament could impeach public officials and private citizens for crimes and, upon conviction, impose various criminal penalities, including death.

Otherwise, there were five major areas of controversy at the convention regarding the nature and scope of the federal impeachment power. Two of these disputes—the proper forum for impeachment trials and the means for judicial removal—overlapped, because they both involved similar aspects of each of the four main plans before the constitutional convention.

For example, Edmund Randolph made the first significant proposal regarding the proper court for impeachment trials by suggesting as part of his proposed Virginia Plan the creation of a national judiciary, which would hold its offices during "good behavior" and have the power to impeach "any national officers."[16] The Randolph Plan became the order of business the next day when the convention resolved itself into a Committee of the Whole to begin serious deliberation. On the same day, Charles Pinckney of South Carolina proposed a draft of a federal constitution,[17] which was also referred to the Committee of the Whole.[18] Randolph's resolutions became, however, the focus of the convention's discussion and, as amended, the substance of the first report of the Committee of the Whole to the convention on June 13. Randolph and Madison agreed that the convention should give the power of impeachment to the national judiciary.

In the middle of June, William Paterson, who also was the attorney general of New Jersey, proposed the New Jersey Plan as an alternative to Randolph's Virginia Plan. The New Jersey Plan gave the national judiciary "the authority to hear and determine in the first instance on all impeachments of federal officers."[19] It further provided that Congress could remove the executive upon the application of a majority of the state governors but it could not impeach. Shortly after the introduction of the New Jersey Plan, James Wilson of Pennsylvania contrasted the two plans' treatment of impeachment.[20] He noted that the Virginia Plan provided for removal of officers upon impeachment and conviction by the federal judiciary, while the New Jersey Plan neglected to include impeachment by the lower house and provided for removal only through application of a majority of the state governors.

On June 18, Alexander Hamilton entered the debate on the proper court for impeachments. He proposed a plan modeled on the British system and the New York Constitution. Under his plan, the chief executive, senators, and federal judges were to serve during good behavior.[21] It further provided that

[t]he Governor, Senators and all officers of the United States were to be liable to impeachment for maladminstration and corrupt conduct; and upon conviction to be removed from office, and disqualified for holding any place of trust or profit—all impeachments to be tried by a Court to consist of the Chief or Judge of the Superior Court of Law of each state, provided such judge shall hold his place during good behavior and have a permanent salary.[22]

In late July, while Madison still pushed for the national judiciary as the body to be empowered to try impeachments, the Committee of Detail,[23] responsible for putting all resolutions and suggestions into draft form, considered a compromise solution to allow trial "before the Senate and the judges of the federal judicial Court."[24] But, on August 6, the committee released its official report proposing in part that the House of Representatives "shall have the sole power of impeachment"[25] and that the president "shall be removed from his office on impeachment by the House of Representatives, and conviction in the Supreme Court. . . ."[26] The committee further suggested giving the Supreme Court original jurisdiction of "the trial of impeachments. . . ."[27]

On August 27, the convention, at Gouverneur Morris's request, postponed consideration of the inclusion of impeachment trials within the Supreme Court's jurisdiction. Morris viewed the Supreme Court as unsuited for that purpose, "particularly, if the first judge was to be of the [P]rivy Council."[28] John Dickinson of Delaware moved to provide that judges should serve "during good behavior" but "may be removed by the Executive on the application [of] the Senate and House of Representatives."[29] Gerry seconded the motion, but Morris argued against Dickinson's motion on the ground that it was contradictory to "say that the Judges should hold their offices during good behavior, and yet be [removable] without a trial."[30] Roger Sherman of Connecticut disagreed, noting that a similar provision was contained in the British statutes.[31] James Wilson responded that such a provision was less dangerous in England because it was unlikely the House of Lords and the House of Commons would ever concur on judicial removal. But, "[t]he judges would be in a bad situation," Wilson warned, "if made to depend on every gust of faction which might prevail in the two branches of [the American] government."[32] Randolph and John Rutledge agreed with Wilson and objected to Dickinson's motion. By the time the motion came to a vote, only Connecticut voted for it, while seven states opposed it.[33]

On September 4, the Committee of Eleven, which the convention commissioned to report on those parts of the Constitution that had been postponed or not yet acted upon, urged the convention to accept the proposal that "[t]he Senate of the United States shall have power to try all impeachments. . . ."[34] The committee agreed to designate the Senate as the body to conduct *all* impeachment trials after concluding that the president would not be selected by the Senate but rather by a college of electors, thereby removing what the committee had perceived as the troublesome conflict of granting both the trial and appointment powers to the same body.

In the ensuing convention debate, Madison objected to the Senate as the forum for trying impeachments because it would make the president "improperly dependent" on the Senate "for any act which might be called a misdemeasnor [*sic*]."[35] He proposed the Supreme Court, acting either alone or in conjunction with another body, as the more appropriate forum.[36] Morris favored the Senate, maintaining that "there could be no danger that the Senate would say untruly on their oaths that the President was guilty of crimes. . . ."[37] He thought the Supreme Court "might be warped or corrupted" if it had the power to try impeachments, particularly in a case involving a president who had appointed any of its members.[38] Pinckney agreed with Madison that empowering the Senate to try impeachments would make the president too dependent upon the legislature.[39] Hugh Williamson of North Carolina argued that the Senate would be too lenient in presidential impeachments because it shared various powers with the president, while Sherman contended that the Supreme Court was an improper body for trying impeachments because the president appointed its members, at least some of whom might feel some loyalty to him for having selected them.[40]

The delegates ultimately agreed that the Senate posed the fewest problems of the various proposed trial courts. When the full convention voted on the Senate as the trial body for impeachments, only Pennsylvania and Virginia dissented from the proposal to make the Senate the "sole" court for impeachment trials.[41]

The third major controversy regarding impeachment at the convention involved the impeachability of the president. Even though almost all state constitutions had provided that governors may be impeached, many delegates became concerned with impeachment as a check on the president.[42] For example, on July 19, Morris had warned that the prospect of impeachment would "render the [president] dependent on those who are to impeach."[43] The next day the convention engaged in its most extensive discussion of the propriety of presidential impeachment. Pinckney expressed agreement with Morris's position, but George Mason, James Wilson, Elbridge Gerry, William Davie of North Carolina, and Benjamin Franklin argued in favor of presidential impeachment. Davie considered it "an essential security for the good behavior of the Executive."[44] Dr. Franklin pointedly remarked that history showed "the practice before this in cases where the chief Magistrate rendered himself obnoxious [was to make] recourse . . . to assassination in [which] he was not only deprived of his life but of the opportunity of vindicating his character. It [would] be the best way therefore to provide . . . for the regular punishment of the Executive when his misconduct should deserve it, and for his honorable acquittal when he should be unjustly accused."[45] Madison thought it was "indispensable" to provide for presidential impeachment.[46] Otherwise, he argued, the president "might pervert his administration into a scheme of peculation and oppression. He might betray his trust to foreign powers."[47] Randolph added that "tumults and insurrections" would inevitably result if the Constitution provided no mechanism for punishing a president's abuse of power.[48] Rufus King took the position that impeachment was inappropriate in the case of an officer who served for a fixed term but would be appropriate in the case of the judiciary, since they would hold their offices during good behavior. Thus, in his opinion, "[i]t is necessary therefore that a forum should be established for trying misbehavior."[49] Near the end of the debate, Morris admitted he had been convinced presidential impeachment was necessary for ensuring that the president would not be above the law.[50] Following this discussion, the convention tentatively agreed to a clause providing for the president's removal for "malpractice or neglect of duty."[51] On July 26, the convention reaffirmed the provision that the president shall be "removable on impeachment and conviction of malpractice or neglect of duty."[52] At the end of the convention, only South Carolina and Massachusetts voted against making the president impeachable.[53]

The fourth major dispute was over the scope of impeachable offenses. Throughout the early debates on this issue, every speaker agreed that certain high-ranking officials of the new government should not have immunity from prosecution for common-law crimes, such as treason and murder.[54] Many delegates also envisioned a body of offenses for which these federal officials could be impeached. They referred to "mal-" and "corrupt administration," "neglect of duty," and "misconduct in office" as the only impeachable offenses and maintained that common-law crimes such as treason and bribery were to be heard in the courts of law.[55] Paterson, Randolph, Wilson, and Mason each argued that the federal impeachment process should apply only to misuse of official power in accordance with their respective state constitutions and experiences. As late as August 20, the Committee of Detail reported that federal officials "shall be liable to impeachment and removal from office for neglect of duty, malversation, or corruption."[56]

Yet, in its report on September 4, the Committee of Eleven proposed that the grounds for conviction and removal of the president should be limited to "treason or bribery."[57] On September 8, Mason opened the discussion on this latter proposal by questioning the wisdom of limiting impeachment to those two offenses. He argued that "[t]reason as defined

in the Constitution [would] not reach many great and dangerous offences."[58] He further contended that "[a]ttempts to subvert the Constitution may not be Treason as . . . defined" and that, since "bills of attainder
. . . are forbidden, . . . it is the more necessary to extend the power of
impeachments."[59] Mason then moved to add "maladministration" in
order to permit impeachment upon less conventionally defined common-
law offenses.[60] Gerry seconded the motion. Madison objected that "[s]o
vague a term will be equivalent to a tenure during pleasure of the Senate."[61] Recalling an earlier debate on July 20 in which he had asked
for more "enumerated and defined" impeachable offenses, Morris agreed
with Madison.[62] Mason thereupon withdrew his motion and substituted
"bribery and other high crimes and misdemeanors," which he apparently
understood as including maladministration.[63] The motion carried without any further discussion of the new phrase by a vote of eight to three.[64]

The final major dispute in the convention regarding impeachment involved the number of votes necessary for conviction and removal. As it
turned out, this dispute was closely linked to the convention's decision
regarding the proper forum for impeachment trials. The resolution of this
issue required the delegates to consider the special qualities and constitutional duties of the Senate, particularly as they related to impeachment.

One of the first references to the concept of the two-thirds vote was on
June 6, when Hugh Williamson urged the convention to require that *all*
congressional acts pass a two-thirds vote of the Senate.[65] Shortly thereafter, the Committee on Detail restricted Senate treaty ratification and
confirmation of appointments to two-thirds vote.[66] Although it is not
clear who was responsible for applying this rule to Senate impeachment
trials, the Committee of Eleven (with no formal expression of dissent)
proposed doing so on September 4 as a part of its official report.

The supermajority vote had no "parallel in pre-revolutionary constitutionalism."[67] In fact, the first serious debate about the utility of such a
requirement was made with respect to John Dickinson's original 1776
draft of Article 18 for the Articles of Confederation, which would have
required two-thirds approval of the states for assent to certain important
matters of business, particularly treaties. Ultimately, Article 18 was a
compromise that survived various attacks in later drafts of the Articles
of Confederation. By 1781 "when the articles were finally adopted in
Congress, the deliberative principle behind the two-thirds vote was inte-
grated with the majoritarian practical outcome of it. Even outspoken
majoritarians agreed that important matters ought to require a two-
thirds majority."[68]

The significance of the two-thirds vote is directly traceable to the
convention's special view of the Senate.[69] The constitutional convention
delegates saw the Senate as composed of well-educated, wealthier, more

virtuous citizens, who would be capable of making sound judgments with the nation's best interests in mind. The delegates viewed the House as being more subject to factions and more inclined than the Senate to hasty and intemperate action.[70] They structured the Senate to counterbalance the House's bad tendencies and, particularly when acting alone, to deliberate carefully on the most important political questions. In other words, the framers adopted the two-thirds vote to ensure that the normally deliberate Senate would be most careful when considering issues of critical importance. The convention's sentiment, according to Professors Hoffer and Hull, was that "[t]he Senate sat to hear treaty ratification, executive appointments, and impeachment trials without the concurrence of the lower house for the same reason that all three types of business required two-thirds votes. These issues should not be 'popular.' The Constitution assigned this labor to the Senate because the delegates expected [it] to rely upon its own wisdom, information, stability, and even temper."[71] With respect to the Senate's role in impeachment proceedings, Alexander Hamilton later suggested that there was no situation in which the Senate should be more cautious and insulated from popular sentiment than when it sat to try an impeachment. Hamilton explained that "impeachment hearings were not trials in which the senators were jurors, despite the fact that they sat upon oath or affirmation, so much as deliberative sessions, when they decided whether an official had betrayed his public trust."[72] In other words, the supermajority vote required for a conviction in a Senate impeachment trial ultimately "emerged as part of the revolutionary republican compromise between representative assemblies and deliberative councils. The association of impeachment with the two-thirds rule signified a final Americanization and republicanization of the impeachment process."[73] In short, the two-thirds requirement reflects the framers' efforts to "republicaniz[e]" impeachment by ensuring that the Senate would be as thoughtful and deliberate in its consideration of such matters as the House of Lords had been (but without the latter's patricianism).

Even though many of the delegates were familiar with the English experience with impeachment,[74] their general agreement to deviate from English impeachment is noteworthy because it shows that from the convention's outset the delegates put a uniquely American stamp on the federal impeachment process.[75] For example, the delegates vigorously debated the definitions for impeachable offenses, whereas the English Parliament had always refused to constrain its jurisdiction over impeachments by restrictively defining impeachable offenses. The delegates also agreed to limit impeachment to officeholders, but in England, anyone, except for a member of the royal family, could be impeached. Whereas the English House of Lords could convict upon a bare majority, the

American delegates required a supermajority vote of the members of the Senate present. In addition, the House of Lords could order any punishment upon conviction, but the delegates limited the punishments in the federal constitution to those typically found—removal and disqualification—in state constitutions.[76] Moreover, the English people had no means by which to discipline their king, while the framers agreed to make the president impeachable for certain offenses.[77] Thus, the constitutional convention debates about impeachment confirm that the federal impeachment process is, in many critical aspects, uniquely American. The next chapter on the impeachment debates in the ratifying conventions depicts even further the contemporaneous common or public understanding of the federal impeachment process as an unusual political mechanism for disciplining and removing a special set of federal officials for certain kinds of misconduct. The next chapter also considers the implications of the framers' and ratifiers' understandable precoccupation with working out many of the fundamental aspects of this unique disciplinary mechanism rather than with addressing the kinds of impeachment problems that would be of concern to subsequent generations.

Chapter Two

THE IMPEACHMENT DEBATES IN THE
RATIFYING CONVENTIONS

THE FRAMERS agreed that the Constitution took its authority from its adoption by the sovereign People of the United States in the ratification process. Moreover, the early case law in this country recognized that the records and other publicly available authorities on ratification offered a contemporary and relevant explanation of the meaning of the Constitution.[1] If the ratifiers had or expressed any shared understanding of the meaning of the Constitution, such as with respect to the federal impeachment process, then it would heavily influence, if not control, subsequent readings of relevant portions of the document.

In forming their impressions of the Constitution, the ratifiers had access only to personal reports about the constitutional convention (constrained by the secrecy of its proceedings), pamphlets or letters for or against the new Constitution, and their readings of the document's plain language. What we know about the ratifiers' understandings, however, is limited because of evidentiary problems with the surviving records, including the varying shorthand skills of the people who transcribed the ratification debates, the note takers' partisanship or incompetence, and the difficulty of achieving consensus on how (or even whether) it is possible to aggregate the various views of different ratifiers (even at a single state convention) to determine their collective intent.[2]

Probably the most prominent ratification document discussing the federal impeachment process was *The Federalist Papers*. It consists of a series of essays written strictly for the purpose of securing ratification of the Constitution in New York.[3] Nevertheless, the views expressed in the essays are often attributed generally to the ratifiers, because its principal authors—James Madison, Alexander Hamilton, and John Jay—are commonly viewed as being among the most thoughtful, insightful, and authoritative commentators on the Constitution during ratification. Moreover, even though the prevailing ratifiers rarely attributed the sources of their comments on the Constitution, they often made arguments to explain or defend the proposed federal impeachment process similar to those asserted in *The Federalist Papers*. Thus, the parts of *The Federalist Papers* discussing impeachment may provide some insight into many of the ratifiers' common attitudes about impeachment.

In fact, Hamilton wrote the principal essays on impeachment. Because many of his arguments on behalf of the federal impeachment process remain influential, they should be put into some perspective. Hamilton disagreed with the final version of the federal impeachment process,[4] and he left the constitutional convention long before the Constitution was formally approved. Moreover, his contentions sometimes were specious, made against complaints never actually lodged against the Constitution, and based on dubious historical analogies. Yet, Hamilton often followed the general practice of the times by basing many of his insights into the framers' purposes in designing the impeachment process on inferences from the text and structure of the Constitution. In addition, his discussions of federal impeachment were not only the most extensive of any during the ratification campaign but also still make sense today. Thus, examining Hamilton's major arguments on behalf of the federal impeachment process provides important background material for better understanding its fundamental nature.

For example, in *Federalist No. 65*, Hamilton explained the framers' choice to make the Senate the forum for impeachment trials. First, he suggested the decision was not novel because it followed the generally respected conventions of Great Britain and several states, which had "regarded the practice of impeachments as a bridle in the hands of the legislative body upon the executive servants of the government."[5]

Second, Hamilton favored the designation of "a numerous court for the trial of impeachments."[6] He explained that such a body would be well suited to handle the unique procedural demands of an impeachment trial, in which it, unlike the Supreme Court, should "never be tied down by such strict rules, either in the delineation of the offence by the prosecutor, or in the construction of it by the judges, as in common cases serve to limit the discretion of courts in favor of personal security."[7]

In other words, Hamilton believed that judges lacked the kind of skills, judgment, and public accountability that the body empowered to try impeachments needed to have. In conducting civil or criminal proceedings, judges apply and are supposedly constrained by legal principles adopted by a politically accountable body, such as a legislature. At least at the federal level, judicial decisions are most problematic when judges do not abide by the boundaries set by some lawmaking authority, because judges are not subject to the same kinds or range of political reprisals for their mistakes or policy decisions as the latter. In contrast, an impeachment trial requires the body in charge to formulate rules or set policy—for example, defining impeachable offenses—that is more akin to legislative policymaking than to adjudication performed by judges. The larger the body empowered to try impeachments, the less susceptible it will be to political intrigue or domination by a small faction. The political accountability of the members ensures further that they take due care in developing and applying standards. As Hamilton suggested, "[t]he awful discretion which a court of impeachments must necessarily have to doom to honor or to infamy the most confidential and the most distinguished characters of the community forbids the commitment of the trust to a small number of persons."[8]

Another reason the framers chose the Senate as the forum for impeachment trials, Hamilton explained, was that they thought designating the likeliest alternative—the federal judiciary—as the impeachment trial body would be less fair to an impeachable official. Because judges would then be authorized to oversee an impeachable official's impeachment trial and civil or criminal proceedings, "those who might happen to be the objects of prosecution would, in a great measure, be deprived of the double security intended them by a double trial."[9] Hamilton suggested further that empowering the judiciary to try impeachments, even in conjunction with the Senate, would still allow federal judges to engage in "double prosecution," thereby enabling judges to aggrandize themselves at the expense of the other branches.[10] Hamilton also explained the framers' opposition to allowing juries to try impeachments, because they believed judges could easily influence juries and, thus, unfairly direct the outcomes of both the impeachment and common-law or legal proceedings in which an impeachable official could be punished.[11]

In *Federalist No. 66*, Hamilton responded to what he called the four major objections to the proposed federal impeachment process. Although the substance of these complaints no longer seems relevant, they still merit consideration because Hamilton's responses clarified the framers' reasons for structuring the federal impeachment process in the way that they did. The first complaint was that the granting of the impeachment power—consisting of a combination of some judicial and legislative authority—to Congress upset the balance of powers between the three different branches. Hamilton countered that there were two structural impediments to the abuse of the impeachment power. First, the division of impeachment authority between the House of Representatives and the Senate, "assigning to one the right of accusing, to the other the right of judging, avoids the inconvenience of making the same persons both accusers and judges; and guards against the danger of persecution, from the prevalency of a factious spirit in either of those branches."[12] Second, "the security to innocence, from th[e] additional [prerequisite of two-thirds concurrance of the Senate for a conviction], will be as complete as itself can desire."[13]

The second objection was that empowering the Senate to try impeachments would make the Senate too powerful.[14] The essence of this complaint, which was frequently made in the ratification process, was that removal power enabled the Senate to control its objects, including the president. Hamilton offered no satisfactory response to this objection; he merely claimed that it was unclear and should not have precluded the framers from deciding "on general principles, where [the impeachment power] may be deposited with most advantage and least inconvenience[.]"[15]

Hamilton offered two responses to the third objection to the proposed federal impeachment process, that the Senate could not be trusted to try the impeachments of officials whom it had confirmed. First, he claimed that no such difficulty had ever occurred in the states that had a similar system.[16] Second, Hamilton emphasized that, as a practical matter, the Senate would feel little loyalty to the officials it had confirmed. Because the Senate did not have the authority to direct such appointments but rather could only "ratify or reject the choice of the president," it was not likely "the majority of the Senate would feel any other complacency towards the object of an appointment than such as the appearances of merit might inspire, and the proofs of the want of it destroy."[17]

The fourth objection addressed by Hamilton was a common complaint made against the proposed federal impeachment process during ratification. The claim was that authorizing the Senate to ratify treaties and to try impeachments made "the senators their own judges, in every case of a corrupt or perfidious execution of that trust."[18] Many ratifiers feared that the Senate would be the only body authorized to punish the president for his misconduct but would shirk its duty to do so in those instances in which it had advised or encouraged him to "betray" national interests "in a ruinous treaty,"[19] because the senators would have ratified his abuse of power.

Hamilton responded that the requirement of a supermajority of senators for treaty ratification made such treachery unlikely, particularly because he expected that the senators chosen "by the collective wisdom of the legislatures of the several States" would have sufficiently good "character" to protect the public from corrupt presidential agreements with foreign interests.[20] He admitted, however, that impeachment could not protect the nation from a conspiracy between a faction of the Senate and the president because members of Congress could not be impeached.[21] Rather, the security was to be found in an informed citizenry willing to protect "the public good" in the electoral process.[22] Nor should the public discount the willingness of senators "to punish [the president for his] abuse of their confidence" or "to divert the public resentment from themselves by a ready sacrifice of the authors of their mismanagement and disgrace."[23]

In *Federalist No. 69*, Hamilton addressed another issue of modern concern—the preferred order for the impeachment and criminal prosecution of the president. The Constitution sets forth the grounds for impeaching the president[24] in a different place from its provision that every impeachable official, including the president, is "liable and subject to Indictment, Trial, Judgement, and Punishment, according to law."[25] Yet, Hamilton read this text as providing that a president would first be impeached and removed from office and "would afterwards be liable to prosecution and punishment in the course of law."[26] Given that the constitutional convention delegates did not discuss the preferred order of impeachment and legal actions and that the Constitution does not state in so many words that a president's liability at law should attach only after he has left office, Hamilton's reading seems to have assumed its conclusion.

In fact, Hamilton's reading reflected his personal agenda. Although he did not offer a proposal to the constitutional convention making impeachment a prerequisite to criminal indictment of the president, he gave Madison in the closing days of the convention a paper that "delineated the Constitution which [Hamilton] would have wished to be proposed by the Convention."[27] Under its terms, the president would have been elected for life[28] and would have had a more royal character than what the actual Constitution proposed. This is reflected by Hamilton's use of the word *abdicate* rather than *resign* to describe a relinquishment of office by the president's own act.[29] Furthermore, a king's immunity from ordinary legal process would have been bestowed upon this president-for-life, but, unlike a king, the president would have been subject to impeachment. If convicted and removed from office, the president could, according to Hamilton's plan, "be afterwards tried & punished in the ordinary course of law."[30] None of these features of Hamilton's plan received, however, any significant support in the constitutional convention. Also, the constitutional convention rejected a motion to suspend the president pending final judgment in any common-law or criminal action brought against him while he was in office.[31]

In *Federalist No. 79*, Hamilton discussed the nature of judicial tenure and removal under the Constitution. First, he explained the meaning of the clause providing that federal judges should serve "during good behavior." In his opinion, this provision did not set forth a basis for removing federal judges, that is, bad behavior or misconduct, but rather was intended to distinguish judicial tenure from the more limited terms of elected federal officials. Thus, the framers used this phrase to ensure that "the judges, . . . if they behave properly, will be secured in their places for life[.]"[32] Hamilton suggested further that Article III's guarantees of undiminished compensation "and permanent tenure" for federal judges would protect judicial independence.[33] He explained that the clause authorizing judicial impeachments was not a threat to judicial independence because it set forth a difficult process for judicial removal and, thus, was "the only provision on the point which is consistent with the necessary independence of the judicial character, and is the only one which we find in our own Constitution in respect to our judges."[34]

In the next passage, Hamilton explained that even in the impeachment process there were limits on the grounds for which a federal judge could actually be removed from office. He approved of the absence of *any* provision in the Constitution for removing federal judges on the basis of senility, because the difficulty for achieving consensus on its occurrance would either preclude the provision from being enforced or make it "more liable to abuse than calculated to answer any good purpose. The mensuration of the faculties of the mind, has, I believe, no place in the catalogue of known arts."[35] Nevertheless, Hamilton asserted that insanity could constitute a basis for "virtual disqualification" from office.[36]

Finally, Hamilton explained in *Federalist No. 81* that the division of impeachment authority between the House and the Senate "is alone a complete security" against congressional retaliation against judicial review of legislative enactments.[37] He explained that the threat of impeachment would check judicial "encroachments on the legislative authority," because judges interested in preserving their positions would not abuse their authority and thereby "hazard the united resentment of the body [e]ntrusted with . . . the means of punishing their presumption, by degrading them from their stations."[38]

Ironically, despite Hamilton's extensive arguments in *The Federalist Papers* on behalf of the federal impeachment process, his fellow essayist James Madison believed that the most reliable source of the ratifiers' views on any aspect of the Constitution was in the resolutions passed by the state ratifying conventions.[39] Madison thought that these official declarations comprised relatively reliable records of the collective attitude of an assembly of ratifiers on some specific part of the Constitution because the resolutions were issued primarily to communicate such intent to the other states as well as the general public during the ratification campaign.

There were, however, only two noteworthy state resolutions regarding impeachment. They each addressed an issue—the impeachability of members of Congress, particularly senators—that was not discussed in the constitutional convention but was of concern to many ratifiers in several states. In particular, the Virginia and North Carolina ratifying conventions both formally proposed to amend the new Constitution to provide "[t]hat some tribunal other than the Senate be provided for trying impeachments of senators."[40] Obviously, this proposal reflected the shared objection of a majority of delegates from the North Carolina and Virginia conventions to what they regarded as the Constitution's improper authorization of the impeachment of senators.

The impeachability of senators was also discussed at some length in at least two other state ratifying conventions. For example, in the Massachusetts convention, which ratified the Constitution, two delegates defended the document in part on the ground that the impeachability of senators was a check against legislative abuse of power.[41] Meanwhile, in the Pennsylvania convention, which also ratified the Constitution, John Smilie wondered whether members of Congress could be impeached and, if so, whether they would be reluctant to punish any of their colleagues for their official misconduct.[42] James Wilson responded that he did not believe members of Congress could be impeached.[43] He explained that the Constitution made legislators accountable through the constitutional requirement of having one-third of the Senate subject to change every two years. Moreover, he argued, legislators "may not be convicted on impeachment before the Senate, [but] they may be tried by their country; and if their criminality is established, the law will punish [them]. . . . This is all that can be done under the [Constitution], for under it there is no power of impeachment."[44] Wilson went further to suggest that "[w]hen a member of the Senate shall behave criminally, the criminality will not expire with his office. The Senators may be called to account after they shall have been charged."[45] Wilson added that, even though federal judges were impeachable, they should not be impeached for legitimately exercising judicial review, because, he asked rhetorically, "What House of Representatives would dare to impeach, or Senate to co[nvict] judges for the performance of their duty?"[46]

The most substantial discussions on other aspects of the proposed federal impeachment process occurred in Virginia and North Carolina. In the Virginia ratifying convention, James Madison responded to arguments from George Mason[47] and future presidents John Tyler (also a constitutional convention delegate)[48] and James Monroe[49] that empowering the Senate to ratify treaties and to try impeachments made it too powerful. They asserted that there was "a twofold security" in the Constitution to ensure that the Senate could fairly try a corrupt president.[50] Madison explained that the president could be tried by those senators who had been "a part of the Senate" at the time of the president's misconduct but who had not been parties to his misconduct *and* "other members [who had] come into the Senate, one third being excluded every second year."[51]

The North Carolina convention also featured substantial discussion about the scope of impeachable offenses, especially with respect to whether they were limited only to actual or indictable crimes. For example, James Iredell, who would later serve as an associate justice on the Supreme Court, called attention to the complexity, if not impossibility, of defining the scope of impeachable offenses any more precisely than to acknowledge that they would involve serious injuries to the federal government. He understood impeachment as having been "calculated to bring [great offenders] to punishment for crime which it is not easy to describe, but which every one must be convinced is a high crime and misdemeanor against government. [T]he occasion for its exercise will arise from acts of great injury to the community[.]"[52] Iredell explained further that "the person convicted [in an impeachment trial] is further liable to a trial at common law, and may receive such common-law punishment as belongs to a description of such offenses, if it be punishable by that law."[53] As examples of impeachable offenses, he suggested that "[the] president must certainly be punishable for giving false information to the Senate"[54] and that "the president would be liable to impeachments [if] he had received a bribe or had acted from some corrupt motive or other."[55] He warned, though, that the purpose of impeachment was not to punish a president "for want of judgment" but rather to hold him responsible for being "a villain" and "willfully abus[ing] his trust."[56] Governor Johnston, who would subsequently become the state's first U.S. senator, agreed that "[i]mpeachment . . . is a mode of trial pointed out for great misdemeanors against the public."[57]

In the Virginia convention, several speakers asserted that impeachable offenses were not limited to indictable crimes. For instance, James Madison argued that, if the president were to summon only a small number of states in order to try to secure ratification of a treaty that hurt the interests of the other unrepresented states, "he would be impeached and convicted, as a majority of the states would be affected by his misdemeanor."[58] He suggested further that, "if the president be connected, in any suspicious manner with any person, and there be grounds to believe that he will shelter him," the president may be impeached.[59] George Nicholas agreed that a president could be impeached for a nonindictable offense.[60] John Randolph explained that "[i]n England, those subjects which produce impeachments are not opinions. . . . It would be impossible to discover whether the error in opinion resulted from a willful mistake of the heart, or an involuntary fault of the head."[61] He stressed that only the former constituted an impeachable offense.[62] Edmund Randolph agreed that no one should be impeached for "an opinion."[63]

The discussions in the various state ratifying conventions and the two formal resolutions on the scope of impeachable officials reflect the framers' and ratifiers' preoccupation with clarifying the fundamental aspects of the federal impeachment process, especially with respect to those features that looked innovative or novel, such as presidential impeachment or the relationship between federal impeachments and the removal and disciplining of misbehaving state officials, or drew on familiar state practices but to an uncertain degree, such as the propriety of using a legislative body—the Senate—as the impeachment trial body. For the modern

reader, many of the subjects of these early discussions seem obvious and the concern about them misplaced, while other discussions, such as about the scope of impeachable offenses, still seem relevant but inconclusive. Moreover, the framers and ratifiers had only limited foresight and did not discuss other issues, including the justiciability of impeachment challenges, the applicability of the Fifth Amendment due process clause to the federal impeachment process, and the severability of impeachment sanctions, that arose after ratification and preoccupy impeachment scholars and participants. Consequently, the challenge for the modern reader is to figure out the relevance of the framers' and ratifiers' often incomplete discussions, silence, and limited foresight to contemporary debates about the scope of the federal impeachment power.

In the decade following ratification, the federal impeachment process continued to be the subject of much debate and concern. For instance, in the First Congress, then Representative James Madison tried to calm fears about possible presidential abuse of authority to remove certain executive officers by suggesting that "he will be impeachable by the House before the Senate for such an act of maladministration; for I contend that the wanton removal of meritorious officers would subject him to impeachment and removal from [office]."[64] Although one could construe Madison's comment as meretricious because it supported a position he had taken in a partisan debate rather than as a framer, it is consistent with a stance he took in the Virginia ratifying convention to support presidential impeachment for nonindictable abuses of power.[65]

Within a year, the First Congress passed the Bribery Act of 1790 providing that upon conviction in federal court for bribery, a federal judge shall "forever be disqualified to hold any office."[66] The significance of this enactment is that it might reflect the views of some of the framers on whether impeachment is the only means for disqualifying federal judges, because many members of the First Congress had attended the constitutional convention or participated in the ratification campaign.[67] Even so, the Bribery Act of 1790 was never enforced, in part because of concerns about its constitutionality,[68] which remains in doubt to this day.[69]

In the meantime, James Wilson continued to explain to the Pennsylvania citizenry the new Constitution, including the nature of the impeachment process. His views are often given special weight (at least with respect to impeachment) by constitutional scholars because of his familiarity with the original design of the Constitution, as reflected in his writings on British constitutional law as applied to the colonies,[70] service as a delegate to the constitutional convention, reputation among his contemporaries as one of the principal architects of the federal Constitution,[71] and appointment as one of the first justices on the Supreme Court. Immediately following his appointment to the Court, Wilson gave a series of lectures as a professor of law at the College of Philadelphia to clarify the foundations of the American Constitution. In these talks, delivered in 1790–1791 but published posthumously in 1804, Justice Wilson described impeachments as "proceedings of a political nature . . . confined to political characters, to political crimes and misdemeanors, and to political punishments."[72] He emphasized that the framers believed that "[i]mpeachments, and offenses and offenders impeachable, [did not] come . . . within the sphere of ordinary jurisprudence. They are founded on different principles; are governed by different maxims; and are directed to different objects: for this reason, the trial and punishment of an offence on an impeachment, is no bar to a trial and punishment of the same offence at common law."[73]

Consequently, it is fair to say that, to a significant degree, ratification opened the door to virtually endless debate about certain features of the federal impeachment process. In fact, as part II demonstrates, the very first attempted federal impeachment, in 1798, which involved the impeachment of a U.S. senator, and many subsequent exercises of the federal impeachment power, have raised complex issues that have confirmed as well as surpassed the framers' and ratifiers' concerns and expectations regarding the federal impeachment process.

PART II

TRENDS AND PROBLEMS IN

IMPEACHMENT PROCEEDINGS

IN *Democracy in America*, Alexis de Tocqueville predicted that the relative mildness of the penalties available in impeachments—limited "to tak[ing] away the power from him who would make a bad use of it and to prevent[ing] him from ever acquiring it again"[1]—would make impeachment relatively easy and popular to use.[2] The actual impeachments conducted in American history do not, however, confirm de Tocqueville's prophecy. Since the Constitution's adoption, the House of Representatives has only impeached fifteen people.[3] Of those fifteen officials, the Senate convicted seven,[4] acquitted five,[5] dismissed two impeachments for reasons not directly related to the innocence or guilt of the impeached officials,[6] and never proceeded against one who had resigned prior to the beginning of his impeachment trial.[7]

In a number of other instances, the House of Representatives initiated but did not conclude impeachment proceedings because of the intervening resignation of the targeted official. The most famous of these cases involved President Richard M. Nixon. He resigned from office in 1974 after the House Judiciary Committee approved three articles of impeachment (charging obstruction of justice, abuse of presidential power, and unconstitutional defiance of House subpoenas) based partly on his involvement with a burglary of the Democratic Party headquarters at the Watergate Hotel.[8] In the first case of an impeached official resigning to evade a Senate impeachment trial, the House voted in 1873 to impeach Mark W. Delahay, U.S. district judge for the District of Kansas, for unsuitable personal habits and questionable financial dealings, but he resigned from office before the House had formally approved articles of impeachment against him.[9] In 1876, Secretary of War William Belknap resigned from office two hours before the House voted to impeach him. Subsequently, many senators questioned the jurisdiction of the Senate to try an individual no longer in office, and the Senate failed to convict

Belknap.[10] In 1926, the House impeached George W. English, U.S. district judge for the Eastern District of Illinois, for habitual malperformance, but he resigned from office six days before his Senate impeachment trial was scheduled to begin.[11]

Drawing on the impeachment proceedings referenced in the two preceding paragraphs, this part explores the more significant practices, trends, and problems in the House and Senate's respective impeachment activities. Chapter 3 examines the procedures and difficulties in House impeachment proceedings, while chapter 4 provides a similar analysis for Senate impeachment trials. Chapter 5 identifies other trends and issues involving the House and the Senate or the relationship between Congress and the other two federal branches. Chapter 6 suggests that the soundest approach for clarifying the legal difficulties with the federal impeachment process requires recognizing the limits of conventional sources of constitutional decision making, such as original understanding, and reconciling to the extent possible what each of the relevant constitutional authorities, including text, history, structure, and precedent, have to say about the problem at hand. This analysis clarifies impeachment as a unique component of the Constitution's system of checks and balances, which normally involves dialogues among the three branches about constitutional interpretation, but which, in the area of impeachment, involves a dialogue that purposefully excludes the judiciary largely if not entirely.

Chapter Three

IMPEACHMENT PROCEEDINGS IN

THE HOUSE OF REPRESENTATIVES

A T THE TURN of the century, Lord James Bryce suggested impeachment was "like a hundred-ton gun which needs complex machinery to bring into position, an enormous charge to fire it, and a large mark to aim at."[1] As Professor Warren Grimes has aptly observed, it is the House of Representatives that is empowered constitutionally to "light[ ] the fuse" to this weapon.[2]

The House's authority to initiate impeachments derives from Article I, section 2, which provides that the House "shall have . . . the sole power of impeachment."[3] Article I also provides a general grant of authority to the House to determine the rules of its proceedings.[4] The House has used its impeachment and rule-making powers to develop special rules for its impeachment proceedings, which have been modeled on the impeachment practices of the states and the English parliament prior to the constitutional convention.[5]

THE BASIC PROCESS

The impeachment process begins with the lodging of a complaint of official misconduct in the House.[6] As a practical matter, anyone, including any representative, the president, a state legislature, or grand jury, may request that the House begin an impeachment investigation.[7]

In addition, there are two statutory mechanisms for facilitating the initiation of an impeachment proceeding in the House. First, the Judicial Councils Reform and Judicial Conduct and Disability Act of 1980 created a vehicle for transmitting a request for impeachment proceedings directly from the federal judiciary.[8] Pursuant to the act, the Judicial Conference may forward a certification to the House that "consideration of impeachment may be warranted."[9] In the 1980s, the Judicial Conference transmitted such certifications to the House regarding Judges Harry Claiborne, Alcee Hastings, and Walter Nixon, each of whom was subsequently impeached and removed from office.[10] Second, the Independent Counsel Act[11] provides that information gathered in the prosecution of certain high-ranking government officials[12] may, at the discretion of a special prosecutor appointed by a three-judge panel or of the panel itself, be forwarded to the House for consideration of possible impeachment action.[13]

Pursuant to the House rules, impeachment resolutions are referred to the Judiciary Committee, while resolutions calling for an investigation by the Judiciary Committee or a select committee are referred to the Rules Committee.[14] Complaints of judicial misconduct are sent directly to the Judiciary Committee, or are referred to the Judiciary Committee by any members of the House or the Senate who have received them. In addition, impeachment resolutions referred to the Judiciary Committee are ordinarily directed to one of its subcommittees. For example, responsibility for the 1980s impeachment inquiries was spread among three of the Judiciary Committee's standing subcommittees.[15] The designated subcommittee has the discretion—under the leadership of its chair—to proceed with the investigation of the charges of misconduct referred to it.

Once initiated, impeachment investigations have tended to vary. For example, the three impeachments conducted by the House in the 1980s differed from previous ones in that a federal criminal trial had preceded each of them, allowing the relevant subcommittees to make use of the record of relevant court proceedings, including prior grand jury investigations. The Eleventh Circuit Judicial Council also submitted a report of its own investigation of Judge Hastings after a jury had acquitted him.[16] Thus, the House's primary investigatory task in each of these impeachments partially consisted of gathering and analyzing the full record from the three judges' prior proceedings.

Once the House has completed its impeachment investigation, its next step is to vote on the articles of impeachment. In this century, this vote has coincided with the House's vote on impeachment.[17]

Subsequently, the House designates the house managers to present the articles of impeachment before the bar of the Senate. In the words of traditional English parliamentary practice, which the states prior to 1787 also followed,[18] the managers orally "impeach"—or accuse—the impeached official (or respondent) in the Senate.[19] In practice, this has meant that the house managers have also overseen and often participated directly in the prosecution of the impeached official in the Senate. Up until the 1980s, the House chose its managers in one of three ways: (1) election by majority vote of the House;[20] (2) by resolution naming them;[21] and (3) by resolution authorizing the Speaker to appoint them.[22] In each of the three 1980s impeachments, the leadership of the House Judiciary Committee in consultation with the House leadership chose the house managers.[23]

THE MAJOR PROBLEMS ARISING IN HOUSE
IMPEACHMENT PROCEEDINGS

There have been four major problems with the House's impeachment activities over the years. I consider each in turn.

The Decline in House Impeachment Activities

Warren S. Grimes has determined that if one measures constitutional history "in four fifty-year increments, impeachment investigations grew from seventeen during the first period to twenty-three during the third period, then fell sharply to only seven during the period ending in 1989."[24] Since 1936, the House has initiated only five impeachment investigations: one involving Justice William O. Douglas in 1970 (not resulting in the filing of any formal charges by the House); another involving President Richard Nixon in 1974 (culminating in his resignation in 1974 a few days after the House Judiciary Committee had formally approved three articles of impeachment against him); and the three proceedings in the 1980s against Judges Claiborne, Hastings, and Nixon. The decrease in the House's impeachment activity is especially striking if one considers that the size of the federal judiciary increased more than fortyfold during that same period.[25]

There may be several interrelated causes for the relative decline in House impeachment activity. First, it is possible that the House may lack the time or interest to conduct impeachment proceedings. At least with respect to the relatively low-profile impeachments, such as those involving lower federal court judges, there is little likelihood for House members to gain some political advantage and, thus, hardly any, and perhaps no, incentive for them to make time for impeachments given the other issues, such as the budget, national defense, and health care that compete for their limited attention and are likelier to be of concern to their constituencies. Although the situation is apt to be different in a high-profile impeachment, such as a presidential impeachment, in which representatives are likely to feel pressure from several sources, including their constituencies, the media, and the opposition party, those kinds of proceedings are relatively rare and, based on the attempted impeachments of Presidents Johnson, Nixon, and Reagan (the latter because of his alleged involvement with the Iran-Contra affair), are likely to capture the attention of House members if the president's popularity is already declining. In any event, members of the House who are concerned with their reelections may not be eager to forgo chances to deal with the matters likely to make them popular with their respective constituencies and to get them votes. Moreover, the enthusiasm of House members for conducting an impeachment, especially for a low-profile impeachable official, will probably be low or at least take a while to take hold in a case in which they must handle the first full investigation of the targeted official's alleged misconduct.

Second, it is often easier for other means of disciplining impeachable officials to be implemented than it is for the House to conduct an impeachment. For instance, it is easier for the Justice Department to initiate a criminal prosecution than it is for the House to commence an impeachment. The initiation of a criminal prosecution generally will require the consent of only a small number of people, while the commencement and completion of an impeachment proceeding in the House requires support from key congressional leaders and, if it is to be done right, ultimately from most representatives. Hence, someone with a grievance against an impeachable official may turn initially to a prosecutor rather than to the House for the simple reason that the former may be likelier to take some action in the near or foreseeable future. Moreover, the House can save itself valuable time to spend on other matters by forgoing or at least delaying impeachment proceedings until other means of disciplining the impeachable official have run their course—other means that can build a record on which the House can later rely to expedite its own investigation, or that can exonerate the individual or force a resignation (either of which could obviate the need for an impeachment). For example, judges may be disciplined not just by impeachment but through criminal proceedings and the internal disciplinary process available to the judiciary under the Judicial Disability Act of 1980. Both mechanisms might have enabled the House to avoid unnecessary or unwarranted judicial investigations that it may have undertaken during earlier periods. Of course, they also may have developed in part to occupy the vacuum left by the House's failure to impeach (at least in a timely fashion).

Third, the process for selecting qualified, honest federal officials, including federal judges, has generally improved. Increasingly rigorous scrutiny of people in the confirmation and electoral processes has generally brought about the appointment or election of more qualified or distinguished individuals to office (or perhaps people who are simply more skilled at concealing their indiscretions).

Fourth, it is possible that more intense media scrutiny of the conduct of impeachable officials in office has helped to hinder concealment and avoidance of public accountability for misbehavior and to provoke resignations from officials who might otherwise have had to face impeachment. At the same time, the publicity given to impeachment hearings may partially account for a decline in impeachments initiated for purely partisan reasons. Even if it is not possible to determine precisely the degree to which media coverage has helped to depoliticize impeachments, the decrease in impeachment activity has coincided with a decline in politically motivated impeachments.[26] In contrast, the first three completed impeachments in the House, which occurred during the first half of the nineteenth century, reflected the animosity between Federalists and Jeffersonian Republicans and their mutual desire to keep each other's members out of federal offices, including judgeships.[27] In contrast, the House Judiciary Committee's investigation of William O. Douglas may have begun for partisan reasons, but it ended in a report that found no grounds for impeachment. Although Justice Douglas's life-style, including his four marriages, and much of his decision making provoked hostile reactions from many Republicans, the impeachment investigation ultimately exposed and perhaps even diffused the personal or partisan motivations for his attempted impeachment.[28]

Delays in Initiating Impeachments

Several factors have also led the House to delay the initiation of such hearings. First, the House Judiciary Committee lacks sufficient resources to conduct in-depth inquiries of official misconduct on its own. In the twentieth century, most impeachment proceedings have begun only after the Judiciary Committee has received substantial, well-documented information of misconduct from some investigative body. The House substantially delayed the three 1980s impeachments, until other proceedings against the targeted judges were completed.[29] In fact, the only impeachment investigation initiated by the Judiciary Committee in the past fifty years without a prior referral by a law enforcement agency (or a prior prosecution) was the unsuccessful one against Justice Douglas in 1970. Even in the case of President Nixon, the House began its inquiry after a special prosecutor had begun to investigate his possible criminal activities.

A second factor explaining delays in initiating House proceedings is that the House has used some antiquated procedures. For example, the House has traditionally filed a "replication" to the answer filed by the respondent.[30] In the system of common-law pleading widely used in the nineteenth century, a replication was one of a series of pleadings used to narrow the legal and factual issues in dispute. In modern civil practice, those functions are addressed by more flexible devices, including discovery, pretrial motions (such as summary judgment), and pretrial conferences. Nevertheless, in the 1980s impeachments, the House managers continued to file replications.[31]

Third, for almost half a century, the Justice Department has not shared with the House pre-indictment materials indicating the possible need for an impeachment. Pre-indictment cooperation between the House and federal prosecutors may no longer exist in part because it raises potentially serious separation of powers and institutional concerns. It is not likely that the Justice Department or the House Judiciary Committee is welcome in the other's constitutional domain. Moreover, Justice Department prosecutors and House members are each probably sensitive to the practical ramifications of any allegations that politics played a role in the decision to initiate or stall a criminal prosecution or impeachment. In addition, the Justice Department might have concluded that referring a criminal matter to the House Judiciary Committee could complicate a prosecution and perhaps jeopardize a defendant's right to a speedy trial or diminish the department's initiative to prosecute.

Moreover, prior to the 1980s, the Justice Department may well have thought that such cooperation was not necessary because it believed a criminal prosecution would have been likely to expedite a judge's resignation, as it did with Judges Albert Johnson of the Middle District of Pennsylvania in 1945,[32] Otto Kerner of the Seventh Circuit in 1974,[33] and Herbert Fogel of the Eastern District of Pennsylvania in 1978.[34] Yet, this assumption proved false in the 1980s, when the Justice Department criminally prosecuted three federal district judges—Harry Claiborne, Alcee Hastings, and Walter Nixon—none of whom resigned from office. Thus, the House was forced in each case to initiate impeachment proceedings well after the completion of each judge's criminal prosecution. Given the House's relative lack of resources and interest in conducting impeachment inquiries, it should not be surprising to find that the House has yet to initiate impeachment proceedings against two other federal judges— Robert Aguilar, who faces an impeachment resolution against him filed in 1993 but all of whose criminal convictions were ultimately overturned by the Ninth Circuit,[35] and Robert Collins,[36] whose criminal convictions were upheld on appeal but who is incarcerated but still receiving his judicial salary.

The Competence of House Members to Handle Impeachment Matters

A common concern about the House's impeachment proceedings is that they put House members into positions for which the representatives are neither trained nor prepared. For example, the subcommittee's role in an impeachment is akin to that of a prosecutor, requiring its members to construct (or oppose the compiling of) a carefully documented case through the filing of appropriate briefs, direct questioning of witnesses, cross-examination, and oral advocacy. However, many House members are not lawyers, much less experienced in litigation or trial tactics.

The participation of experienced trial lawyers as counsel for the targeted officials further complicates House impeachment proceedings. For example, in the pretrial proceedings for the Claiborne, Hastings, and Nixon impeachment trials, there was an extensive motion and pretrial practice directed to narrowing the issues before the trial committees.[37] Moreover, in the Hastings trial, depositions were conducted, and the Senate filed a collateral enforcement action in the courts to require the attendance of a witness.[38] The house managers delegated many of the tasks involved in these matters to outside counsel and permanent staff, reserving for themselves oversight responsibility and all arguments made before the full Senate.[39]

Moreover, the house managers, who have the heaviest workload of any representatives in the impeachment process, probably have more substantial nonimpeachment, legislative duties than was the case in earlier impeachments. House managers found little need in the nineteenth century to abandon impeachment proceedings for other legislative business. In contrast, the Claiborne trial committee called a recess or adjourned early on at least four occasions to allow the house managers to cast votes on the floor of the House.[40] To avoid these interruptions, the Hastings trial committee agreed that it would try to continue proceedings while the house managers were absent for a House vote.[41]

Doubts about the Fairness of House Impeachment Proceedings

A final issue raised in House impeachment inquiries is whether they have adequately protected the independence of the federal judiciary in general and of the targeted judge in particular. This is a potential problem because the House has not investigated claims concerning judicial independence, in spite of the fact that all three of the district judges impeached in the 1980s claimed that there had been prosecutorial misconduct.[42]

Yet, the 1980s impeachments also sparked substantial concern from members of Congress, federal judges, and many citizens about the unseemly fact that a convicted and imprisoned felon was still receiving a salary and possibly might continue to sit as a judge after his term of imprisonment.[43] The heavy pressure on the House to impeach the three judges in the 1980s, combined with the relative ease of deferring to another body's fact-finding, arguably accounts for the overwhelming committee and House votes to impeach Claiborne, Hastings, and Nixon. The investigating subcommittee unanimously approved the articles of impeachment for each of the three respondents; and the Judiciary Committee approved the impeachment articles unanimously against Judges Claiborne and Nixon and had only a single dissenting vote against its recommendation to impeach Judge Hastings.[44] In the full House, there were no opposing votes against the impeachments of Judges Nixon[45] and Claiborne,[46] and only three opposing votes against Judge Hastings' impeachment.[47] With the possible exception of the vote to impeach Judge Archbald in 1912 (in which there were 223 in favor of his impeachment, with only 3 opposed to it),[48] the massive majorities in the 1980s have differed sharply from the votes on the impeachment of every other official in this century.

Contrasting the Ritter and Claiborne impeachments provides further reinforcement of the influence of a prior conviction on an impeachment proceeding. Both judges were charged with underreporting their income tax returns. The nondisclosed income in Ritter's case was an alleged kickback received from a former law partner whom the judge had appointed as a receiver. In contrast, Judge Claiborne was accused of underreporting income that had no connection with his judicial function.[49] Judge Ritter's conduct arguably conflicted more clearly with the duties of an Article III judge, yet the House impeached Ritter by the slim majority of 181 to 146 as compared to its vote of 406 to 0 to impeach Claiborne. The outcome of Claiborne's impeachment is consistent with the House's having given substantial deference to his prior conviction.

Even more pressure was placed on the House to impeach President Nixon. No doubt, the pressure was compounded by national televising of the Judiciary Committee's proceedings. Despite any concern over whether the president was unfairly railroaded as a result of the great public outcry for his ouster, the House moved with some dispatch to approve three impeachment articles against him.[50] Nevertheless, any concern about a rush to judgment in some impeachments must be balanced against the founders' expectation that the intemperate action of the House in the impeachment process would be checked by the Senate's deliberation. Thus, even if one were to concede that the impeachment proceedings of the three federal judges in the 1980s and of President Nixon in 1974 were somehow tainted by pressure applied to the House from the outside, the Senate still had a role to play in each of those actions, one that at least would have allowed for further consideration of the impeached official's innocence.[51] Although President Nixon's resignation obviated the need for further action, the Senate conducted hearings for each of the impeached judges in the 1980s. The next chapter explores the quality of and problems with these and other impeachment trials.

Chapter Four

THE SENATE'S ROLE IN THE FEDERAL

IMPEACHMENT PROCESS

W HILE the House of Representatives has the exclusive authority to initiate impeachments, the Senate has the "sole power to try all impeachments."[1] Like the House, the Senate is constitutionally authorized to determine the rules for its respective impeachment proceedings.[2] Pursuant to this power, the Senate has developed *Rules of Procedure and Practice in the Senate When Sitting on Impeachment Trials*.[3] Having changed very little since President Andrew Johnson's impeachment trial in 1866,[4] these rules govern removal proceedings before the full Senate unless a majority of senators decides otherwise. To the extent that its impeachment rules are silent, the Senate's general rules for legislative business apply.

THE BASIC PROCESS

The Senate's role begins after receipt of the impeachment articles from the House at the bar of the Senate.[5] The chairman of the house managers asks the Senate to order the appearance of the accused to answer the charges, demands a conviction and appropriate judgment, and presents the articles of impeachment. Unless a special trial committee is appointed, the Senate by resolution sets a date and time for proceeding to consideration of the articles. The Senate has regarded its jurisdiction as the court of impeachment as having been narrowly circumscribed to the articles brought before it by the House.[6]

Throughout its first 150 years, the Senate exercised its trial authority by conducting proceedings on the Senate floor as a plenary court of impeachment. Under the present system, the Senate as a whole may take evidence, or if the Senate so asks, a committee of senators may be appointed under rule XI of the impeachment rules,[7] to collect evidence in the case. If the Senate forgoes, as it did in the impeachment trial of Judge Halsted Ritter in 1936, using a trial committee,[8] then the house managers and the impeached official's counsel present evidence and make their motions and arguments on all evidentiary and constitutional questions before the full Senate. Debate by Senators on any question is not allowed in open session. Rule XXIV of the Senate's impeachment rules explicitly directs that all "the orders and decisions [in a removal trial] shall be voted on without debate."[9] Thus, senators are not permitted, unless they suspend or modify the applicable rules by a majority vote, to engage in colloquies, or to participate in any argument in impeachment trials.

In each of the three impeachment trials in the 1980s, the Senate designated twelve senators under rule XI to act as a special trial committee to receive and report evidence pertaining to the misconduct of the impeached official. Rule XI developed as a response to complaints about the complexity and time-consuming nature of, and senators' consistently poor attendance at, impeachment trials. Concern about such attendance first arose in the Belknap trial in 1876, and reached its apex in Judge Harold Louderback's impeachment trial in 1933.[10] The Louderback proceeding lasted for seventy-six of the first one hundred days of President Franklin D. Roosevelt's first term, one of the busiest legislative periods in American history. Subsequently, at least forty Senators urged the Senate Judiciary Committee to consider "whether a committee could be appointed to take evidence."[11] After considering various proposals, the Senate passed Resolution Number 1878,[12] which authorized a committee of twelve senators to receive evidence and take testimony. In 1935, the resolution became rule XI, which was revised in 1986 to require that the committee consist of an unspecified number of senators.[13]

Subject to contrary vote by the Senate, a trial committee functions as the Senate would, with the same investigatory powers, in gathering evidence and taking testimony.[14] For its procedure, the committee follows the Senate's impeachment rules unless the Senate orders otherwise. When the Senate's impeachment rules are silent on a matter, the Senate's legislative rules govern the committee's proceedings.[15] Otherwise, the trial committee's chair (chosen by the committee members) retains the authority to rule on motions, but, at the request of any senator on the committee, the chair's ruling(s) may be appealed to, and affirmed or overturned by, a majority of the full Senate. The committee prepares a transcript of the entire hearings before it, a neutral statement of the facts, and a summary of the evidence that the parties have introduced on the contested issues of fact.[16] Neither the transcript nor the summary contains any recommendation from the trial committee as to the impeached official's guilt or innocence. Nevertheless, both documents are distributed to the full Senate. In addition, the trial committee's proceedings are recorded and videotaped for other senators to review if they so desire.

Following a period sufficient for the remaining senators to study the record, the full Senate reconvenes to determine the "competency" and "relevancy" of the evidence submitted and to decide whether to call any witnesses or to have all of the evidence resubmitted to the entire body.[17] After the parties make their closing arguments, the full Senate debates the impeachment in closed session, during which the committee members may express their opinions as to guilt or innocence. This is the only opportunity for the trial committee members to express openly their views on the impeachment under consideration. After full debate, the Senate votes on the guilt or innocence of the accused. A vote of two-thirds or more on any article results in the official's conviction and automatic removal from office. The Senate's practice is to vote separately or not at all on whether to disqualify the convicted official from holding future office. Moreover, any issue with the potential of depriving the full Senate of a chance to judge the guilt or innocence of the impeached official, regardless of whether it has been raised in proceedings before a trial committee or the full body, is usually referred to the full Senate and resolved by a majority vote. A majority of the Senate may also revise the rules governing impeachment trials, if it deems such action proper. It is not unprecedented for reconsideration or revision of the rules to occur either when an impeachment trial is expected or at an early stage of a Senate proceeding.

TRENDS AND PROBLEMS IN SENATE REMOVAL PROCEEDINGS

In contrast to the House, the Senate has been increasingly criticized for its handling of impeachment matters. Such criticisms, though, need to be evaluated in light of the fact that the data obtainable about the Senate's impeachment proceedings differs from what is available for the House's impeachment hearings. Whereas the latter sessions are open to the public and fully recorded, senators may not debate many issues in impeachment trials; and, even at the times in which debate is permitted, it must be done in closed session. As a result, the reasons for certain decisions in an impeachment trial may not be reflected in the public record. Instead, the only information from which the senators' reasoning on an issue can be gleaned will probably be any motions and supporting memoranda submitted by the parties or the ultimate resolution of the issue through the actual admission or exclusion of the evidence involved. This final disposition may be reflected in a roll-call vote on the motion or objection, or it may be inferred from the subsequent conduct of the trial with regard to that evidence. Consequently, the following analysis relies on anecdotal evidence; the published records of removal proceedings; historical, political, and scholarly commentary on impeachment trials; and the responses of twenty-one senators to a survey conducted by the National Commission on Judicial Discipline and Removal.[18]

Systemic Problems with Senate Removal Proceedings

The three most common complaints about the Senate's impeachment trials, regardless of whether they are conducted before the full Senate or a trial committee, are (1) they may be cumbersome and disrupt legislative business; (2) the senators arguably lack the requisite experience, expertise, or training to deal competently with impeachment matters; and (3) existing impeachment rules may not foster fair proceedings. I consider each criticism in turn.

THE REMOVAL PROCESS AS ARGUABLY CUMBERSOME

A few statistics on the resources expended on the Claiborne, Hastings, and Nixon removal proceedings may provide some helpful background on the debate over whether the removal process is cumbersome and interferes too much with the Senate's other legislative business. For example, the trial committee's reception of evidence and taking of testimony regarding Judge Claiborne's removal took eight days;[19] and debate, closing arguments, and voting before the full Senate filled the bulk of three legislative days.[20]

Judge Hastings' removal proceedings substantially exceeded these totals. To assist the trial committee's members, the Senate hired nine full-time people and reassigned many staffers.[21] Pretrial proceedings required the issuance of seven pretrial orders on such subjects as discovery, evidentiary principles, pretrial statements, legal fees, and stipulations on the authenticity of documents.[22] At trial, the committee limited each side's evidentiary presentations to thirty-eight hours (including direct and cross-examination).[23] The evidentiary hearings took eighteen full days during which fifty-five witnesses testified.[24] The full Senate spent almost four legislative days hearing preliminary motions and closing arguments, debating, and voting on eleven of the seventeen articles of impeachment.[25]

Judge Nixon's removal proceedings consumed less of the Senate's time than the Hastings hearings did. The difference in the length of the two proceedings resulted in part from the fact that the Nixon trial committee often considered its Hastings counterpart's disposition of similar procedural issues as controlling precedents. Nevertheless, the Nixon trial committee's hearings took almost four days.[26] The Senate spent portions of three legislative days deliberating Nixon's removal.[27]

Based on these statistics, a number of people cite three related reasons for the unworkability of impeachment trials. First, they argue the size of the Senate makes removal proceedings unworkable.[28] As early as the 1900s, senators complained that a full Senate trial was unwieldy. By 1936, almost half of the Senate claimed that the increase in the size of the body, from the original twenty-six to ninety-six at that time made a full Senate trial unworkable.[29] They argued that it was unreasonable to expect ninety-six people to operate efficiently as a court of impeachment and to be equally prepared or interested in impeachment trials.

Second, some senators and commentators claim that the Senate's increase in size has coincided with a rise in the Senate's level of business.[30] The problem for the Senate is that it is politically costly for it to suspend other business for the sake of a removal proceeding. As early as the impeachment trials of Judge Harold Louderback[31] and Judge Halsted Ritter,[32] many senators expressed their displeasure with the process, particularly its tendency to interfere with the Senate's consideration of other important issues involving national security and the economy. Over the years, the problem has been that time spent on impeachment proceedings is time lost for other legislative business. Given the limited number of legislative working days for each session of Congress,[33] senators are hard pressed to determine which of those days needs to be set aside for a federal judge's removal proceeding.

Yet another factor critics have cited as undermining the Senate's capacity to effectively handle impeachment matters is the growing size of the federal judiciary. This growth may correspond to an increase in the number of judges who engage in misconduct, justifying their removal and more impeachment trials. For example, prior to 1985, only nine judges had been tried for impeachment,[34] but there were three impeachment trials from 1986 to 1989[35] and two others are likely at some point in the future.[36]

In contrast, the defenders of the status quo generally argue that an unwieldy, drawn-out process assures an impeached official the greatest possible chance to prove his or her innocence. As Sen. Charles McC. Mathias, the chair of the Claiborne trial committee, suggested, "I don't think the removal of a federal judge is necessarily one of those things that ought to be either fast or easy no matter how pressing the times are. If the process is difficult, I think it helps to give the sense of independence that is important to the judiciary. The fact that judges know this is going to be a cumbersome and important process is part of the insulation that gives them their sense of independence."[37]

THE SENATORS' ARGUABLE LACK OF EXPERIENCE WITH AND EXPERTISE IN CONDUCTING IMPEACHMENT TRIALS

Senators tend to divide into two groups over their competency to handle impeachment trials. Although senators often agree that impeachments are different from any of their other tasks, they disagree over the significance of this consensus. On the one hand, many senators, particularly during the three 1980s impeachments, claimed that prosecution (as required by the removal process) requires skills many of their colleagues do not have.[38] For example, Senator Howell Heflin, who was a member of the Claiborne trial committee and subsequently a commissioner on the National Commission on Judicial Discipline and Removal, observed that, "[while t]he twelve Senators who comprised th[at] Committee were well aware of the facts and involved[,] it is highly improbable that any Senator had the time to thoroughly review th[e] materials [compiled by the trial committee.]"[39] In fact, Senator Heflin claimed to have found that "[f]ew Senators other than the 12 members of the Impeachment Committee were familiar with all the elements of the case."[40]

On the other hand, many senators feel that most of their colleagues rise to the occasion in impeachment trials. For example, both Senators Arlen Specter and Joseph Lieberman praised the performance of their colleagues on the Hastings Trial Committee. Senator Specter was especially impressed that the Senate devoted its most serious attention to Hastings' removal, in recognition of its uniqueness.[41] Senator Lieberman found "[t]he Senate's closed door deliberations [among] the most thoughtful and impressive moments of my first year in the Senate."[42]

Yet, critics of the Senate's removal process have often pointed to the lack of attendance at impeachment trials as reflecting the Senate's general lack of interest in such proceedings. For example, at the 1913 trial of Circuit Judge Robert Archbald, at which time the Senate had ninety-four members, "Judge Archbald's counsel f[ou]nd that the trial [rarely] attracted the attention of more than 20 Senators and that even the composition of the group attending [constantly] chang[ed:] following their normal routines, the Senators, far from behaving like judges and jurors during a trial, wandered in and out of the Senate chamber at will, often gathering only in response to a quorum call."[43]

During the 1930s, attendance at impeachment trials was also very sparse.[44] At one point during the impeachment trial of Judge Louderback in 1933, only three senators were present.[45] Nor were there any efforts made prior to the adoption of rule XI to require the attendance of a meaningful number of senators.[46] As one commentator observed in describing the impeachment trials conducted during the first half of this century, "the Senators who are sworn wander in and out of the chamber during the taking of evidence, and ultimately vote to convict or acquit without exposing their views as to the law or facts."[47]

Opinions conflict, however, about the quality of the attendance at the full Senate's and the trial committees' proceedings in the 1980s. Indeed, attendance records are of only limited significance because senators can be listed as having attended sessions at which they were present just long enough to have their names recorded. Moreover, Senator Heflin has complained that at no time were a full two-thirds of his colleagues present for full-Senate deliberations for the 1980s impeachments, except for the periods when senators cast their final votes.[48] In contrast, most of the twenty-one senators responding to the 1992 survey conducted by the National Commission on Judicial Discipline and Removal stated that attendance was not a problem during the full Senate's final deliberations on Judges Claiborne's, Hastings', and Nixon's removals. Most of these senators also found attendance for the Claiborne, Hastings, and Nixon trial committees to have been "excellent" or "good."[49]

Nevertheless, senators' preparation for impeachment trials may be hindered by the absence of any official compilation of a comprehensive set of source materials for impeachment trials. Even though several items currently substitute for such a manual,[50] senators generally agree that they lack the time to cull through these documents to find relevant information. The materials also tend to vary in detail and quality.[51] Moreover, the absence of a compilation of precedents has made it harder for senators to benefit from the wisdom or judgment of their predecessors on similar procedural or substantive issues and to make decisions consistent with past trial rulings. The absence of such a document also tends to impede the efforts of impeached officials and their counsels to become fully prepared for and informed about the preferred practices in impeachment trials.

PROBLEMS WITH THE SENATE'S PROCEDURAL RULES

Another major set of concerns about impeachment trials in the Senate involves whether the Senate's impeachment rules foster fundamentally fair proceedings. The debates over fairness diverge over three issues: (1) the applicability of the Fifth Amendment due process clause;[52] (2) the need for set rules of evidence and uniform standards of proof; (3) the propriety of issue preclusion and collateral estoppel for previously convicted impeachable officials. I describe in turn each of these issues as background for my analyses of the major constitutional issues raised in impeachment proceedings in part III and of proposals for reforming the impeachment process in part IV.

Due Process.   In his lawsuit challenging his removal from office, Alcee Hastings argued, inter alia, that the failure of the Senate to conduct his hearing before the full body of the Senate violated the Fifth Amendment due process clause.[53] He claimed he had a "property" interest in keeping his judgeship and salary and that the government could not deprive him of these in an impeachment trial "without due process," that is, without following the proper procedures, including a complete trial before the full

Senate. In granting Hastings' motion to overturn his impeachment trial, Judge Stanley Sporkin of the U.S. District Court for the District of Columbia explained that impeachment trials "must be conducted in keeping with the basic principles of due process that have been enunciated by the courts and, ironically, by the Congress itself."[54] Subsequently, the U.S. Court of Appeals for the District of Columbia reversed and remanded Sporkin's ruling[55] for reconsideration in light of the Supreme Court's decision in *Walter Nixon v. United States*.[56] On remand, Judge Sporkin dismissed Hastings' lawsuit as nonjusticiable but did not comment further on the merits of Hastings' due process claim.[57]

At present, senators decide for themselves on whether the Fifth Amendment due process clause applies to impeachment trials and, if so, what kind of process it requires. In the past, this has sometimes led to inconsistent results. For example, because the Hastings impeachment trial was carried over from the 100th to the 101st Congress, several members of the House who had participated in the impeachment of Alcee Hastings— James Jeffords, Trent Lott, and Connie Mack—had become senators in the meantime and were in a position to participate in Hastings' impeachment trial. In order to avoid any appearance of a conflict of interest, all three senators recused themselves.[58] In contrast, an attempt in Judge Pickering's impeachment trial to disqualify various senators for similar reasons failed. In that proceeding, three senators—Bailey, Condit, and Samuel Smith—had each been members of the House and had voted on Pickering's impeachment. The full Senate never took action on a resolution to disqualify these senators, each of whom voted in Pickering's impeachment trial.[59]

The Need for Uniform Rules of Evidence and Standard of Proof.   Two perennial issues raised in removal proceedings are whether the Senate should adopt uniform rules of evidence or a uniform standard of proof and, if so, which of each kind.[60] I consider each question in turn.

The proponents of uniform evidentiary rules for impeachment trials argue that such proceedings need to make use of the same kind of reliable, nonprejudicial evidentiary rulings as other similar actions, such as criminal trials, currently employ. For example, uniform rules of evidence would give impeached officials notice as to the kind and amount of evidence they are expected to submit in an impeachment trial.

Opponents of the Senate's adoption of set rules of evidence for impeachment trials argue that those proceedings do not have the same needs for such rules as do state and federal courts—to make trials fairer and more efficient and to keep certain kinds of evidence away from the jury, whose members might not appreciate its relevance, credibility, or potentially prejudicial effect.[61] The opponents view impeachment trials as extraordinary hearings conducted by senators who do not need, like a typical jury, to be protected from "hearsay" or prejudicial evidence.[62] Moreover, the opponents of uniform evidentiary rules contend that even if the Senate could agree on such rules for impeachment trials, they would not be enforceable against or binding on individual senators, each of whom traditionally has had the discretion in an impeachment trial to follow any evidentiary standards he or she sees fit.[63]

The absence of any set rules of evidence need not, however, work to the disadvantage of impeached officials. As long as the Senate refuses to establish such rules, then the primary concern of an impeached official's counsel is to address substantive matters. Counsel know they can argue for whatever evidence they believe can benefit their client. As times and membership in the Senate change, defense counsel (as well as the house managers) know that the Senate is open to persuasion on virtually every evidentiary question. Consequently, impeached officials are in a similar position to the defendants in most administrative proceedings in which no set rules of evidence apply.[64]

In practice, the Senate and the trial committees have tended to admit as much evidence as time and relevance have permitted. Consequently, in the 1980s impeachments, each trial committee largely erred on the side of including arguably relevant evidence. In those instances in which inconsistent evidentiary rulings occurred, more often than not the different trial committees reached different conclusions on the relevance of the particular evidence submitted or on how best to enable each senator to decide for himself or herself on the appropriate weight to be given to the evidence submitted. For instance, in Judges Claiborne's and Nixon's removal proceedings, the Senate took the position that the members were free to determine for themselves the relevance of the judges' criminal convictions to their fitness to remain in office.[65] Similarly, the Hastings Trial Committee emphasized that "any Senator remains free to vote to acquit Judge Hastings for any reason, including agreement with his position [that] the jury's verdict shall be given great deference."[66]

In the three impeachment trials held during the 1980s, considerable debate in the Senate focused on (1) whether the Senate should follow or apply a uniform standard of proof for impeachment trials and, if so, (2) which burden of proof ought to apply in such proceedings. The major argument in favor of a uniform burden of proof is that it would put both sides in an impeachment trial on notice as to how best to present their respective cases and would allow for greater consistency in impeachment trials.[67]

Nevertheless, the Senate has refused invitations to apply a uniform standard of proof to impeachment trials. For example, in Judge Claiborne's removal proceedings, the Senate by a 75 to 17 vote rejected his motion to designate "beyond a reasonable doubt" as the standard of proof in the impeachment trial."[68] Subsequently, the Hastings and Nixon Trial Committees both construed that vote as a precedent confirming each senator's freedom to adopt whatever standard of proof he or she preferred.[69]

In any event, the Senate could choose, as individual senators already do, from among three established burdens of proof: beyond a reasonable doubt, clear and convincing, and preponderance of evidence. Some senators favor the "beyond a reasonable doubt" standard, because they believe it makes conviction more difficult and, hence, provides greater protection for federal judges or high-ranking members of the executive branch from politically motivated removal proceedings. Other senators favor the same standard as a jury in a criminal trial must use in an impeachment trial based on a felony conviction, because, in Senator Orrin Hatch's words, "fairness dictates the Senate should use the same standard."[70] In the Hastings impeachment trial, Senator Biden favored the same standard, because a jury had already acquitted Judge Hastings of various felony charges and, thus, fairness dictated that the Senate ought to apply the same burden of proof to protect Hastings from being convicted by the Senate on the basis of the same evidence under a more lenient standard.[71]

Others have argued that the proper burden of proof is clear and convincing evidence of the commission of an impeachable offense. They criticize the "beyond a reasonable doubt" standard as failing to recognize that the purpose of an impeachment is to defend the community against abuse of power by impeachable officials. In contrast, a lower burden, such as preponderance of evidence, fails to respect society's interest in retaining skilled and honest governmental officials and the damage to the innocent jurist's reputation wrought by an erroneous conviction.[72]

Other senators and the house managers have argued that the applicable standard of proof ought to be preponderance of the evidence. In their opinion, this burden is more consistent with the unique nature of an impeachment trial, in which a respondent may lose his livelihood or reputation, as opposed to the tougher standard of proof applicable in criminal trials, in which a court may take away a defendant's life, liberty, or property. In other words, many observers find a lower standard of proof appropriate for impeachment trials given the kind of interests at stake.[73]

The Debate over Issue Preclusion. The impeachment trials of Judges Claiborne and Nixon raised the issue of whether the Senate should give preclusive effect to prior felony convictions or at least to the evidentiary or factual findings underlying such judgments. The debate initially arose in the impeachment trial of Judge Claiborne, who was the first person to stand before the Senate in such a proceeding as a convicted, imprisoned felon. The House subcommittee relied heavily on Claiborne's criminal convictions to shorten its investigation of him. In the floor debate on the proposed articles of impeachment against Claiborne, the third of which urged his conviction and removal solely on the basis of his felony conviction, House Judiciary Committee Chair Peter W. Rodino, Jr. explained his desire to take "legislative notice of the factual finding already determined beyond a reasonable doubt by a jury of Judge Claiborne's peers and sustained at all levels of direct appeal."[74]

When the matter reached the Senate, the house managers filed a pretrial motion seeking summary conviction based upon the third article of impeachment. The managers found support in judicial doctrines of finality, collateral estoppel, and full faith and credit.[75] In a second motion, the managers urged application of collateral estoppel to specific issues alleged in the first two impeachment articles.[76] The house managers argued that neither motion sought to usurp the Senate's obligation to determine whether the particular conduct involved constituted an impeachable offense.[77] Rather, the managers explained that they wanted to avoid fact-finding proceedings before the Senate on issues that they felt had already been fairly and fully adjudicated by a court of law.

The House's two motions were directed to the Senate Trial Committee. At Chairman Mathias's suggestion, the trial committee did not rule on the motion for summary disposition because it had the potential of depriving the full Senate of its duty to render final judgment on whether Claiborne had committed an impeachable offense.[78] Moreover, completion of the evidentiary trial mooted the House's pretrial motions, and the Senate, after lengthy debate, ultimately voted to acquit Claiborne on Article III.[79] Even if Claiborne had been convicted on the third article, the post-trial vote would have meant little. The third impeachment article's value lay in providing a chance for a pretrial summary disposition in a case in which the facts were not genuinely in dispute. The Senate's refusal to consider the motion before trial had several secondary effects, including the House's subsequent decision not to seek a pretrial summary disposition in the impeachment of Judge Nixon, who like Claiborne, had been a convicted, imprisoned felon at the time of his impeachment trial.

Concerns about Rule XI Trial Committees

In the aftermath of the 1980s impeachment trials and the Supreme Court's decision in *Walter Nixon v. United States*[80] holding challenges to the Senate's use of trial committees nonjusticiable, most senators have expressly endorsed the continued use of special trial committees at least for removal proceedings against impeached federal judges.[81] Even so, there are three potential problems with Rule XI trial committees. I consider each issue in turn.

DISCOURAGING THE OTHER SENATORS FROM FAMILIARIZING
THEMSELVES WITH THE RECORD

A particularly serious charge made against rule XI trial committees is that
they may discourage many senators from reading the record and making
their own informed judgments about the credibility of key witnesses. If
most senators fail to become personally familiar with the record, it is
unimaginable that they will adequately protect the integrity of the impeachment process or that impeached officials will receive full and fair
hearings before the Senate.

A powerful piece of evidence in support of this complaint is the comparison made by Judge Nixon's impeachment counsel, David Stewart, of
the voting patterns of committee members and of those not serving on the
committee. To illustrate the inherent unfairness of the trial committee
system, Mr. Stewart argued that the senators who did not serve on the
trial committees in the 1980s voted in favor of conviction in higher
numbers than those who served on such committees. According to Mr.
Stewart, "[f]or 17 of the 18 impeachment articles voted on after a committee trial, the senators who actually heard the evidence supported the
accused in significantly greater proportion than did those senators not on
the trial committee. [Of] the 10 impeachment articles on which Judges
Hastings and Nixon were convicted, nine failed to attract a two-thirds
majority of the committee."[82]

There are at least four possible responses to Mr. Stewart's statistical
argument. First, the committee members' votes conceivably differ for
many reasons, including party affiliation, legal training, region, seniority,
and familiarity with the impeachment process. The variation in voting
patterns cannot conclusively be attributed to any single factor. Second,
regardless of the implications of Stewart's statistics, the fact remains that
more than two-thirds of the senators who served on the trial committee
voted to convict Nixon on the first impeachment article, and conviction
on that article alone was sufficient as a constitutional matter to remove
him from office. Third, at least two-thirds of the members of the Senate
present for final judgment on the Claiborne, Hastings, and Nixon removals voted to remove each of them on the basis of various impeachment
articles. The Constitution does not dictate what each senator must have in
mind when voting on removal; it mandates only that at least two-thirds of
the members present must vote (as they in fact did) to convict in order for
a removal to occur. Fourth, a hearing before a trial committee (at which
attendance is usually excellent or good) is not necessarily less fair to an
impeached official than one conducted before the full Senate, which would
likely mean (if past is prologue) very few senators would actually attend
(perhaps even fewer than would be present at a committee hearing).[83]

Nevertheless, a related problem may be that no formal mechanism is available to familiarize the full Senate with the trial committee members' conclusions on contested issues of fact or recommendations to convict or acquit.[84] Although committee members are free to participate as actively as they wish in the final deliberations, their views are not formally communicated to their colleagues prior to the final deliberations, in order to prevent their discouraging other senators from making up their own minds. Unless some effort is made to encourage committee members to share their opinions with their colleagues, the full Senate may not be able to take advantage of the opinions and judgments of the trial committee members who saw and heard the evidence firsthand.

SCHEDULING CONFLICTS

Like house managers, the members of the 1980s trial committees had to make special efforts to avoid scheduling conflicts. The trial committees tried to solve this problem by adopting a rule providing that a quorum of the committee consists of seven members. The Claiborne committee explained it needed the rule to bolster the constitutionality, fairness, and credibility of the committee system, which would otherwise allow for the receipt of some evidence with perhaps only a single senator present.[85] Nevertheless, all three committees' proceedings had to be continuously interrupted in order for their members to vote on the Senate floor.[86]

RESOLVING DISPUTES OVER PRETRIAL MATTERS,
INCLUDING DISCOVERY

Despite the fact that all three of the impeachment trials in the 1980s involved impeached judges who had had ample discovery conducted as part of their prior criminal trials, pretrial matters consumed a substantial portion of the Hastings and Nixon trial committees' respective work loads. The trial committees' efforts to facilitate pretrial matters, particularly discovery requests and conflicts, exposed two interrelated problems. First, the Hastings trial committee had no strategy, rules, or expertise in dealing with such matters. To some extent, this was understandable because the Hastings' removal provided the first chance a trial committee—or the Senate—ever had to conduct discovery for an impeachment trial.[87] In any event, the Hastings trial committee spent much time and effort in supervising prolonged, heated disputes over a wide variety of discovery matters, including having to issue several orders to resolve such matters as extensions of time, exchanging witness lists, document requests, depositions, and stipulations. It also adopted a rule providing that "one committee member shall constitute a quorum for the purpose of a pretrial examination of witnesses at which sworn testimony is heard and evidence taken."[88] This rule reflected the trial committee members' recognition that they did not all have the time to attend each deposition. The Hastings trial committee's other orders reflect its preference to allow as much discovery as was reasonably possible. Nevertheless, in the aftermath of the Hastings impeachment trial, trial committees remain free, by virtue of the Senate's rules and general practices, to opt for different procedures if they see fit.

Second, the disputes over pretrial matters in the Hastings' removal proceeding illustrate how defense counsel can delay or disrupt committee hearings. Hastings' counsel, Terrance Anderson, aggressively opposed most of the house managers' efforts to expedite discovery (or, for that matter, any other part of the trial).[89] To be sure, the line between a zealous defense counsel acting in good faith and a dilatory one is sometimes quite thin. The problem for senators on the trial committee is that they rarely have to deal with trial tactics. Criminal defense attorneys appearing on behalf of an impeached official may try to transform impeachment trials into the kind of criminal proceedings with which they are more familiar and are likelier to have more experience than any of the members or staff of a trial committee. Under such circumstances, defense counsel can frequently test the committee members' patience and skills.

Moreover, defense counsel and the house managers do not stand on equal footing before a trial committee (or the Senate itself). Trial committees are reluctant to order house managers, because the latter are duly elected members of a coequal branch. Nor is it even realistic for defense counsel to expect to get the same respect the house managers receive from senators. For example, in issuing its orders to resolve various discovery disputes, the Hastings trial committee would "order," "direct," or "require" Counsel Anderson to do things,[90] while it would "recommend," "expect," or "ask" the house managers to perform certain tasks.[91]

The discovery in the Nixon impeachment trial contrasts sharply with the bickering evident throughout the proceedings before the Hastings trial committee. For example, there is no instance in the Nixon proceedings in which the trial committee ever rebuked the parties for failing to reach agreement on discovery or other matters. Moreover, perhaps because Stewart was often willing to reciprocate and not contest each of the house managers' requests, the trial committee granted virtually all of his requests for time delays and broad document production.

Chapter Five

IMPEACHMENT ISSUES INVOLVING
CONGRESS AND THE OTHER BRANCHES

S EVERAL TRENDS or problems with the federal impeachment process have arisen involving the relationship between the House and Senate or between the three branches of the federal government. These include (1) the uncertain precedential value of impeachment proceedings; (2) the increasing influence of the executive branch in initiating or displacing impeachments; (3) Congress's tendencies in defining impeachable offenses; (4) the significance of Congress's general reluctance to overextend or abuse its impeachment powers; (5) the House and Senate's respective failures to consider routinely the propriety of disqualifying convicted officials; and (6) the propriety of reimbursing the defense costs of impeached officials acquitted by the Senate. I consider each development in turn.

THE SIGNIFICANCE AND INFLUENCE OF
IMPEACHMENT PRECEDENTS

The precedential effect of impeachment proceedings is often at its strongest if a question of constitutional interpretation is involved. In such a case, Congress seems to be especially sensitive to the permanent effect of its decisions on the Constitution and its relationship with the other federal branches. There is also a general desire in Congress to provide the parties in an impeachment proceeding consistent, predictable, and stable guidelines and to avoid any practice that might undermine the confidence of the participants in the fairness of the impeachment process. Lastly, members of Congress are aware that they are not only politically accountable for their impeachment decisions but also answerable to the court of history for how they handle the issues or principles at stake in impeachment proceedings.

For example, the subsequent congressional reaction to the outcome of the very first impeachment trial illustrates the potentially lasting influence of a constitutional decision made by Congress in such a proceeding. Then-Representative John Adams initiated that impeachment in 1797 against William Blount, who was a United States senator from Tennessee.

The House impeached Senator Blount for taking various actions to undermine the relationship between the United States and Native Americans
and for conspiring to aid England in its war with Spain despite the United
States' official neutrality.[1] On July 8, 1797—the day after the House had
impeached Blount, the Senate expelled Blount by a vote of 25 to 1.[2]
Blount challenged the Senate's "jurisdiction" to subject him as well to an
impeachment trial,[3] claiming that he was not a "civil officer" of the
United States for purposes of impeachment.[4] He argued that "civil officers" were only those appointed by the president; that only "civil officers" could be impeached; and, thus, that the impeachment process could
not be used to punish a senator.[5] On January 10, 1798, the Senate voted
14 to 11 to defeat a resolution declaring that Blount was a "civil officer"
of the United States and therefore subject to impeachment.[6] By the same
margin, the Senate voted on January 14, 1799, to dismiss the impeachment resolution against Blount for lack of jurisdiction.[7] Ever since, the
House and the Senate have regarded the Blount impeachment as standing
for the proposition that senators are not impeachable because they are
not "civil officers of the United States."[8]

In contrast, the influence of impeachment decisions involving mixed
questions of constitutional interpretation and policy, such as the propriety of using trial committees or reimbursing the defense costs of acquitted
officials, primarily depends on the preferences of current members of
Congress. For example, there are several reasons not to interpret the
Senate's rejection of the third article of impeachment against Judge
Claiborne—asking for issue preclusion based on his prior felony convictions—as a lasting refusal to apply collateral estoppel in an impeachment.
First, the third article did not directly ask the senators about whether
Claiborne's prior convictions settled certain key facts underlying his impeachment. Second, despite the Senate's refusal to endorse the third article, it is unclear whether the prior felony convictions strongly motivated
senators to convict Judge Claiborne on the other two articles. As Senator
Levin has admitted, "[m]y own gut feeling is one way or another, following some fiction or reality, we will find a way to remove somebody from
office who [has] been convicted of a crime [and] who [has] exhausted the
appeal."[9] Third, Judge Claiborne's acquittal on the third article was
made possible by the fact that thirty-five senators voted present rather
than on the merits of the third article.[10] Thus, the rejection of the article
turns on many votes that could be construed as expressing a desire "not
[to] base removal on the conviction itself"[11] or not to do so in Claiborne's
case because of doubts about the conviction's reliability. Lastly, the third
article of impeachment may have asked too much of the Senate by re-
questing it to find that a felony conviction is an impeachable offense
rather than to make an independent judgment on whether, accepting the

facts underlying a felony conviction, the conduct at issue constituted an impeachable offense.[12]

Of course, Congress retains the discretion to reach a different conclusion even about a matter of constitutional interpretation. Yet, impeachments rarely pose pure questions of constitutional law. Instead, Congress usually follows a prior impeachment practice, unless Congress decides to abandon it for the sake of efficiency or fairness. For example, although the Senate approved rule XI in 1935,[13] it did not invoke the rule in Judge Ritter's 1936 impeachment trial in part because many senators expressed doubts about its constitutionality.[14] Nor does the Senate today perceive itself as bound to using rule XI trial committees.

If Congress were disposed, however, to give some precedential effect to its prior decisions in impeachment proceedings, it still must confront the troublesome matter of figuring out the significance of a specific precedent. The difficulty of achieving consensus on the precise meaning of a prior impeachment decision may preclude that precedent from having any seriously binding effect on Congress or may make it easier for subsequent members of Congress to interpret the prior practice in a way that suits their present purposes. Impeachments are further complicated by Congress's penchant to defer to tradition, as reflected in its requirement of unanimous consent for modifying procedural rules[15] and preference for allowing each member to vote his or her conscience on the appropriate law and burden of proof to apply.

Three examples illustrate the dilemmas involved in trying to measure the influence of an impeachment decision. They each show that the likely weight Congress will give to an impeachment precedent depends heavily on the collective will of members of Congress during the relevant period and the political climate of the impeachment action in question, including the extent of media coverage, the popularity or notoriety of the targeted official, and the electorate's interest.

For example, the precedential value of the Blount impeachment is not entirely unclear. The Senate's votes on the impeachment resolution against Senator Blount can be read as reflecting the Senate's view—or at least the view of the fourteen senators who voted against the impeachment resolution and exercise of jurisdiction against Blount—that senators are not impeachable officials. But, the attempt to impeach and convict Senator Blount also arguably reflects the kinds of party divisions and regional antagonisms that existed during the nation's early years. For example, Blount was a Republican, and ten of the eleven senators who voted to assert impeachment jurisdiction over Blount were Federalists, while five out of the six Republican senators rejected jurisdiction.[16] Yet, the fact that nine Federalists voted to reject jurisdiction, combined with the 25 to 1 vote to expel Blount,[17] reflect that something more than partisan politics might have provoked these hearings and that most senators refused to convict Blount for purely partisan reasons.[18] In addition, Blount's popularity in the West, based on his leadership of a movement to separate it from the United States, might have influenced the vote to reject jurisdiction as reflected in the fact that every western senator voted against jurisdiction.[19] The votes rejecting jurisdiction might have been based on the Senate's reluctance to convict someone whom it had expelled or who was not in office at the time of his impeachment trial. Moreover, the latter votes could reflect a sentiment among some senators that impeachment could be based only on indictable offenses. Even though the Senate voted to expel Blount for "a high misdemeanor, entirely inconsistent with his public trust and duty as a Senator,"[20] the term as used in that context does not seem to have meant an actual crime, because no one accused Blount of having committed an indictable crime.[21]

The principle underlying the nation's second impeachment is also disputable in certain respects. It involved United States District Judge John Pickering of New Hampshire, whom the House impeached on March 2, 1803, by a vote of 45 to 8. The impeachment articles charged drunkenness and profanity on the bench and the rendering of judicial decisions based neither on fact nor law.[22] Although Judge Pickering, like Senator Blount, did not appear on his own behalf in the Senate proceedings, his son filed a petition arguing that Pickering was so ill and deranged that he was incapable of exercising any kind of judgment or transacting any business and that he should therefore not be removed from office for misconduct attributable to insanity.[23] Nevertheless, the Senate voted 18 to 12 to accept evidence of Judge Pickering's insanity,[24] 19 to 7 to convict,[25] and 20 to 6 to remove him from office.[26] Consequently, he became the first federal official in American history to have been convicted and removed from office.

There is still controversy over whether Pickering's impeachment establishes that impeachable offenses are not limited to indictable crimes. On the one hand, Simon H. Rifkind, counsel for Justice William O. Douglas during the House's impeachment action against him in 1970, contended that Pickering was charged "with three counts of wilfully violating a federal statute relating to the posting of bond in certain attachment situations, and the misdemeanors of public drunkenness and blasphemy."[27] On the other hand, the authors of one impeachment study claim that "no federal statute made violation of the bond-posting act a crime, nor obviously were drunkenness or blasphemy federal crimes. The Pickering impeachment [confirms] that the concept of high crimes and misdemeanors is not limited to criminal offenses."[28]

Yet, either view could be valid, "because the question of guilt was put in the form of asking senators whether the judge stood guilty as charged,"[29] rather than whether the acts he allegedly committed constituted impeachable offenses. In other words, the Senate's votes to convict may not reflect an acknowledgement by the Senate that violations of impeachable offenses were actually involved. Indeed, five senators withdrew from the court of impeachment when the Senate agreed to put the question in the form of "guilty as charged."[30] Two of the senators—both Federalists—objected to procedural irregularities and claimed the question put to them failed to ask whether the charges actually described high crimes and misdemeanors.[31] John Quincy Adams claimed that the other three senators who withdrew—all Republicans—also objected to procedural irregularities and did not want to separate from their party by voting against the judge's conviction.[32]

Another problem with using the Pickering impeachment as a precedent is that party affiliation seems to have played a major role in the Senate's votes to admit the evidence of insanity and to remove him from office. All nineteen of the Senate's votes to convict the Federalist judge came from Republicans, while all seven of his acquittal votes were from Federalists.[33] Even the bipartisan vote to admit evidence on Judge Pickering's insanity can be explained on partisan grounds: the Federalist senators may have wanted to introduce this evidence because they believed proof of Pickering's insanity would save him from a guilty verdict, given their position that insanity was not an impeachable offense, while the Republicans might have expected the admission of this evidence to lead to the judge's conviction because they thought it demonstrated the need to remove him before he damaged the judicial system any further.

A third impeachment often treated as a significant precedent involved Secretary of War General William Belknap. The House impeached him on March 2, 1876.[34] The formal articles of impeachment charged him with acceptance of bribes.[35] However, he resigned prior to the House's formal vote on impeachment.[36] A lengthy debate ensued over the propriety of impeaching an officer who had resigned. The weight of opinion in the House, as evidenced by adoption of the resolution to impeach,[37] was that a civil officer may not escape impeachment by resignation.[38] Representative Robbins of North Carolina explained, for example, that one purpose of impeachment "is to disqualify from holding office hereafter. [It] is within the power of the Senate sitting as a court of impeachment to impose that penalty, and the officer cannot escape it by hasty resignation, which is virtually a flight from justice."[39]

When the issue was raised again at the Senate trial, it met initially with a similar response. The vote to retain jurisdiction was 37 to 29.[40] The

Senate rejected the argument of Belknap's counsel that such a decision required a concurrence of two-thirds of the senators sitting as a court of impeachment, and the trial proceeded.[41] Yet, even though a majority of the Senate voted Belknap guilty on all the articles of impeachment, the two-thirds required for conviction was not met, and Belknap was acquitted.[42] The report to the House stated that, of the twenty-five senators who voted "not guilty," twenty-two claimed to have done so because they believed the Senate had no jurisdiction over an official who had resigned from office prior to his impeachment trial.[43] The other three senators voting not guilty did so because they thought Belknap was innocent of the charges against him.[44]

The precedential value of Belknap's impeachment is uncertain. On the one hand, the result of the Belknap trial provides a strong argument that the Senate will not convict an official who has resigned prior to his impeachment trial. On the other hand, the House vote could be construed as a precedent supporting impeachment of an official who has resigned from office. Moreover, the Senate vote to accept jurisdiction provides additional support for conducting a postresignation impeachment trial, even though the final Senate vote cuts the other way.

Perhaps the only thing that can safely be said about the importance of the Belknap impeachment is that, in any future attempt to impeach an official no longer in office, the battle lines are clear. On the one hand, those seeking an impeachment will claim that the Constitution permits such a proceeding based in part on its authorizing the punishment of disqualification, which seems fit to punish officials no longer in office. Blount's impeachment may be distinguished on the grounds that it turned to a significant degree on the Senate's opposition to the impeachability of senators. Moreover, Belknap's impeachment could itself be distinguished on the basis that the Senate retains the authority to reach its own, independent judgment on the propriety of a postresignation impeachment trial, particularly because the Senate must determine in any given case the political advantage of conducting such a trial.

On the other hand, those opposing the impeachment of an official who is no longer in office will rely on the Blount and Belknap impeachments—particularly the latter—as establishing the principle that resignation precludes impeachment. They will argue further that impeaching someone who is now a private citizen would also conflict with the basic precept of the impeachment process to punish only officeholders for their official misconduct. The political fallout from punishing a private citizen may well outweigh the fear that a resigned official might resume a public post. Lastly, those opposing postresignation impeachments would argue that there is little to be gained politically through such an action. In their view, the Senate could decide that the most important thing is for an official to leave office and, once that end is achieved, Congress need not forgo its other, important legislative business to conduct an impeachment proceeding against someone who may already have suffered or been punished enough.

CONGRESSIONAL PATTERNS RELATING TO
IMPEACHABLE OFFENSES

Mindful of the problems with relying on impeachment precedents as clear expressions of past, present, or future congressional will, one can still identify some trends in the votes of the House and the Senate regarding the scope of impeachable offenses. First, it is noteworthy that of the fifteen men impeached by the House of Representatives, only four were impeached primarily on grounds constituting a criminal offense;[45] and one of those four was Alcee Hastings, who had been formally acquitted of bribery prior to his impeachment. The House's articles of impeachment against the nine others include misuses of power that were not indictable federal offenses, at least at the time they were approved.

Second, the Senate's tendency is to convict on the basis of indictable crimes or at least to find conviction easier if an indictable offense were involved. To be sure, the Senate has convicted some officials on the basis of nonindictable offenses, including Judge Pickering (public drunkenness and blasphemy),[46] Judge West H. Humphreys (convicted and removed by the Senate for various activities in support of the Confederacy and failing to fulfill his duties as a U.S. District Judge),[47] Judge Robert Archbald (convicted, removed, and disqualified by the Senate for obtaining contracts for himself from persons appearing before his court and for adjudicating cases in which he had a financial interest or received payment—none of which offenses were indictable crimes at the time),[48] and Judge Halsted Ritter (convicted and removed from office on the sole basis that he had brought "his court into scandal and disrepute, to the prejudice of said court and public confidence in the administration of justice therein, and to the prejudice of public respect for and confidence in the federal judiciary[]").[49] Yet, in the 1980s, the Senate convicted Judges Claiborne, Nixon, and Hastings on the basis of indictable offenses.

Third, partisan loyalties and differences of opinion have played a decreasingly important role in the impeachment process. In the nineteenth century, heated partisan differences over the appropriate handling and exercise of federal power motivated the impeachments of William Blount, John Pickering, Samuel Chase, James Peck, West Humphreys, and Andrew Johnson. Yet, it is noteworthy that, no conviction, with the possibility of one exception, has yet been based solely on partisan grounds or at least along the lines of a strictly partisan vote.

The one exception may be the 1936 impeachment of Judge Halsted Ritter. Jacobus ten Broeck has suggested, for example, that the Ritter impeachment's "possible connection with the New Deal attack upon the judiciary, its bearing on the question of feasibility of impeachment as a method of influencing or controlling the judicial department is more immediate and impressive than any of the earlier cases."[50] This conclusion is supported in part by the fact that of the seven charges made against Ritter, the Senate was unable to muster a guilty verdict on any of the six specific counts and convicted Ritter only on the final count, which generally claimed a lack of fitness to occupy office.[51]

The critique of the Ritter impeachment posits that Congress made up impeachable offenses against Ritter that had nothing to do with the real reasons it wanted to remove him. The problem with this view is that it ignores the significance of the formal impeachment article on the basis of which Ritter was convicted and removed. Given that impeachment has been recognized as a political process from the beginning of the Republic, it is not surprising that political differences influenced and perhaps even motivated Ritter's impeachment. Yet, the formal impeachment article against Judge Ritter is the clearest expression of what Congress really accepted as its reasons for impeaching him, because Congress actually voted on them. Particularly in the absence of contemporaneous statements to the contrary, the formal impeachment article upheld against Ritter reflects more reliably than anything else the reasons Congress impeached and removed him.

Even though partisanship may also have influenced the initiation of the impeachment attempts against Justice Chase and President Johnson, it seems to have dissipated or become diffused as those two officials approached the brinks of conviction and removal. Similarly, in the two most high-profile, post–World War II impeachment attempts—against Justice Douglas and President Nixon—partisanship ultimately played no determinative role. Even though the impeachment inquiry initiated against Justice Douglas in 1970 was largely motivated by partisan differences of opinion over the moral tones of his judging and life-style, the House never took any formal action against the justice once it became clear in the investigative stage that his critics lacked any nonpartisan basis for questioning the performance of his official duties.[52]

In 1974, President Nixon received strong support from party loyalists in the House in the early phases of the impeachment investigation against him. By late July and early August of 1974, the House Judiciary Committee approved three articles of impeachment (each opposed by all of the

Republicans on the committee), charging President Nixon with obstruction of justice, abuse of powers, and unlawful refusal to supply material subpoenaed by the House of Representatives.[53] Behind the scenes, though, party loyalists encouraged Nixon to resign based on their belief that he was likely to be impeached and removed from office. By early August, Nixon lost almost all Republican support in Congress after he made public tapes of recorded conversations in which he admitted his involvement in some of the matters giving rise to the impeachment inquiry.[54] The willingness of most Republicans to join in acknowledging a nonpartisan basis for impeaching President Nixon and in encouraging him to resign precipitated his resignation.

CONGRESSIONAL RELUCTANCE TO ABUSE ITS IMPEACHMENT POWER

Another trend in the federal impeachment process is that the House has rarely, if ever, and the Senate has never, successfully committed a serious or extreme abuse of its impeachment authority. The fifth chapter of part III discusses more fully the efficacy of constitutional and other, less formal constraints on congressional impeachment practices. It is nevertheless significant that time and time again Congress, and particularly the Senate, for whatever reason, has not only avoided realizing its critics' worst fears (such as by impeaching or removing people on the basis of their hair color or a coin toss) but also given attention to serious constitutional arguments and consequences in the midst of politically charged proceedings undertaken for the purpose of achieving short-term political gains.

For example, all efforts to use the impeachment process for partisan ends, including those in the nineteenth century, have failed. Indeed, the first impeachment attempt by Congress did not succeed in large part because the Senate, despite its obvious disdain for the target—William Blount—decided not to push the limit of its impeachment power by trying to extend it either to a senator or to an official no longer in office. Not insignificantly, Congress has refused ever since to attempt a similar impeachment. Moreover, regardless of the partisan reasons various senators might have had for voting for or against Judge Pickering's removal, it is clear that at the time of his impeachment he was no longer fit to hold judicial office.[55] The successful removal of Judge Pickering is also consistent with Hamilton's opinion that the federal impeachment process could be properly used to impeach insane (as opposed to senile) judges.

In addition, despite the partisan pressures to remove both Justice Chase and President Andrew Johnson, their respective impeachment trials featured considerable debate about the scope of impeachable offenses and the need to avoid the dangers posed by partisan impeachments to the security of future presidents and federal judges. The Senate acquitted Justice Chase and President Johnson in significant part because their respective defenders ultimately persuaded a sufficient number of their colleagues that the absence of clear proof of the commission of an impeachable offense or of misconduct rising to the level of an impeachable offense should, as a constitutional matter, preclude convicting and removing an unpopular impeachable official.[56]

In this century, Congress has been accused of at least three different kinds of abuses of its impeachment authority, none of which convincingly establishes that Congress has engaged in outlandish malfeasance. First, as the prior section suggested, many people suspect that the Senate had partisan reasons (or less than noble motives) for removing Judge Ritter. Yet, the House approved seven articles of impeachment detailing his misconduct and the Senate convicted him on the basis of one impeachment article in full compliance with all applicable constitutional requirements. Nor is it unreasonable or inconsistent with the structure or original understanding of the Constitution for the Senate to have voted for only one of the impeachment articles against him, apparently as a compromise on the specific grounds for removing Judge Ritter. The only serious question about the propriety of Judge Ritter's impeachment trial is whether the misconduct charged in the only successful impeachment article against him—bringing disrepute to the federal judiciary—could constitute an impeachable offense. Such misconduct, even if phrased in an awkwardly general fashion, is not unrelated to the proper discharge of a federal judge's duties because the latter's authority depends fundamentally on general respect for his or her integrity, even-handedness, and competence. Even if there had not been sufficient consensus among senators on whether Judge Ritter actually engaged in tax evasion or received kickbacks from his case assignments (either of which, standing alone, would surely constitute an impeachable offense), the Senate could have reasonably concluded (as reflected in the formal impeachment article approved by at least two-thirds of its members) that there was enough evidence of Judge Ritter's financial improprieties or misconduct (which were alleged to have been related to his judicial decision making) to undo its confidence in his impartiality. The critical line-drawing on the point at which judicial misconduct leaves an unacceptable or indelible taint on the integrity of the federal bench is left to the Senate to make on a case-by-case basis, and the Constitution does not countenance second-guessing (except, of course, in a reelection campaign) of a senator's reasons for voting for an otherwise acceptable impeachment article, particularly when one of the critical safeguards against impeaching strictly on the basis of partisan or personal animosity—a supermajority vote—has been fulfilled.

A second complaint in this century against the federal impeachment process, as suggested in the second section of the previous chapter, concerns the fairness of Congress's timing in initiating, and procedures used in, impeachments. For example, a popular charge is that Congress took too long in commencing each of the judicial impeachments of the 1980s and, once it started those proceedings, relied on the unfair, if not unconstitutional, mechanism of a Senate trial committee to gather evidence and take testimony. The first problem with this complaint is that the Constitution does not put a time limit (or establish a statute of limitations, for that matter) on the initiation or conduct of an impeachment. Slowness is not necessarily an abuse of power, and, even if it were somehow a defect in the system, it is certainly preferable to the alternative—Congress's moving too quickly in impeachment actions. After all, the framers deliberately made the impeachment process cumbersome in order to make impeachment difficult to achieve. Moreover, Congress's delay in initiating impeachments, as well as the decline in its impeachment activity, conceivably reflects Congress's tendency to underutilize rather than overuse its authority. As for the Senate's use of trial committees, it is far from clear that the Constitution mandates that an impeachment trial must be conducted before the full Senate. (In fact, the Constitution requires a quorum for all legislative business and, thus, the full Senate need not be present for any of its official actions. The Constitution also does not require full attendance as a condition for conviction; it requires that at least two-thirds of the members present must agree for such an outcome to occur.) Moreover, it is not unreasonable for the Senate, given its authority to devise the rules for all of its proceedings, its extensive use of committees to assist it in preparing for a wide range of business entrusted to the full body's consideration, and the fact that the English practice (on which much of the federal impeachment process is partially modeled) allowed for the use of trial committees, to designate a trial committee to perform the useful but limited function of building the record on which the Senate could base its final removal vote.

Third, a common complaint is about senators' poor attendance in and preparation for impeachment trials (giving rise to the need for trial committees in the first place). The Constitution does not, however, require a senator to attend all of an impeachment trial, nor, for that matter, to be present for any particular part of it. The Constitution mentions senators' attendance in only two places, one with respect to establishing that "a Majority of each [chamber of Congress] shall constitute a Quorum to do business,"[57] and the other providing that "no Person shall be convicted [in an impeachment trial] without the Concurrence of two thirds of the Members present."[58] The Constitution is also silent about how well informed a senator must be prior to voting on a removal matter (or, for that matter, on any legislative business). This constitutional design leaves ample room for senators to order their priorities in terms of attendance or preparation as they each see fit and to face the political consequences for their choices.

Consequently, it should not be too surprising to find that senators' attendance at, and preparation for, impeachment trials have risen in almost direct proportion to the visibility of the impeached official involved and the relative magnitude of the likely political fallout from the final Senate vote to convict or acquit. Hence, the attendance and level of preparation for the Chase and Johnson impeachment trials exceeded those for the Louderback and Ritter removal proceedings. Ironically, the fact that the latter trials were perceived by senators and their constituents to be less important than the former (or other conflicting legislative business) means that abuse is likelier to occur in the latter proceedings. Under such circumstances, trial committees are apt to ensure impeached officials with fact-gathering sessions at which well-informed senators are likelier to be present (as seems to have been the case for the Claiborne, Hastings, and Nixon removal proceedings). Senators disagree over the level of preparation for the final Senate votes on Judges Claiborne, Hastings, and Nixon, but the fact remains that virtually every senator was present for the final votes in those and other removal proceedings.

In any event, the attendance at and preparation for high-profile impeachment attempts (such as those involving Justice Chase and Presidents Johnson and Nixon) is strong, particularly in comparison with senators' attendance at and preparation for debates on other legislative business. With respect to lower-profile impeachment attempts, it is noteworthy that, despite claims about poor attendance (as well as partisanship) detracting from the impeachment attempt against Judge Louderback, the Senate did not convict him. Moreover, the final arguments in low-profile impeachment attempts have all been well attended. The preparation levels of senators in these proceedings is more difficult to measure, particularly because not every senator speaks or later publishes his position or views. Even so, the hearings themselves have fully aired the evidence on each impeached official's guilt or innocence.

THE INCREASING INFLUENCE OF THE EXECUTIVE IN TRIGGERING THE IMPEACHMENT PROCESS

Interestingly, the decreasing politicization or partisanship of impeachments (at least with respect to low-level or low-profile impeachable officials) has coincided with an increase in congressional deference to executive efforts to discipline such people. In 1904, the Justice Department concluded that preimpeachment prosecution without congressional authorization was not permissible.[59] The department feared that this practice would displace congressional authority to discipline judicial misconduct and put judicial independence from anything other than impeachment at risk.[60] But, by 1973, this assumption no longer held true, as reflected by the Justice Department's decision to prosecute Seventh Circuit Judge Otto Kerner.[61] When the change in policy occurred is not clear. Although the Justice Department sought indictments against numerous judges in the intervening years, each of those judges resigned prior to prosecution.[62]

In fact, the impeachment of Judge Ritter in 1936 is the last time Congress impeached and convicted a federal official who had not been previously prosecuted for having committed criminal offenses. Since 1980, the Justice Department has prosecuted five federal judges, none of whom resigned from office even after exhausting their criminal appeals.[63] On the one hand, these prosecutions have arguably made the House's task of impeaching these officials easier, because they have created records on which the House could base an impeachment. On the other hand, these prosecutions have complicated the impeachment process, because the House has had to delay initiating any impeachments until the criminal process has run its course because of concerns about the unfairness of requiring an impeachable official to defend himself concurrently in multiple hearings or the likely interference simultaneous proceedings would have with each other.

Moreover, these prosecutions have effectively given the executive branch additional power over judicial tenure. They have also raised the related issue of whether, or the extent to which, the executive may be required to share with the House the information it collected during a criminal investigation, because otherwise, the House may experience delays—like those in the Hastings impeachment—in obtaining relevant documents from grand jury or judicial council investigative files.[64]

In addition, a prior criminal prosecution that does not result in a federal judge's resignation creates enormous pressure for Congress to conduct an impeachment. In the 1980s, the image of a convicted and incarcerated felon continuing to receive the salary of a federal judge upset many politicians and, in the view of some, damaged the credibility of the criminal justice system, the impeachment process, and the federal judiciary. The House's decisions to delay impeachment may arguably have been justified on the ground that it had more pressing business or that it did not want to interfere with ongoing criminal prosecutions. Yet, those decisions also increased the chance of a rush to judgment once Congress got around to impeaching those federal judges.

Finally, the propriety of pre-indictment prosecutions depends in part on their goals. If, for example, the department's aim since 1986 has been to expedite the resignation of the federal judges it prosecuted, it has failed. Indeed, the most recent prosecutions show that a convicted federal judge has little or no incentive to resign. For instance, Judge Claiborne saw the impeachment process as a second chance to vindicate himself.[65] Moreover, if a convicted judge is likely to be disbarred and thus lose his means of making a living, the judge has no motivation to relinquish his salary and benefits. Finally, the prospect of an impeachment proceeding may not intimidate a judge who has already been criminally prosecuted and convicted, in view of the fact that the House has engaged in fifty judicial investigations since 1789, resulting in thirteen resignations, four convictions, four acquittals, and four censures.[66] In any event, as Professor Emily Van Tassel suggests, "[i]f removal is the goal, then the evidence suggests that the big stick of impeachment, prior to prosecution, effectively goads judges to voluntarily resign. It seems likely that impeachment is less of a threat when one has already been prosecuted than it would in the absence of prosecution."[67]

The House's and Senate's Failure(s) to Seek the Imposition of All Available Punishments

In practice, the articles of impeachment offer the House an opportunity to signal the form of relief that it regards as appropriate and likely to get sufficient support in the Senate for a conviction. For its part, the Senate has construed the Constitution to make removal automatic upon a two-thirds vote on at least one article of impeachment. Yet, the Constitution also provides that an impeached officer may be disqualified from holding any "office of honor, trust, or profit under the United States." By a separate majority vote following conviction, the Senate has only imposed this additional sanction twice—against Judges Archbald and Humphreys.[68] The House has, however, not taken advantage of its chance to use the impeachment articles to influence the punishment imposed by the Senate. For example, in the Ritter impeachment, each impeachment article asked only that the judge be found "guilty of high crimes and misdemeanors in office."[69] Similarly, in the 1980s, each article adopted by the House asked that the judge be removed from office, not mentioning disqualification from future office, and the Senate issued orders removing each convicted judge from office without voting on whether to disqualify him from future office.[70]

The Senate's failure to impose both punishments in the 1980s impeachment trials has, however, already produced one awkward situation. In the fall of 1992, Alcee Hastings was elected to and sworn in as a member of the House of Representatives. He is the first individual to join the House after having been impeached by it.

The Hastings situation raises two difficult questions, apart from the constitutional issues—discussed in the first chapter of part III—over whether officials who have resigned or left office may be impeached and whether the Senate may impose the punishments of removal and disqualification separately. The first issue posed by the Hastings case is whether impeachments may be brought more than once against the same individual for the same misconduct in office, that is, whether double jeopardy applies to impeachment proceedings. Double jeopardy is a concern in federal trials because the Constitution provides in the Fifth Amendment that no one "shall . . . be subject for the same offence to be twice put in jeopardy of life or limb."[71] Impeachment imposes different kinds of punishment from those exercisable by federal courts, nor can the targets of impeachments be pardoned.[72] Whereas the Constitution expressly prohibits double jeopardy in criminal proceedings, no constitutional provision clearly restricts the Congress to impeaching someone only once. The framers' failure to prohibit Congress from doing in an impeachment what they had explicitly barred the courts from doing may reflect the framers' desire to allow Congress to bring a second set of impeachment proceedings if it saw fit to do so.

The major concern is whether a second set of impeachment proceedings against a person removed from office is fundamentally unfair. With its considerable resources, Congress could, at least theoretically, persecute impeachable officials almost endlessly if there were no prohibition against doing so. If *res judicata* were applicable under these circumstances, an impeached official might then be precluded from arguing that his initial case might have been decided differently by a different Congress. Lastly, fundamental fairness might allow an officer to argue that, whatever the merits of his or her conviction, he or she is entitled to a second chance to serve the public.

A second issue raised in the Hastings situation is whether the Senate could have claimed in 1992 that it still retained jurisdiction over Judge Hastings' impeachment, so that it could make a judgment on his disqualification in spite of its having previously decided to convict him in 1989. The Senate has traditionally viewed its jurisdiction in an impeachment to begin only after it has received formal impeachment articles from the House and to expire automatically once it has decided on guilt or innocence and punishment and adjourned as a court of impeachment.[73] This opinion is reinforced by the division of impeachment authority between the House and the Senate, making one formal check against the Senate's abuse of its impeachment power the need for initial action by the House. Hence, the Senate's adjournment at the close of the Hastings impeachment trial in 1989 arguably marked the end of its jurisdiction as a court of impeachment over Alcee Hastings. This circumstance precludes the

Senate from claiming that it could reassert jurisdiction over Hastings to disqualify him at least in the absence of any further House proceedings against the former judge. In short, the Senate could have disqualified Hastings only if it had done so as part of his 1989 impeachment trial or if it had subsequently received another set of articles of impeachment in 1992, enabling it to impose an additional punishment.

As a practical matter, the chance of a second set of proceedings succeeding are remote and unlikely to attract much political support. The impeachment process is cumbersome, and the practical impossibility of displacing for a second time precious congressional resources from other pressing legislative business might account for the fact that no such proceeding has ever occurred. Given that the Senate left open the door for Alcee Hastings to occupy another federal office by not disqualifying him from doing so, it should not have been surprising for him to have argued in his campaign for Congress that the people in his Florida district could ratify his misconduct, express their own opinion as to his innocence, or give him another chance to serve the public.

DEFENSE COSTS

Judges Hastings and Nixon were the first impeached officials to ask the Senate to reimburse their respective defense costs. First, they argued that fundamental fairness required such reimbursement, because, otherwise, the "independence of the judiciary would be compromised if the Congress could simply bulldoze a federal judge off the bench by creating greater defense costs than the judge could meet without pauperizing himself."[74]

Second, they contended that having to spend money to defend their status reduced each person's judicial salary in violation of Article III's guarantee of undiminished compensation. Each of the relevant trial committees decided that it did not have the authority to grant a reimbursement request, nor even to recommend to the full Senate that the latter should grant such a request. The full Senate took no action on either request.[75]

Subsequently, Judge Sporkin denied Hastings' motion for reimbursement of his defense costs. Judge Sporkin explained that "[t]he requirement that a judge's compensation not be diminished during his tenure in office, does not require that the government insulate judges from expenses, especially those involving acts they did not undertake in their official capacity. There is no basis for the plaintiff's claim that he was entitled to have the Senate contribute to his legal fees."[76]

A further argument supporting Judge Sporkin's conclusion is that, even if impeached officials should be reimbursed for their expenditures in defending their status, the Constitution does not compel one branch to pay for expenses incurred in proceedings brought by another, especially when each is acting pursuant to a separate constitutional authorization. If an impeached official could show malicious prosecution, then that individual would have a remedy in the court system. If an official acquitted in the Senate could show that the House erred in impeaching him, then it is unclear why the Senate should have to pay for the House's mistake. By acquitting the individual, the Senate has checked the House's action to the full extent recognized by the Constitution.

Otherwise, the only constitutionally recognized remedy for defects in the impeachment process is political. If the Senate were to acquit, the impeached official could then ask either or both chambers of Congress to reimburse him for his troubles as a matter of good policy. Just as the House and the Senate make special expenditures to cover the costs of their respective impeachment proceedings, each retains the discretion to reimburse the costs of individuals subjected to such proceedings. Under such circumstances, the only other recourse left to an individual injured by defective impeachment proceedings is to turn to the electorate. Ironically, in this sense, Alcee Hastings' election to the House was his only, best revenge.

Chapter Six

MAKING SENSE OF THE FEDERAL
IMPEACHMENT PROCESS

THE PRECEDING CHAPTERS on past impeachment practices have exposed a number of constitutional issues, such as the scope of impeachable offenses or officials. These problems have long defied systematic analysis and divided constitutional scholars and commentators for several reasons. Perhaps most seriously, each of the traditional sources of constitutional decision making, including both the text and history, are often indeterminate on the impeachment issues of contemporary concern. For example, the constitutional text tells us plainly that the House has the power to impeach,[1] the Senate has the power to try impeachments,[2] the president and the vice-president each may be subjected to impeachment for certain reasons,[3] the chief justice must preside in a presidential impeachment,[4] senators must be on oath or affirmation in an impeachment trial,[5] at least two-thirds of the senators present must concur in order to convict an impeached official,[6] and removal and disqualifications are the only punishments the Senate may impose on a convicted official.[7]

Yet, as we have already seen, the constitutional text also does not resolve many questions about the impeachment process. As even the debates among the ratifiers reflected, the text does not clarify which officials, such as members of Congress, are impeachable. The text does not define "officers of the United States."[8] Nor does it clarify the scope of impeachable offenses; the terms "high crimes or misdemeanors"[9] are hardly self-defining. Moreover, Article III's guarantees that federal judges may serve "during good behavior" and may not have their compensation diminished[10] do not definitively answer whether federal judges are impeachable, whether impeachment is the exclusive means for removing them, or whether federal judges may be disciplined for general misbehavior or only for impeachable offenses. Even the constitutional language limiting the punishments the Senate may impose in an impeachment trial[11] does not preclude disputes over whether they may be applied separately or, in the case of disqualification, after an official has left or resigned from office. Moreover, the text does not indicate the preferred order for criminal prosecutions and impeachment proceedings directed against the same official.[12] In yet another place, the text even seems peculiarly silent by providing that the vice-president should preside over all but presidential impeachments,[13] implying that the vice-president may preside over his or her own impeachment trial. In short, the text of the Constitution gives us only limited guidance in trying to answer or resolve the perennial constitutional issues involving the federal impeachment process.

Similarly, history, which is often thought to provide a reliable guide to unclear constitutional language, does not answer all or most of the contemporary concerns about the nature or scope of the impeachment process. Constitutional historians and scholars have long disagreed over the degree to which the original understanding of, and the national government's consistent practices pursuant to, the impeachment clauses are relevant or essential for clarifying them. While the views of the framers' generation are relatively clear as to some questions its members actually discussed in the constitutional convention and ratification campaign, it is unclear how those discussions relate to the proper resolutions of issues they did not discuss in whole or in part. For instance, neither the constitutional convention nor the ratification debates settled whether legislators, including senators, are impeachable; whether the Fifth Amendment due-process clause applies to the impeachment process; or whether challenges to the impeachment process are justiciable. Moreover, even though the delegates at the constitutional convention debated the inclusion of the phrase "other high Crimes and Misdemeanors" in the Constitution, they failed to categorize fully the offenses that it would cover and their discussion does not clearly invoke any contemporary analogue.

The failures of the text and history to provide clear answers to some of the critical questions about the impeachment process have compelled constitutional scholars to look elsewhere for guidance. Typically, their next choice is between two basic approaches to structural reasoning, both of which involve drawing inferences from the government structures and relationships created by the Constitution. First, some scholars have advanced a "formalist" approach that is "premised on the beliefs that the text of the Constitution and the intent of its drafters are controlling and sometimes dispositive, that changed circumstances are irrelevant to constitutional outcomes, and that broader 'policy' concerns should not play a role in legal decisions."[14] This approach is often associated with the view that the Constitution not only grants to each branch distinct powers but also sets forth the maximum degree to which the branches may share those powers. Second, other scholars argue for a "functional" approach to separation of powers cases that focuses on "whether present practices undermine constitutional commitments that should be regarded as central."[15] This approach involves balancing competing values or interests in separation of powers cases.

Yet, it is far from clear that either of these approaches fully clarifies the impeachment process. On the one hand, formalist arguments may be attractive because functionalist debates over government struture often seem to be open-ended and thus easily subject to manipulation and because creativity in construing the text that sets forth the government's mechanisms for checks and balances seems at odds with a fundamental premise of the constitutional framework—that checks and balances are firmly established to preserve our government as one of enumerated or limited powers.[16] Thus, a problem with functional analysis is that it involves the balancing of competing values without offering much of a clear sense grounded in a legitimate source of constitutional authority, such as the text or history, as to what should serve as a tie-breaking or guiding principle. On the other hand, formalism seems limited, at least in part because it heavily relies on the text and history, neither of which, as we have seen, offers clear answers to many of the interpretive questions posed by the impeachment clauses. In short, the structural analysis of the Constitution is limited by doubts about the reliability or authority of its operating premises.

Yet another factor complicating the task of figuring out the precise scope of the constitutional limitations on the federal impeachment power is that the relevant constitutional clauses are not subject to authoritative resolution through the usual processes of constitutional decsion making. This is reflected by the Supreme Court's ruling in *Walter Nixon v. United States*[17] to treat as nonjusticiable any claims regarding the procedural propriety of judicial impeachment trials. In other words, after *Nixon*, debates about constitutional interpretation in the context of the impeachment process are likely to occur without benefit of Supreme Court input.

The challenge of clarifying the federal impeachment process is compounded even further by the fact that ambiguous or vague constitutional language permits an interpreter to use some discretion in choosing among different plausible readings of the relevant text. In making this choice, each interpreter must rely at some point on his or her own values, particularly his or her moral and political judgments on the nature of our system of government. As Stephen Carter has explained,

> The words of the Constitution do not, by themselves, determine everything, and all who must strive to interpret and apply the text . . . must at some point make leaps of faith not wholly explicable by reference to standard tools for interpretation. . . . All [interpretive] questions require judgment in the finding of answers, and in every exercise of interpretive judgment, there comes a crucial moment when the interpreter's own experience and values become the most important data.[18]

In the impeachment context, this phenomenon is no less true.

It is possible, however, to surmount these difficulties in interpreting the impeachment clauses through three steps. First, each interpreter should disclose to the extent possible the values that guide his or her reading of the relevant text. The point is to disclose as much as possible the premises of one's analysis, for the sake of opening all aspects of a constitutional opinion or decision to the fullest discussion possible. With respect to impeachment, my operating assumption is that it is a unique check on executive and judicial abuse of power. This notion of impeachment seems not only common to all relevant sources of constitutional decision but also to work better than any alternative to tie these together.

The second, more complex step, which keeps the first in check, is to identify the limitations of each of the traditional sources of constitutional decision, such as the constitutional text, structure, and history. The point of this second step is to arrive at a construction of the Constitution that reconciles to the fullest extent possible the different sources of constitutional decision. The idea is that each source serves to supplement or reinforce the others. Such reconciliation is important as a means of increasing the odds of arriving at a reading of the relevant text that is persuasive, reliable, and capable of withstanding the test of time.

Of course, the difficulty is that, as we have already seen, the language in the Constitution often raises but does not answer various questions about the scope of a particular constitutional provision or guarantee. Usually, this aspect of the text requires constitutional decsion makers to undertake the formidable task of resolving ambiguities, gaps, or conflicts in the language or design of the Constitution. Such readers may not be confined *by* particular constitutional language, but they are confined *to* the language. In trying to identify which concepts may be consistent or compatible with indeterminate constitutional language, constitutional decsion makers logically turn most often for guidance to history, which may within certain boundaries provide a context to aid understanding of some constitutional provisions—such as the impeachment clauses—that do not explain themselves, particularly to the modern reader.

For example, construing the constitutional language "high crimes and other misdemeanors" requires looking outside the Constitution itself for guidance, but that search is limited to the clarification of those specific terms. History obviously could facilitate that inquiry. Although the meaning of the phrase "other high Crimes and Misdemeanors" is not self-evident, history helps to provide a frame of reference that gives meaning to it. The goal is to use history not as an end in itself but only as an additional guide in the search for the meaning of an ambiguous constitutional provision.

In resorting to history, however, it is important to avoid constructing data that never existed. A critical problem with relying on original understanding is that the framers' silence on the scope of permissible practices pursuant to a broad grant of power to the national government does not mean they necessarily disapproved or sanctioned such practices.[19] Instead, the silence probably means the framers neither conceived nor addressed the particular exercise of power in question and necessarily left subsequent generations to figure out in which form and in which particular ways the national government may exercise such broad authorizations. Thus, there is no obvious reason to concentrate exclusively on the framers' specific views regarding impeachment in figuring out the constitutional implications for impeachment-related issues that the framers did not consider. If the aim is to clarify as much of the text as possible, it may make more sense to consider not only the impeachment clauses, but also those values and policies reflected in other parts of the Constitution that deal with the distribution of analogous governmental power.[20]

The task, at this juncture, is to coordinate the relevant text and history with the Constitution's design. This endeavor requires two additional steps. First, those attempting to interpret the Constitution should identify those aspects of our constitutional scheme of separation of powers that are immutable in the absence of constitutional amendments. Second, they should define and explain how the three branches of government may deal with the mutable aspects of separation of powers.

In defining the immutable aspects of separation of powers, one should keep in mind that separation of powers is a system designed to limit the three branches to their assigned responsibilities so that no one branch may grow too powerful or infringe on individual liberties.[21] The actual scheme of checks and balances in the Constitution is, however, incomplete. The framers defined the checks and balances for each branch only at its apex.[22] They left the task of structuring the lower parts of the branches to subsequent generations because they understood that the demands on government would change over time and realized that an immutable structure of government from top to bottom would hinder progress.[23]

Any deviations from the immutable allocation of powers within the Constitution are plainly unconstitutional.[24] In fact, many of the major debates in separation of powers cases are over the scope of the so-called immutable allocations of power within the Constitution.[25] In such cases, it seems appropriate to use formalist reasoning, because historical evidence, including the framers' views on the relevant principles, is often clear, as reflected in such authoritative materials as the constitutional text, the debates in the constitutional and state ratifying conventions, and the records of the First Congress.

In those instances involving mutable aspects of separation of powers, it may be more appropriate to use functional analysis. In other words, where neither the text nor the original understanding clearly preclude a branch (or an agent thereof) from exercising a certain power, then a functional approach seems appropriate. The latter would require balancing competing interests to provide the national government with some flexibility to resolve new crises and to protect the fundamental values the relevant constitutional structure was established to guarantee. Functional analysis is particularly useful in cases involving the mutable allocation of powers, because the relevant sources, particularly the text and original understanding, are unclear or silent, or could be reasonably read to reflect a preference for flexibility in this area.[26]

Other sources support using functionalism under the latter circumstances. For instance, this approach is consistent with the Supreme Court's practice of adopting functionalism within appropriate boundaries as an expression of its deference to the constitutional interpretations of Congress and to legislative experimentation in structuring government in those instances in which the innovation does not undermine a clear textual prohibition or the values or principles that the original checks and balances were designed to guarantee.[27] Moreover, a functionalist approach also avoids constitutional inertia by preventing the structure at the top from blinding constitutional interpretation to the realities of government and to the possibilities for change not envisioned or addressed by the framers but still consistent with their handiwork. Finally, functionalism avoids unbounded congressional deviations by delineating the outer limits of permissible tinkering with the structure of government short of the amendment process.

To be sure, congressional innovation with constitutionally mutable allocation of powers is not boundless, because the innovation may still violate values or principles that the original allocation of powers was structured to protect and preserve. The framers may have failed to discuss the permissibility of the specific alteration at issue, but the original values embodied in the constitutional structure obviously remain viable. For example, even though neither the text nor the debates in the constitutional and ratifying conventions clearly resolve whether impeachment is the sole constitutional mechanism for disciplining or removing federal judges, any other means for doing the same things still must preserve both collective and individual judicial independence and integrity—the primary goals of Article III's guarantees of life tenure and undiminished compensation for federal judges.[28]

A major concern with functionalist analysis is, however, that it seemingly conflicts with the notion expressed by Chief Justice John Marshall in *McCulloch v. Maryland*[29] that our national government is "one of enumerated powers."[30] To some, this observation means that government is empowered to do only those things it is specifically authorized to perform by the Constitution and that, in the absence of such permission, the government is not licensed to act. Arguably, a functionalist approach stands the concept of enumerated powers on its head by deferring to Congress in those cases in which there are no specific constitutional constraints preventing it from doing so, rather than acknowledging congressional power only when there is a specific constitutional authorization supporting it.

The problem with this argument is that it essentially ignores the holding as well as the significance of *McCulloch* itself. The Court in *McCulloch* never held—nor, for that matter, has the Court ever held—that Congress only has a specific power to do something as long as it is expressly authorized by the Constitution to have such authority. The judgment in *McCulloch* to uphold the constitutionality of the Bank of the United States ultimately rested not just on Chief Justice Marshall's interpretation of the necessary and proper clause[31] but also on his understanding of the more general need to infer certain congressional powers from the unique nature of the Constitution itself. In Marshall's view, interpreting a constitution, particularly in a case involving an issue about the legitimate reach of the new national government's powers,

> requires, that only its great outlines should be marked, its important objects designated, and the minor ingredients which compose those objects be deduced from the nature of the objects themselves. That this idea was entertained by the framers of the American constitution, is not only to be inferred from the nature of the instrument, but from the language. [In] considering [a] question [about the legitimacy of a congressional exercise of power,] we must never forget, that it is a constitution we are expounding.[32]

Marshall's point was that the structure and original understanding of the Constitution indicate that interpreting "a constitution intended to endure for ages to come and, consequently, to be adapted to the various crises of human affairs[,]"[33] requires reading the document broadly to allow Congress some flexibility in effectuating its enumerated powers. This historic view is reinforced, as I have discussed, by subsequent Supreme Court decisions using a balancing approach in separation of powers cases in which there is no clear textual prohibition or original understanding to the contrary.[34]

Moreover, the assumption that the federal courts may preclude Congress from taking advantage of ambiguous or open-ended language, structure, or history in cases involving the mutable allocation of powers ironically violates the notion of a national government of limited powers. In such a government, the federal courts, too, are limited, and one constraint might well be that the federal judiciary is not necessarily empowered to intervene or to overturn the policy decisions or innovations made by the other branches in every separation of powers dispute.[35] Of course, part of the task of constitutional interpretation is to figure out the appropriate times for judicial action and restraint.

The final step in clarifying the constitutional system of impeachment is to understand what, if anything, construing the impeachment clauses suggests about constitutional interpretation in general. Interpreting those provisions demonstrates the limits of superimposing certain theories onto particular constitutional provisions. Common sense suggests that before manipulating a particular constitutional provision to fit a particular theory of constitutional interpretation, it is better first to assess whether a particular constitutional provision is compatible with any preexisting theory of constitutional interpretation. If a theory does not fit or cannot explain the nuances of a particular constitutional provision, then that theory should not be used to explain that particular provision. Constitutional decsion makers and commentators should examine each constitutional provision on its own terms, recognizing the provision's special his torical and structural contexts. Such contextual interpretion necessarily means that interpreting different constitutional provisions depends on different configurations of the relevant sources of constitutional decision.[36] Although this methodology will not make constitutional interpretation as predictable as it would likely be under a theory attempting to organize constitutional law in terms of a single unifying concept, it at least reduces the possibility of distorting or manipulating the Constitution by construing constitutional provisions on their own terms as opposed to the terms of some unrelated theory. Thus, the critical question is whether there is an appropriate guiding principle that is specially suited to interpret one or all of the impeachment clauses or that is common to (or links) other analogous or relevant provisions. As part III demonstrates, the answer brings us full circle: back to the importance of coordinating as many legitimate sources of constitutional decsion making as possible to clarify the particular problem, area, and power(s) involved.

PART III

CLARIFYING THE CONSTITUTIONAL

ASPECTS OF THE FEDERAL

IMPEACHMENT PROCESS

THIS part seeks to resolve some of the perennial constitutional difficulties identified in part II regarding the federal impeachment process. Its five chapters examine in turn the scope of the officials subject to and the punishments available in impeachment proceedings; whether impeachment is the exclusive means for removing or discipling impeachable officials, especially federal judges; the scope of impeachable offenses; the proper procedure for impeachment hearings and trials; and the justiciability of constitutional or other challenges to impeachment procedures or decisions.

These issues require Congress to wrestle with and give meaning to broad constitutional language or authorizations. They also compel Congress to consider the extent to which it is or should be bound by prior congressional interpretations of the Constitution. Consequently, the resolutions of these issues have enormous ramifications for our understandings of the Constitution, the scope of Congress's impeachment authority, and Congress's ability to rise above narrow-minded or short-sighted partisan politics to engage in reasonably principled constitutional interpretation.

Chapter Seven

THE SCOPE OF IMPEACHABLE OFFICIALS

AND APPLICABLE PUNISHMENTS

T HE CONSTITUTION limits the impeachment power to "[t]he President, Vice President and all civil Officers of the United States."[1] A tough interpretive question posed by this provision is which officials qualify as "civil officers of the United States." Even though the Constitution makes no express reference to the removal of federal judges, the constitutional convention assumed,[2] *The Federalist Papers* expressly acknowledged,[3] and the federal government has acted from its inception as if the "civil officers" subject to impeachment include federal judges.[4] Otherwise, neither the text nor the constitutional convention debates addressed the meaning of the phrase "civil officers of the United States." Moreover, the scattered discussion in the ratifying conventions about the scope of impeachable officials settled little, except perhaps for the applicability of the impeachment process to the president, federal judges, and other high-level but otherwise unspecified federal, as opposed to state, officials.

In an effort to define "civil officers of the United States" and therefore the range of impeachable officials, this chapter examines the impeachability of senators and officials who resigned from or left office office at the time of their impeachments. Given that the impeachability of the latter officials depends on the Senate's authority to impose the punishment of disqualification separately (because it would not make sense to remove an official who was no longer in office), this chapter also considers the severability of impeachment sanctions.

THE IMPEACHABILITY OF U.S. SENATORS

Raoul Berger has made the most forceful argument for the impeachability of senators.[5] He contended that the framers were in all probability familiar with the English practice in which "the vast bulk of impeachments" were against members of the House of Lords[6] and that the fact that the state ratifying conventions regarded senators as impeachable is evidenced by their concern over the Senate's being empowered to try its own members.[7]

Yet, constitutional language, structure, and history support different inferences from the framers' familiarity with English impeachment procedures and the state ratifying conventions' debates about the impeachability of senators. First, in three different places, the text of the Constitution suggests that legislators are not officers of the United States and are thus not impeachable. Article II, section 3 provides that the president "shall Commission all the Officers of the United States."[8] Obviously, members of Congress, including senators, are not so commissioned.[9] Moreover, Article 1, section 6 provides that "no person holding any office under the United States shall also be a member of either house during his continuance in office."[10] This clause plainly prohibits someone who has accepted an appointment as an "officer of the United States" from also serving in the House; however, the conflicts it seeks to eliminate can only be avoided if it also bars any member of Congress from accepting a position as an "officer of the United States." Lastly, the appointments clause in Article II, section 2, indicates legislators are not officers of the United States. It speaks of two kinds of federal officers, neither of which likely includes members of Congress. It provides that

> [the President] shall nominate, and by and with the Advice and Consent of the Senate, shall appoint [all] other offices of the United States, whose Appointments are not herein otherwise provided for, and which shall be established by Law; but the Congress may by Law vest the Appointment of such inferior Officers, as they think proper, in the President alone, in the Courts of Law, or in the Heads of Department.[11]

This clause implies that "officers of the United States" are presidentially appointed officials who occupy positions created by Congress; that "inferior Officers" are less important federal officials whose appointments Congress may vest in in certain other, nonlegislative bodies; and that senators, who are not appointed by the president nor occupy positions created by the Congress, do not fit into either category of federal officials.

Bolstering the arguments based on the constitutional text, the constitutional structure also seems to bar the impeachability of members of Congress. Article I, section 5 provides that "each House shall be the Judge of the Elections, Returns and Qualifications of its own Members. . . . Each House may . . . punish its members for disorderly behavior, and, with the concurrence of two thirds, expel a member."[12] It seems illogical for the framers to have given Congress two separate methods by which to punish or remove its members, both of which suffer from the same defect—the unlikely prospect of either chamber deciding to move against one of its own. Alternative or multiple mechanisms for removing legislators might have made sense if each sought to make up for the other's deficiencies, a prospect that expulsion and impeachment fail to achieve. Instead, the expulsion power given to Congress most logically qualifies as Congress's analogue to impeachment for the purposes of disciplining its members.

Moreover, fairly read, the original understanding hardly supports the impeachability of national legislators. Although several ratifiers accepted the impeachability of senators, their arguments met resistance in every instance, including the rejoinder (cutting against Berger's assumption about the framers' knowledge) that there were no known instances of impeachments of legislators.[13]

Even so, the critical question is whether it is reasonable to infer the impeachability of senators from the uniqueness of the punishments available in an impeachment proceeding. In other words, the basic issue is what are the appropriate inferences to draw from the absence of a clear constitutional prohibition against the Senate's exercising expulsion and impeachment powers against its own members and from the inclusion of a punishment unavailable in an expulsion in the impeachment process.

Various sources of constitutional authority suggest that it would be improper to read the Constitution as allowing the Senate to exercise expulsion and impeachment powers against its members. First, the plain meaning of constitutional provisions prohibiting service as both a legislator and officer of the United States and as suggesting "officers of the United States" are presidentially appointed officers (subject to impeachment) in positions created by the Congress, combined with the bizarre prospect of allowing the Senate to have multiple powers to discipline its members, make a strong case against interpreting the Constitution as permitting the Senate to expel and to impeach its members. Second, in relevant precedents, the Supreme Court has consistently construed the phrase "civil officers of the United States" to cover a category of federal officials appointed by the president to offices created by Congress.[14] Third, even though the House of Representatives impeached Senator Blount,[15] the Senate's failure to convict him *and* Congress's subsequently unbroken practice of treating senators as unimpeachable raises a reasonable expectation on the part of national legislators that they are not impeachable and that they may rely on this judgment as presumptively constitutional in the absence of clear evidence to the contrary. Moreover, the suitability of using disqualification to punish otherwise impeachable officials who have resigned or been expelled or forced from office hardly constitutes a sensible or sound basis on which to impeach a senator who is still in office.

The Nature of Impeachment Punishments

This section examines two questions about the constitutional limitations on the available sanctions in impeachment proceedings: whether the Senate may impose the punishments of removal and disqualification separately and, if so, whether the Senate may disqualify a convicted impeachable through a majority vote.

In fact, the Constitution mentions impeachment sanctions in only two places. Article II provides that all civil officers of the United States "shall be removed from Office on Impeachment for, and Conviction of, Treason, Bribery, or other high Crimes and Misdemeanors."[16] The most natural reading of this language seems to provide for a nondiscretionary sanction. If someone is impeached, he or she must be removed from office (assuming of course the person does not first resign).

In Article I, the Constitution further provides, however, that judgment in impeachment cases "shall not extend further than to removal from Office, and disqualification to hold and enjoy any [federal] Office."[17] Reading this language in conjunction with the relevant Article II clause quoted above, a Senate judgment against the civil officer apparently must lead to removal, but the Senate has discretion to impose any bar—permanent, temporary, or none whatsoever—to holding any further office.[18]

In practice, the Senate has followed these readings.[19] It treats the punishment of removal as automatically following from its conviction of an impeachable official by two-thirds vote of the members present. It also has taken the position that it may then, if it sees fit, take a separate vote on whether to impose the sanction of disqualification against the convicted official.

Because the Senate treats removal as the automatic consequence of a two-thirds vote to convict, it obviously regards a two-thirds vote as a prerequisite to the imposition of the punishment of removal. Yet, on each of the two occasions on which the Senate imposed the punishment of disqualification,[20] it did so after a simple majority vote. The Senate defends this practice on its reading of the relevant text as described in the preceding paragraph and on its belief that the officials subjected to a separate disqualification vote are adequately protected from abuse through the requirement of a supermajority vote prior to a conviction and through the political accountability of senators.

The Senate's practice, however, does justice to neither the relevant constitutional text nor structure. First, the fact that removal follows automatically from an impeachment conviction by a two-thirds vote does not suggest anything determinative about the requisite vote for disqualification. The Senate's authority for its custom of conducting different votes is premised on a dubious inference from the facts that the Constitution mentions removal twice, once in connection with a conviction, which admittedly may occur only through a two-thirds vote, and disqualification only once, as one of the two punishments permissible in an impeachable proceeding. Yet, an equally reasonable inference from the relevant text is that, given the framers' expectation that the two-thirds vote requirement would make it less likely for impeached officials to be convicted and punished for improper motives, both punishments should be applied by similar votes. Otherwise, letting a simple majority of the Senate choose to disqualify a convicted official eliminates the important protection the framers sought to provide against intemperate impeachment by empowering at least one-third of the body to check its wanton use. The Senate's current practice precludes a significant number of senators, who would normally have the power to prevent a conviction, from blocking the harsh punishment of disqualification if they saw fit.

THE POSSIBILITY OF POSTRESIGNATION IMPEACHMENT

Since the Senate refused to convict either Senator Blount, who had been expelled from office at the time of his impeachment trial, or Secretary Belknap, who had resigned prior to his impeachment trial,[21] Congress has not brought impeachment actions against any officials after they left office. This practice alone stands as a formidable obstacle to any future attempt to initiate an impeachment against such officials. Yet, there is a surprising consensus among commentators that resignation does not necessarily preclude impeachment and disqualification.[22]

In fact, Congress's practice of not pursuing the impeachments of officials who have left office can be explained more easily as an expression of Congress's judgment that impeaching such officials is not worth the political costs involved rather than as an outcome dictated by constitutional history, text, and design. First, Congress's practice of not impeaching officials no longer in office "has no substantial historical foundation and is not supported by a single authoritative and unequivocal decision of recent times."[23] Prior to the constitutional convention, Parliament and several states allowed impeachment of officials no longer in office. For example, several constitutional convention delegates acknowledged that in April 1787 the House of Commons had voted to impeach Warren Hastings for improprieties he had committed as the governor-general of India, a position from which he had resigned two years earlier.[24] Moreover, the delegates at the constitutional convention indicated no intention of abandoning the English practice or the provisions of many state constitutions, such as those of Virginia and Delaware, that allowed postresignation impeachments.[25]

Second, the Constitution does not restrict the time at which an impeachment proceeding may be brought and includes language consistent with impeachments after departures from office. Although Article II refers to all civil officers, this reference means only that those who are still civil officers at the time of conviction of the impeachment must be *removed*. Article I does not refer to "all civil Officers" and provides only a limitation on the penalty in an impeachment proceeding rather than a limitation on jurisdiction.[26] According to the conventional rule of constitutional analysis, which gives meaning to each word of the Constitution, the inclusion of both present removal and future disqualification as penalties for impeachment suggests that they are two separate penalties that may be separately applied. If the punishments may be levied apart, there is no logical impediment to Congress's attempting to disqualify, whenever it chooses, someone who is or was a civil officer of the United States.

Third, the delegates at the constitutional convention seemed to accept that impeachment may take place after departure from office. On the only occasion when the timing of impeachment was discussed at the convention, most delegates proceeded as if the president would be impeachable after he left office.[27] The question that preoccupied the delegates was whether the president should also be impeachable while in office. By a vote of eight to two, the convention made the President impeachable while in office, without giving the slightest indication that this action constituted any grant of immunity after leaving office.[28]

Shortly after the convention, two prominent commentators took the position that resignation or departure from office did not preclude impeachment. In *Federalist No. 39*, James Madison compared the impeachment provisions of Virginia and Delaware with those in the new Constitution, stressing that the latter extended, rather than curtailed, the liability of the president by denying him immunity "during his continuance in office."[29] Similarly, in 1846, long after he had left the White House, John Quincy Adams declared on the floor of Congress that "I hold myself, so long as I have the breath of life in my body, amenable to impeachment by this House for everything I did during the time I held any public office."[30]

The critical element guiding the timing of impeachments is that the checks regarding impeachment ultimately are political, not constitutional. No doubt, there are numerous reasons not to move for impeachment against an official after resignation, but none of these are constitutionally mandated. For example, Congress may well figure that political support for a postresignation impeachment is unlikely or that such a proceeding would be futile, unnecessary, or unduly harsh.

Justice Story made perhaps the best-known argument in favor of "confining the impeaching power to persons holding office" by stressing that the framers did not intend for any private citizens to be subjected to impeachment,[31] but his argument was misplaced. In context, Justice Story appeared to be concerned primarily with distinguishing the American impeachment practice from the contemporaneous British practice, which allowed impeachment against private citizens, including all peers and commoners.[32] Moreover, one can accommodate Justice Story's concern without going so far as to argue that postresignation impeachment is impermissible. By subjecting only the president, the vice-president, and "officers of the United States" to impeachment, the constitutional language itself makes clear that the framers rejected impeachment against private citizens for acts done as such,[33] but allowed impeachment of private citizens for misconduct relating to or previously committed during their occupancies of certain offices.[34]

Chapter Eight

IMPEACHMENT AS THE SOLE MEANS OF
DISCIPLINING AND REMOVING
IMPEACHABLE OFFICIALS

A PERENNIAL QUESTION is whether impeachment is the only means of removing "all Civil Officers of the United States," including federal judges. This issue raises two basic problems involving the extent to which (1) one branch of the federal government may discipline or remove the members of another branch and (2) the members in a branch have removal power over other members in the same branch.

THE REMOVAL POWER OF ONE BRANCH OVER THE MEMBERS OF ANOTHER BRANCH

Removal authority is a critical element of separation of powers. Whoever exercises the power to remove may also be able to control the actions of the officials subject to it. For example, the impeachment power enables Congress to exercise extraordinary influence over federal judges, the president, and other high-ranking executive officials. This power is particularly intimidating to federal judges, because they have been the targets of its exercise more than any other class of impeachable officials, they do not have any comparable power over members of Congress, and they lack the means available to the president (or those of his subordinates he chooses to defend) to ward off an impeachment, such as the bully pulpit or the granting of political favors. If, however, impeachment is the sole means by which the political branches may discipline or remove federal judges, then the members of the judiciary at least may feel more secure from the partisan retaliation or arbitrary dismissals they might otherwise suffer.

Judicial Tenure, Discipline, and Removal

The issue of whether impeachment is the sole or exclusive means of disciplining or removing a federal judge requires clarifying (1) the nature of judicial tenure and (2) the propriety of disciplining or removing a federal judge through some means other than by an impeachment. I consider each of these related problems in turn.

THE RELATIONSHIP BETWEEN THE GOOD BEHAVIOR CLAUSE
AND THE IMPEACHMENT PROCESS

Defining the nature of judicial tenure requires reconciling the impeachment clauses with the constitutional provision that federal judges "shall hold their Offices during good Behavior."[1] This effort leads one to ask whether misconduct that would not constitute an impeachable offense might still violate the "good Behavior" standard and thus subject a federal judge to removal or at least discipline through some process other than impeachment. This issue arises because the Article III formula could sensibly be read either as (1) setting a substantive standard of conduct on which judicial tenure is contingent, or as (2) employing an eighteenth-century term of art to signal that federal judges shall hold tenure for life unless impeached and, thus, that the good behavior clause itself does not establish a separate or independent basis for removal other than those specified in the impeachment clauses.[2]

The second reading essentially takes the position that the impeachment and good behavior clauses together mean that the life tenure of a federal judge may be prematurely interrupted only by an impeachment for the commission of an impeachable offense, not misbehavior of just any kind. The first reading is that those clauses provide that federal judges may serve for life, subject to removal either through impeachment for having committed an impeachable offense *or* through impeachment and possibly some other means of removal for having engaged in misbehavior not rising to the level of an impeachable offense. In effect, the latter view is that, because federal judges are removable for misbehavior including but not limited to the commission of impeachable offenses, they may be ousted under a looser standard than other impeachable officials, whom Congress may remove only by impeachment for "Treason, Bribery, or other high Crimes or Misdemeanors."[3]

The major problem with the latter reading of the good behavior and the impeachment clauses is that it is less consistent than is the former with relevant constitutional history and structure. First, the framers included the phrase "during good Behavior" in the Constitution to contrast the unlimited term of federal judges with the fixed terms for the president, vice-president, and members of Congress.[4] Under the more historically accurate view of the good behavior clause, federal judges with unfixed terms and high-level officials with fixed terms may have their terms of office ended prematurely if there is a Senate conviction for "Treason, Bribery, or other high Crimes and Misdemeanors." In this sense, the phrase "during good behavior" is a term of art primarily describing the length of a federal judge's tenure.

Second, it was generally accepted during and after the constitutional convention that federal judges should have life tenure and that such status was crucial to the independence of the federal judiciary.[5] The delegates at the convention never abandoned their desire to eliminate the problem they had experienced in the colonies of having judges who were dismissed unless they did what the king told them to do. Such judges rarely had the courage of their convictions. In Article III, the framers solved this problem by guaranteeing federal judges life tenure and undiminished compensation, measures that the framers considered integral to securing the judiciary's place in the new national government's system of checks and balances. The framers recognized that life tenure and irreducible compensation were indispensable if federal judges were to have the freedom to exercise truly independent judicial review. As Alexander Hamilton explained, the federal judiciary needed special status to serve as a necessary bulwark against legislative aggrandizement and the tyranny of the majority.[6] The framers envisioned the federal courts as a safe haven for people trying to protect their civil liberties against actions by either the president or Congress. There never was any serious question at, during, or after the constitutional convention that the judiciary's role in the new system of checks and balances would be to protect the people themselves from the excesses of other branches. To achieve that end, the framers sought to insulate federal judges from political reprisals for unpopular decisions by narrowing the bases for judicial removal to "high crimes and misdemeanors" rather than to the more broadly phrased "provisions of the seven states constitutions that provided for impeachment, five of which made 'maladministration' a ground of impeachment, while New York proceeded for 'malconduct' and North Carolina for 'misbehavior.'"[7] As Madison warned, "so vague a term [as maladministration] will be equivalent to a tenure during pleasure of the Senate."[8] In short, "no evidence exists that the framers desired to compromise the independence of federal judges by making it easier to remove them."[9]

The original understanding of the framers and ratifiers regarding the good behavior and impeachment clauses reflects the founders' common perception that impeachment is the only mechanism with which the elected branches are empowered to remove federal judges.[10] It is far less clear whether the founders intended to preclude altogether judiciary-dependent mechanisms for judicial discipline or those methods that the elected branches cannot fully execute because the judiciary itself must play an important role in their implementation.[11]

In fact, there were three models of judicial discipline with which the framers were familiar.[12] They were aware of systems within the states and in England under which judges could be removed by the executive at will,[13] by the executive upon "address" from the legislature,[14] or by legislative bodies through impeachment.[15] The susceptibility of judges to discharge at the whim of the Stuart monarchs had been a major grievance among the English in the seventeenth century.[16] The colonists expressed their own displeasure over the vulnerability of their judges to removal at the king's pleasure in the Declaration of Independence.[17] Indeed, many colonists envied the terms of judicial tenure—"during good Behavior"— used in the Act of Settlement, which the Parliament devised at the turn of the century to provide life tenure for judges in England.[18]

The constitutional convention considered and rejected the second political mechanism for judicial removal—legislative address to the executive—which had been used in four states (as opposed to the six states that provided for impeachment).[19] On August 27, 1787, Delaware's John Dickinson proposed that judges be removeable by the executive "on the application by the Senate and House of Representatives."[20] Dickinson's proposal tracked the typical system of address, which consisted of a formal request made by a legislature to a chief executive, asking him to agree to the removal of a judge. Legislatures and executives were not necessarily constrained in their reasons for making or responding to an address. After brief debate, the motion failed by a vote of one in favor, three abstentions, and seven opposed. Gouverneur Morris, John Rutledge, and Edmund Randolph explicitly opposed the motion as inconsistent with the intended independence of the judiciary.[21]

Moreover, many commentators at or around the time of the Constitution's drafting and ratification referred to impeachment as the only means by which the political branches could remove judges. For example, Alexander Hamilton argued that the "article respecting impeachments" in the Constitution was the "only provision on the point which is consistent with the necessary independence of the judicial character, and is the only one which we find in our Constitution in respect to our own judges."[22] The Anti-Federalist essayist Brutus agreed that the "only causes" for which federal judges could "be displaced" would be impeachable offenses.[23]

Both the relevant text and original understanding support viewing impeachment as the only political means for judicial removal.[24] The Constitution erected and the framers understood the federal impeachment process as a highly deliberative, cumbersome decision-making mechanism. It defies common sense for the framers to have taken great pains to have purposefully designed such an awkward system for remedying judicial misconduct but then implicitly left Congress and the president free to remove judges on identical or more lenient grounds through some other, nonspecified, more efficient devices.

Moreover, this conclusion is consistent with analogous Supreme Court opinions on separation of powers. For example, the Court has described impeachment as the only mechanism by which Congress may remove executive officers.[25] The Court has also determined that allowing Congress to exercise any other direct control over the removal of executive officers would give Congress too much dominion over the exercise of executive power,[26] even though this control would have been over policy matters on which legislative influence is ordinarily considered to be proper. As Peter Shane has explained, "[g]iven that the legitimate purview of congressional politics is presumably narrower in adjudication than in executive administration, it is inconceivable that the Court would permit Congress to exercise a greater role in dismissing judges than it performs in supervising executive officers."[27]

With respect to structural analysis, formalist separation of powers theory, drawing on relatively unambiguous original understanding, argues in favor of protecting judicial independence by prohibiting political mechanisms for judicial discipline other than impeachment. The framers clearly intended separation of powers to preclude any possibility of adjudication by Congress except in cases of impeachment.[28] Moreover, the exercise of direct influence over the judiciary by the executive except through the expressly conferred powers of appointment and faithful enforcement of the laws—that is, prosecution—would clearly have frustrated the framers' desire, reflected as early as the Revolutionary Constitutions, to divide executive and legislative powers.[29] The framers sought such separation to protect the people from judges who "might behave with violence and oppression."[30] In other words, "[t]he obvious potential for subjugation of the judiciary that would result from placing disciplinary power over judges in the hands of the Executive alone would manifest an abuse about which the founders were self-consciously and explicitly concerned."[31] Hence, any proposal for subjecting federal judges to removal at the whim of the president or Congress through some means other than impeachment plainly violates immutable principles of separation of powers limiting the political branches' removal of federal judges.

THE CONSTITUTIONALITY OF JUDICIARY-DEPENDENT MECHANISMS FOR JUDICIAL DISCIPLINE AND REMOVAL

There are four judiciary-dependent mechanisms for disciplining or removing federal judges that have been used at some point in American history: (1) the Bribery Act of 1790,[32] which automatically disqualified any federal judge convicted of bribery; (2) the indictment, prosecution, conviction, and imprisonment of executive officials or federal judges prior to their impeachments; (3) Judicial Councils, operating pursuant to the judiciary's claimed inherent administrative authority over the operations of the federal courts; and (4) the Judicial Disability Act of 1980, which established a process within the judiciary for investigating and disciplining federal district and circuit court judges for certain kinds of misconduct. This section considers the permissibility of the first two of these methods, while the constitutionality of the other two are considered in the next section on judicial self-regulation.

The absence of any relatively clear textual mandate or original understanding on the legitimacy of judiciary-dependent removal mechanisms permits a more flexible or functionalist analysis of their constitutionality. The framers said virtually nothing about whether the criminal prosecution of an impeachable official should take place before or after his or her impeachment.[33] Moreover, even though the writ of *scire facias* was available at common law as a judicially operated mechanism for removing judges for misbehavior,[34] there is no indication the framers intended to include that writ within the "judicial power" conferred by Article III.[35] Thus, one must be prepared to make reasonable inferences from other sources, such as the structure of the Constitution and precedent, in trying to determine the legitimacy of judiciary-dependent modes of judicial discipline.

The Constitutionality of Pre-Impeachment Criminal Prosecutions.   In recent years, pre-impeachment criminal prosecutions of impeachable officials have occurred under two different systems. The Independent Counsel Act[36] permits the appointment of a special prosecutor to prosecute certain high-level executive officials, including the president. Otherwise, federal judges have been prosecuted since Watergate by Justice Department lawyers from the Public Integrity Section of the Justice Department.[37] I consider below the constitutionality of each kind of criminal prosecution.

CRIMINAL PROSECUTIONS OF FEDERAL JUDGES.   The textual argument against pre-impeachment criminal prosecutions of federal judges is based on Article I, section 3, clause 7, which provides that "[j]udgment in cases of impeachment shall not extend further than to removal from office and disqualification to hold and enjoy any office of honor, trust or profit under the United States; but the party convicted shall nevertheless be liable and subject to indictment, trial, judgment and punishment, according to law."[38] The specific reference to the criminal liability of a "party convicted" has been read by some as implying that the "cases of impeachment" to which the prior clause refers need always precede prosecution. At least superficially, the provision would not be limited to federal judges but would treat prosecutions of sitting judges or other impeachable officials identically. Even so, the problem with allowing pre-impeachment prosecutions and imprisonments is particularly serious with respect to federal judges, because the constitutional guarantees of life tenure and undiminished compensation militate in favor of allowing them to continue receiving their salaries until such time as they are formally removed from office.

Construing the Constitution as barring pre-impeachment prosecutions of federal judges is problematic for three reasons. First, the operative language could also be construed as merely anticipating (but not requiring) that impeachments would precede criminal prosecutions but that, regardless of the order in which they proceed, an impeachable official may be subjected to both in appropriate cases. Second, the Bribery Act of 1790 conceivably reflects the understanding of the First Congress—commonly regarded as representative of the framers' generation—that criminal prosecutions could occur prior to impeachment proceedings, because it is premised on such a sequence.[39] Third, reading the pertinent constitutional language as mandating that impeachments must precede criminal prosecutions would produce some odd results, such as barring any criminal prosecution of an impeached judge who was acquitted on facts that would support a criminal conviction.[40]

Perhaps an even more serious problem with this reading is that it conflicts with the original understanding of the relationship between impeachments and criminal prosecutions and relevant precedents.[41] The framers did not regard impeachment and the criminal law as serving the same ends. The function of the first half of paragraph 7 is to signal the framers' intention to distinguish the American system from the British practice, under which it was permissible to impose criminal sanctions in an impeachment. The second half of paragraph 7 of Article I, section 3 clarifies further that the exclusion of criminal sanctions from the impeachment process separates impeachment from criminal law, but does not immunize impeachable or impeached officials from criminal prosecution.

On three separate occasions, federal appellate courts have adopted this latter construction of Article I, section 3, and rejected arguments that impeachment of federal judges must precede their indictment, prosecution, and conviction and imprisonment. The claimants in these cases maintained that indictment, prosecution, and imprisonment of a federal judge should be prohibited prior to an impeachment because the targeted judge is effectively removed in violation of the constitutional principle that impeachment is the only constitutionally permissible means of removing federal judges.

United States v. Isaacs[42] was the first case in which a defendant claimed that indictment prior to impeachment was tantamount to removal without an impeachment conviction. Denying Judge Otto Kerner's application to stay his prosecution for criminal activities committed before he had entered judicial office, the Seventh Circuit in *Isaacs* explained that "[p]rotection of tenure is not a license to commit crime or a forgiveness of crimes committed before taking office."[43] The court also rejected the argument that judicial independence could only be protected by recognizing impeachment as the only means by which to punish judicial misconduct, because judicial independence "is better served when criminal charges against [judges] are tried in a court rather than in Congress. With a court trial, a judge is assured of the protections given to all those charged with criminal conduct."[44]

More recently, in *United States v. Claiborne*,[45] the Ninth Circuit rejected Judge Claiborne's claim that his conviction *and* imprisonment prior to his impeachment were unconstitutional because they violated the constitutional ban against judicial removal through any means other than impeachment.[46] Judge Claiborne buttressed his claim with three arguments. First, he argued that the "Party convicted" language in Article I, section 3, clause 7, presupposes that any disruption of a federal judge's life tenure should occur first through impeachment and only later through criminal prosecution; otherwise, the past tense "convicted" has no meaning.[47] The problem with this reading is that it conflicts with the framers' view of impeachment and criminal proceedings as separate actions unfolding in no particular sequence.

Second, Claiborne argued that prosecuting judges subjects them to a level of intimidation that violates their independence.[48] In his view, even if one were exonerated, the rigors and expense of a criminal investigation are so great as to give the executive leverage over federal judges. To be sure, there is little doubt that the vulnerability of sitting judges to criminal prosecution potentially could compromise judicial independence by effectively subjugating judges to the political branches. Indeed, the ability of federal prosecutors to use criminal investigations or prosecutions to pressure or intimidate federal judges hostile to the administration is well documented.[49]

The problem with this second argument is that judicial independence is not the only constitutional value relevant to judicial performance. The framers also sought to secure judicial integrity. In fact, every federal court ever asked to consider the constitutionality of pre-impeachment prosecutions of federal judges has deemed the impropriety of placing judges "above the law" to be the dominant constitutional value involved.[50] In other words, these courts concluded that judicial vulnerability to criminal prosecution prior to impeachment does less to compromise judicial independence than immunity does to undermine legal accountability.[51]

Claiborne's final argument was that imprisoning him while he was still a federal judge effectively removed him from office.[52] He maintained that his pre-impeachment imprisonment skirted the constitutionally man-

dated procedural safeguards for removal and created a "constitutional
. . . collision between two branches of our government" by compelling an
Article III judge "to surrender to the custody of the attorney general, an
officer of the executive branch; . . . [and to] be confined outside his district, disenabled from performing judicial functions."[53] This argument
rests on the belief that life tenure means that "a judge has judicial authority unless and until that power is stripped by congressional impeachment."[54] According to Claiborne, Congress alone has been charged with
judicial removal; therefore, the attorney general's bypass of the impeachment process violated separation of powers principles.[55] He concluded
further that because criminal prosecution necessarily presupposes the potential for imprisonment (a de facto removal from office), prosecution
must be prohibited.

The Ninth Circuit found an unusual basis on which to reject Judge
Claiborne's third argument that impeachment of federal judges must precede their prosecution and imprisonment. Maintaining that "federal
judges [may] be removed from office only by impeachment," the court
reasoned that because the Seventh Circuit had ruled in *Isaacs* that criminal prosecution and conviction of a senator does not ipso facto "vacate
the seat of the convicted Senator, nor compel the Senate to expel him or
to regard him as expelled by force alone of the judgment," neither were
judges automatically removed "by force alone of the judgment."[56]

Critics of *Claiborne* find this analogy unpersuasive because they do not
believe it definitively answers the question of whether imprisonment (as
opposed to conviction) prior to impeachment is constitutionally permissible.[57] In addition, they argue, the analogy disregards the key protections
uniquely conferred upon the judiciary collectively and individually.
Claiborne critics contend that the protections accorded by Article III to
ensure that judicial independence require that judges must be treated differently for purposes of criminal prosecution and imprisonment. In sum,
these critics argue that in the area of criminal prosecution and imprisonment, senators are not analogous to judges, because senators lack an
equivalent of judicial independence.

The latter contention, though, does not comport with constitutional
structure or history. First, just as judges are protected in their official
status by Article III's guarantee of judicial independence, senators enjoy
immunity for their official acts through the speech and debate clause.[58]
Neither judicial independence nor the speech and debate clause, however,
protect judges or senators, respectively, from prosecution for violating
the criminal law.[59] In effect, the *Claiborne* critics contend that judges
should have a special immunity from criminal prosecution until they are
impeached, but there is no textual support for such an argument. The
concept of judicial independence protects judges *only as judges*. Judges

may have the power to interpret the criminal law, but their official status does not immunize them from complying with it.

Second, imprisonment is not the same as removal. Imprisoned judges retain their titles, salaries, pensions, benefits, and, most importantly, their ability to return to the bench with full authority to decide cases and controversies.[60] No doubt, imprisonment is an impediment to exercising the duties of a federal judge, but it does not have the same permanent or functional consequences as removal and disqualification pursuant to impeachment conviction. In fact, the term *removal* had a specific, formal meaning in 1789, limited to the termination of one's tenure in office.[61] In light of various references made in public documents at or around 1787 strongly indicating that the framers did not equate criminal liability with removal, Stephen Burbank has concluded that "[i]n the case of 'removal from office,' the framers had in mind the formal termination of a commission or of tenure in office. Yes, they were very concerned about judicial independence and yes, the Constitution should be interpreted so as to accommodate situations unforeseen and unforeseeable in 1787. But criminal proceedings were not a threat to judicial independence unknown to the framers, and . . . they were not a threat the framers deemed serious enough to foreclose."[62]

CRIMINAL PROSECUTION OF HIGH-RANKING EXECUTIVE OFFICIALS.   Anxiety over prosecution of impeachable executive officials as constituting an illegitimate bypass of the impeachment process reached its climax in *Morrison v. Olson*.[63] There, the Court considered whether the Independent Counsel Act[64] was unconstitutional because it enabled Congress to assert pressure on the president—pressure that the Constitution permits only through the impeachment power. According to the solicitor general, the act was a congressional attempt "to bypass the impeachment process that the Framers designed to [ensure] that high officers of government could be investigated and removed from power."[65] In the same vein, Justice Scalia in dissent suggested "[h]ow much easier for Congress, instead of accepting the political damage attendant to the commencement of the impeachment proceedings against the president on trivial grounds . . . simply to trigger a debilitating criminal investigation of the Chief Executive under this law."[66]

There are three reasons supporting the *Morrison* Court's rejection of the characterization of the act as an illegitimate bypass of impeachment. First, Congress has no power under the act to "trigger" an investigation by a special prosecutor.[67] The act gives the attorney general unreviewable discretion to deny any request by Congress to initiate an investigation.[68] Indeed, Congress has the same power under the act to request an investigation by the attorney general as it would have in the absence of the statute to informally pressure the attorney general to commence an investigation. In addition, although the act requires that the special prosecutor turn over evidence that Congress could then use as grounds for an impeachment, the act is not an expansion of congressional power to impeach because it is merely a reporting device rather than a substitute for an impeachment proceeding.

Second, the provisions in the act authorizing investigation and prosecution of impeachable executive officials are neither novel nor unique. Federal prosecution of impeachable officials within the executive branch did not begin with the Independent Counsel Act. Federal prosecutors in the Justice Department have prosecuted impeachable officers, such as federal judges, for years. If those prosecutions are not unconstitutional bypasses of the impeachment process, it is difficult to conceive how the prosecutions of other impeachable officials could be. In addition, prior to enactment of the Independent Counsel Act, the president and the attorney general frequently named special prosecutors pursuant to regulations or statutes that put constraints on their removal by the president.[69] In short, the act does not interfere with the impeachment process any more than these various law enforcement schemes, whose constitutionality has never been seriously challenged.

Third, the act and impeachment are not directed at the same class of individuals. The class subject to investigation under the act is both broader and narrower than the class of officers subject to impeachment. The act covers a broader range of officials than impeachable officials because it requires the appointment of a special prosecutor to investigate former senior administration officials, senior officials of the president's political campaign, and any other person with whom the Justice Department has a conflict of interest. Conversely, only certain high-ranking executive officials are impeachable. The scope of the act is narrower in the sense that, absent an extraordinary finding of a conflict of interest, it does not apply to most government officers, including those in the executive branch, whereas the impeachment power by its terms applies to "all Civil Officers of the United States," including federal judges.

The Constitutionality of the Bribery Act of 1790.   Ironically, the First Congress suggested its own solution to the problem of imprisoned federal judges continuing to receive their salaries by passing the Bribery Act of 1790, which automatically disqualified any federal judge convicted of bribery. The constitutionality of this act has, however, confounded scholars for years. For one thing, the act was never enforced.[70] Nor does it have any legislative history illuminating the motives of its drafters or the specific problems the First Congress was trying to resolve by enacting it.

Nevertheless, the Bribery Act could be justified as the First Congress's reasonable attempt to achieve one or both of at least two legitimate objectives by combining its powers under the necessary and proper[71] and the impeachment clauses. First, the First Congress might have been trying to clarify the impeachment procedure established in the Constitution by categorically declaring that a conviction in federal court for one of the impeachable offenses specifically listed in the Constitution—bribery—always justifies disqualifying a federal judge from office. In other words, the act might reflect Congress's expression of its intent to conduct impeachment trials for any federal judges convicted of bribery when it was convinced that it would disqualify any such judges. This conclusion would have no bearing, however, on the permissibility of statutory removal or disqualification for any other crime besides treason, the one other ground for impeachment that the Constitution specifically mentions.

Second, the First Congress might have been delegating some of its impeachment authority to criminal juries in a manner designed to work to the advantage of federal judges. Although the framers had taken great pains in the Constitution to distinguish impeachment proceedings from criminal trials,[72] the First Congress might have passed the act of 1790 with the expectation that the values of judicial independence and integrity normally protected through the supermajority vote required in an impeachment trial would be more than adequately protected through the special procedural safeguards unique to criminal proceedings. In a typical impeachment proceeding, the targeted official is usually not entitled to the kinds of elaborate procedural safeguards applicable in criminal proceedings.[73]

Moreover, the First Congress might have viewed the delegation entailed in the act as constitutional because it rested on the idea that judges are not immune from the criminal law. Such a notion does not threaten judicial independence because the Bribery Act of 1790 was not directed at any essential judicial activity. Rather, the act focused on judicial misconduct that violated a specific criminal law. The constitutional duties of a federal judge do not require or necessitate any kind of criminal misconduct. In other words, the First Congress might have believed that the act did not threaten judicial independence, because it did not punish or prohibit federal judges for any conduct central to the performance of their constitutional obligations.

Nevertheless, two objections to the constitutionality of the Bribery Act of 1790 merit special consideration. First, as Walter Dellinger has suggested, the constitutionality of the Bribery Act of 1790 should be evaluated in terms of whether it is any more legitimate than a statute that automatically disqualified the president or the vice-president once they were convicted in federal court of criminal misconduct equivalent to an impeachable offense.[74] Based on the premise that impeachment is the sole means of disciplining and removing the president, vice-president, and all federal judges, Dellinger's contention is that such a statute applied to the president and vice-president would be plainly unconstitutional, because it would substantially disrupt the administration of justice and domestic tranquility; deprive the president and the vice-president of the special securities of an impeachment proceeding, such as a supermajority vote of the Senate prior to a conviction; and redefine the balance of power at the top of our government. A similar statute directed at federal judges would, in Dellinger's opinion, likewise be unconstitutional, because it would deprive judges of the unique protections available in an impeachment for ensuring judicial independence, including the chance to give Congress reasons not to remove if it sees fit.

Although intriguing, Dellinger's argument is flawed. As I have previously suggested, impeachment is the sole *political* means for disciplining and removing federal judges, whereas judiciary-dependent mechanisms for judicial discipline, such as the Bribery Act of 1790, might be constitutional as long as they do not violate the special values Article III sought to guarantee. Given that the Bribery Act of 1790 could reasonably be read as subjecting federal judges in limited circumstances to disqualification in a forum in which they could take advantage of greater procedural safeguards than those available in impeachment trials, the act does not necessarily conflict with separation of powers, at least in cases involving federal district and circuit court judges. If Supreme Court justices were subjected to this statute, a different situation might occur, because they operate, like the president and the vice-president, at the apex of their respective branch. Consequently, separation of powers concerns are at their most sensitive in those instances in which the removal, disqualification, and disciplining of the most powerful federal judicial officers are at stake.

Moreover, subjecting the president or vice-president to similar legislation poses different or heightened separation of powers concerns: they occupy unique positions under the Constitution as the top two officials in the executive branch; and it is especially important to preserve their relationship with, and status vis-à-vis, the other branches by limiting the means by which they may be disciplined, removed, and disqualified by the impeachment process. Also, the automatic disqualifications of the president or vice-president would certainly produce political repercussions that no forum could reasonably diffuse, except for the impeachment process in which the key decision makers are not only politically accountable but also amenable to considering the legal *and* political consequences of their decisions.[75]

The second objection to the constitutionality of the Bribery Act of 1790 is that one of the specific safeguards set forth in the Constitution for the disqualification of federal judges is that at least two-thirds of senators must agree on the propriety of a conviction and the imposition of such a penalty. The statute, which needs only a majority vote of both the House and the Senate for passage, would deprive an impeached official of the constitutional safeguard of allowing formal disqualification only through a supermajority vote of the Senate. In other words, upholding the constitutionality of this statute would allow a majority of the Congress to defeat or frustrate the power guaranteed to at least one-third of the Senate to defeat whenever it saw fit a conviction or the imposition of the punishment of disqualification.

There are two possible responses to this latter complaint. First, the two-thirds requirement might restrict only the Senate's imposition of the punishment of disqualification in the aftermath of an impeachment trial. An alternative disciplinary mechanism, such as the Bribery Act's reliance on juries in criminal trials, might be constitutional as long as that system protected the values the original structure was designed to safeguard. Second, if the Bribery Act of 1790 were narrowly construed to represent nothing more than the First Congress's declaration that any federal judge convicted of bribery deserved automatic disqualification, then it would be consistent with a strict reading of the two-thirds concurrence of the Senate as a prerequisite to any judicial disqualification formally understood. Under this construction, the statute merely expresses the attitude of a majority of Congress about what Congress is likely to do in an impeachment proceeding against a federal judge convicted of bribery and leaves to Congress the responsibility for ultimately bringing, when it sees fit, an appropriate impeachment proceeding.

In any event, it is not insignificant that, as circumstances developed, the First Congress never expressed its understanding of the act, nor was the act ever enforced. It is unlikely any future Congress would be any more willing to pass a similar statute in light of its uncertain constitutionality and the political fallout its use would surely engender by circumventing the procedures set forth in the Constitution for judicial disqualification through impeachment.

Each Branch's Removal Powers over Its Own Members

Easy Removal Cases

The judiciary has the least power of any of the three branches to discipline and remove its own members. The Constitution expressly grants to each chamber of Congress the power to expel its respective members for "disorderly conduct."[76] Although the Constitution provides for the impeachment, removal, and disqualification of certain officials in the executive branch by the Congress, there is little doubt that executive officers may be removed in ways other than impeachment. For example, under the doctrine of *Myers v. United States*[77] and *Humphrey's Executor v. United States*,[78] the president, incident to his power to appoint and to his constitutional duty to faithfully execute the laws, may remove subordinate officers who perform executive functions and who are also subject to impeachment. Other executive or quasi-executive officials who are not appointed by the president are removable by the person or agency[79] entrusted with their appointment, subject to the regulations of Congress.[80]

The powers of Congress and the president over the removal of the members of their respective departments provide useful insights into whether the judiciary has the power to remove its members. First, if legislators are not impeachable officers, then the fact that Congress has the power to expel its own members for "disorderly conduct" sheds no light on the propriety of allowing judges to remove other judges. The Constitution explicitly grants the political branches only one method—expulsion—for removing legislators.

Second, a reasonable assumption is that if the framers desired the members of one branch to have the power to remove other similarly situated or equally powerful members in the same branch, then the framers would have made this desire explicit. Explicitly granting Congress expulsion power over its own members suggests that Congress would not have had this power absent a constitutional grant. Likewise, the absence of any grant of similar expulsion power to the judiciary raises the inference that federal judges do not have an impeachment-like power to remove each other, precisely because the Constitution fails to grant this power.

In the executive branch, the president's removal power extends to subordinates, but they are not his equals in a constitutional or practical sense: they serve in the federal government to assist him in discharging *his* constitutional duties.[81] Yet, in a different branch in which all members have similar tenure and wield the same kind of power as every other member of that branch, the Constitution seems to grant self-disciplining authority only explicitly. In short, the framers may have felt that a grant of such removal power by some members of Congress over equally powerful members of the same branch was so unusual and potentially divisive that it required explicit constitutional authorization.

Third, judges differ from the president, Congress, and other members of the legislative and executive branches, because only the federal judiciary has life tenure. Of course, life tenure alone does not suggest that federal judges are removable only by impeachment. It does suggest, however, that federal officials with radically different tenure from the president and members of Congress may well have to be treated differently *for removal purposes.* The question is whether popularly elected and life-tenured officials should be treated the same under the Constitution for purposes of removal.

Morrison demonstrates that the rationale for presidential removal of impeachable officers performing executive functions does not apply to judicial removal of judges. The president needs removal power to ensure that his subordinates uniformly apply the laws, protect the civil liberties of all citizens, and enforce the laws faithfully. In contrast, the federal judiciary does not need removal authority to ensure that each judge performs his or her constitutional duty. Judicial review exists to provide protection against mistaken interpretations or applications of the law. Although confidence in one's independence facilitates the exercise of judicial review because it enables each judge to reach the result that he or she believes is dictated by applicable law rather than political expediency, independence is not necessarily a virtue in the executive branch, where the knowledge that one serves at the president's pleasure keeps a subordinate in line.

Similarly, the president's ability to remove officials exercising executive functions allows the president alone to direct them in the exercise of their executive functions. The specter raised by allowing federal judges to remove other federal judges is that such removal power may include the potential to control the exercise of Article III judicial power.

From a separation of powers standpoint, a major difficulty with allowing the federal judiciary to remove its own members is fashioning a principled approach to innovations to, or deviations in, the allocation of removal powers, including impeachment, set forth in the Constitution. These changes are the result of congressional enactments or, much more rarely, judicial initiatives. If the congressionally devised or judicially enforced removal scheme is a departure from the Constitution's mutable structure, it is constitutional only if it does not violate the values furthered by ensuring federal judges have life tenure and undiminished compensation—judicial independence and integrity.

Judicial Self-Regulation

Over the years, Congress has made many attempts to involve judges in monitoring, disciplining, and sometimes even removing their peers.[82] These attempts have often involved the judicial councils, groups of sitting judges originally established by the Congress to deal with administrative problems within the court system, which the judges properly administer. The two major constitutional questions that have emerged regarding judicial councils are whether they constitutionally may monitor caseloads and discipline poor judicial performance as an administrative matter and whether they constitutionally may investigate, discipline, and make recommendations to Congress regarding impeachment for certain judicial misconduct.

THE SIGNIFICANCE OF *CHANDLER*

One of the first debates about the constitutionality of allowing judges to discipline other judges arose in *Chandler v. Judicial Council of the Tenth Circuit*.[83] Acting pursuant to a 1948 law empowering it to make appropriate rules for the proper administration of its court business,[84] the judicial council of the Tenth Circuit had determined that Judge Stephen Chandler, then chief judge of the Western District of Oklahoma, was "unable or unwilling to discharge efficiently the duties of his office."[85] The council ordered him to take no further action in any pending case, distributed his caseload to the remaining judges of the district, and directed that no new cases be assigned to him until further notice. Judge Chandler challenged the council's actions in court, but the Supreme Court denied his application for a stay of the council's order, characterizing the council's action as "entirely interlocutory in character" pending prompt inquiry by the council into the administration of judicial business in the Tenth Circuit.[86] After a hearing, the council ordered that Judge Chandler could retain some of his original caseload. On a second appeal, the Supreme Court decided that because Judge Chandler might have had other avenues of relief left open to him, it was relieved from having to review the merits of the council's order.[87]

Dissenting, Justices Black and Douglas asserted that the Constitution established Congress, "acting under its limited power of impeachment," as the *sole* agency of government that may hold a federal judge accountable for the administration of his court and effectively deprive him of his office, even temporarily.[88] Providing only marginal support for their claim, Justices Black and Douglas argued that full judicial independence could only be maintained through recognizing impeachment as the exclusive means for removing or disciplining individual federal judges.[89]

The problem with the *Chandler* dissent is that claiming impeachment is the exclusive means, political or otherwise, for removing federal judges is not inconsistent with allowing judicial councils broad power to deal with administrative matters within their jurisdictions. No doubt, the judicial councils could rearrange or reschedule much of a judge's caseload if the judge were either slow or critically ill. As a matter of common law in both this country and England—which the framers never evidenced any intent to abrogate—judges have historically had the power to make administrative decisions regarding the operation of the courts that they supervise.[90] It logically follows that if a judge suffered from some infirmity such as a heart attack, then the appropriate judicial council has the power to transfer that judge's caseload, at least temporarily, to someone else. For all practical purposes, the Judicial Council for the Tenth Circuit did just this by temporarily depriving Judge Chandler of his caseload because of his persistent failure to diminish his backlog.

The key for reconciling *Chandler* with the Bribery Act of 1790 is to recognize the formal meaning of removal. Removal results in the permanent loss of the judge's power to decide cases or controversies and to receive a salary for such work, as well as the forfeiture of any pension, benefits, and opportunity to serve on judicially related panels such as a judicial council. Displacing a caseload because of illness or a backlog is not the same as permanent removal as the result of a successful impeachment and conviction. Acknowledging that judicial councils might make administrative decisions curtailing a judge's responsibilities does not mean that judges lose their titles or have been rendered permanently disabled from discharging their constitutional duties as federal judges. Judicial councils have administrative responsibility for the smooth functioning of a court system, and the councils' managerial obligations must necessarily include the power to move caseloads and sometimes diminish them to ensure orderly administration. While it may be difficult to draw a bright line between administrative convenience and outright removal, it is clear that removal through impeachment has a distinct meaning and that what happened to Judge Chandler was not, in intent or effect, the functional equivalent of removal through impeachment.

Equally important, the administrative power wielded by the judicial councils does not threaten judicial independence. Although the framers explicitly discussed only the problem of judicial independence from the other branches, real judicial independence also rests on freedom from coercion by one's fellow judges. Granting sitting judges the power to evaluate the propriety of allowing other judges to retain their office certainly has the potential to inject an element of intimidation that, no doubt, can threaten not only collegiality among judges but also independent judicial decision making itself.[91] The point is that the power to remove or even the authority to initiate a removal injects insecurity among those targeted by such power, and once those targeted officials feel compromised by the exercise of removal power, judicial independence is chilled, if not directly violated.

An appellate court's power to review lower court rulings is quite different from a special judicial tribunal's power to make decisions about whether a lower court judge may formally remain in office. The appellate court's review of lower court rulings merely directs lower courts on the proper application or interpretation of the governing law, but granting removal power to an appellate court inevitably suggests that it can retaliate against anything arguably improper a lower court judge has personally or professionally done. Consequently, the administrative action undertaken by the Tenth Circuit Judicial Council in *Chandler* was constitutional because the power it wielded did not send a signal to other judges in the circuit that personal animosity or partisan disagreements might lead to disciplinary actions. The council's action merely indicated that sometimes a drastic but temporary action must be taken to ensure the speedy, efficient, and timely disposition of a district's caseload.

The Judicial Disability Act of 1980

Whereas *Chandler* involved legislation empowering the judicial councils to deal solely with administrative matters relating to the federal courts, including sick or unusually slow judges, the Judicial Councils Reform and Judicial Conduct and Disability Act of 1980[92] further authorized the judicial councils to investigate the professional conduct of and, where appropriate, to discipline, but not to remove, federal district and circuit court judges. The act provides that anyone can file a complaint against a federal district or circuit court judge with the clerk of the appropriate court of appeals.[93] A special committee investigates complaints that cannot be resolved by the chief judge.[94] When the special committee concludes that there is merit to a complaint, the judicial council is then directed to take appropriate action, which may include censure, reprimand, temporary suspension, and transfer of cases, but *not* removal from office.[95] If the judicial council believes that it has uncovered grounds for impeachment, it is empowered to report its findings to the Judicial Conference of the United States, which, after an investigation, may report its findings to the House of Representatives.[96]

The constitutionality of this act does not turn, however, on formal separation of powers analysis. The Constitution does not expressly prohibit judicial self-regulation: it defines judicial tenure as "during good behavior" and makes judges impeachable as "officers of the United States," but it does not definitively answer (at least explicitly) whether judicial self-regulation is appropriate even to remedy misconduct falling short of an impeachable offense. Moreover, original understanding suggests at most that impeachment is the sole political mechanism for judicial discipline and removal. Otherwise, the framers did not discuss the propriety of judicial self-regulation. The lack of clarity on whether the framers knew about or intended to reject *scire facias* judicial removals— that is, the English practice under which judges could remove other judges for misconduct—makes the textual silence on the propriety of judicial self-regulation a dubious basis to bar Congress from considering its authorization.

Consequently, the constitutionality of the Judicial Disability Act turns on functionalism. This approach recognizes that proposals for judicial self-regulation are more attractive today than at any previous time in our history because of increased public demands for official accountability, greater judicial capacity (and reduced legislative ability) to perform a policing function, and the increased complexity of quality control in a vastly larger judiciary subjected to a much broader range of ethical considerations. Moreover, functional analysis allows Congress to authorize judicial self-regulation within the bounds of a balancing test that the Supreme Court has used to settle those separation of powers disputes that the Court cannot resolve on more categorical historical or textual grounds.[97] Under this test, Congress may authorize a system of judicial self-regulation as long as it does not undermine the judiciary's ability to discharge its constitutional functions, or as long as any risk posed to judicial power is outweighed by some other constitutional value that Congress is empowered to protect, such as judicial integrity. Thus, the constitutionality of the act depends on whether it seriously threatens individual judicial independence or expands judicial powers at the expense of the other branches.

The first major concern about the act is that the prospect of judges evaluating each other's integrity risks chilling to an extreme degree an individual judge's exercise of independent judgment as a matter of fairness to litigants. This concern is, however, misplaced for two reasons. First, temporary suspension as authorized by the act is not the functional equivalent of removal as the framers understood that concept. Critics might counter, though, that it is unfair to use *functional* analysis to uphold suspending a judge through some means other than impeachment by making recourse to a *formal* argument about the term *removal*. The point is that these approaches are analytically incompatible: functional analysis calls for balancing the likely benefits of a government practice against its potential threat to constitutional values, whereas formal analysis treats explicit constitutional structure and values as inviolate. Formalism would view, for example, one constitutional ideal as the framers' desire to maximize judicial independence by making impeachment the only permissible mechanism for judicial removal and discipline. But the act is not designed to sanction judges' impeachable misconduct. The Constitution sets forth removal as a disciplinary mechanism for the commission of impeachable offenses. The act aims, however, to establish a special procedure for sanctioning misconduct that does not rise to the level of impeachable conduct. This conclusion is reinforced by Congress's explicit decision to exclude judicial removals as a permissible sanction in the act.[98]

Second, the extent to which the act creates a realistic threat that individual chief judges and judicial councils might use their disciplinary powers to chill the independence of individual judges depends on how much the judiciary may be trusted to protect the values of judicial independence and integrity in each disciplinary hearing. The practice under the act to date suggests this risk is more hypothetical than real.[99] The vested interests of federal judges in making judicial removal as difficult as possible and in preserving the general perception of the integrity of the federal judiciary have thus far prevented the act's disciplinary process from being overused. Yet, this outcome suggests that another potential danger of the act is that the judicial councils might be lenient on some judges and allow some misconduct to go unpunished. Even so, the fact that the judicial council's recommendations do not bind Congress in any way suggests that this latter risk at least is not an impediment to the impeachment process.

The act also does not expand nor alter the supervisory authority of the president or Congress over the federal courts—the president by virtue of his nomination and prosecution powers and Congress through its powers to confirm judges and to regulate federal jurisdiction. Both the substantive judgments authorized by the act, and the procedures for its enforcement, are to be designed by the judiciary. Moreover, the act's provision authorizing the judicial conference to report possible impeachable misconduct to the House of Representatives does not empower it to do something it would be unable to do in the act's absence. Even if this provision did not exist, federal judges would have the same power as anyone else to complain to the House that there are grounds for impeaching a judge (or some other impeachable official). If the act codifies something that could otherwise legitimately occur, then the act is, at least to that extent, constitutional. Nor does the Constitution require the House to perform alone all investigatory work for an impeachment. As with the Independent Counsel Act's provisions, the Judicial Disability Act simply provides a reporting mechanism rather than a substitute for impeachment.

Chapter Nine

THE SCOPE OF IMPEACHABLE OFFENSES

IN ATTEMPTING to persuade the House of Representatives to impeach Justice William O. Douglas in April 1970, then-Representative Gerald Ford maintained that an impeachable offense "is whatever a majority of the House [considers it] to be at a given moment in history; conviction results from whatever offense or offenses two-thirds of the other body considers to be sufficiently serious to require removal of the accused from office."[1] Numerous commentators have taken issue with this statement, which candidly concedes that impeachments may be motivated or resolved by political concerns.[2] Yet, Ford's observation captures the practical reality of impeachment, and subsequent attempts to circumscribe the scope of impeachable offenses have not succeeded in eliminating any role for political factors.

The major disagreement is not over whether impeachable offenses should be strictly limited to indictable crimes,[3] but rather over the range of nonindictable offenses on which an impeachment may be based.[4] The text and the history of the impeachment clauses provide some useful insights into the scope of impeachable offenses. First, the Constitution provides that "all civil Officers of the United States, shall be removed from Office on Impeachment for, and Conviction of, Treason, Bribery, or other high Crimes and Misdemeanors."[5] The Constitution defines *treason* as "consist[ing] only in levying War against [the United States], or in adhering to their Enemies, giving them Aid and Comfort."[6] *Bribery* has also been understood as encompassing an indictable crime, even though Congress did not make it an indictable crime until 1790.[7] The document does not, however, define any other impeachable offenses.

Second, in the English experience prior to the drafting and ratification of the Constitution, impeachment was considered a political proceeding, and impeachable offenses were political crimes. For instance, Raoul Berger found that the English practice treated "[h]igh crimes and misdemeanors [as] a category of *political* crimes against the state."[8] Berger supported this finding with quotations from relevant periods in which the speakers used terms equivalent to *political* and *against the state* to identify the distinguishing characteristics of an impeachable event.[9] In England, the critical element of injury in an impeachable offense was injury to the state.[10] The eminent legal historian, Blackstone, traced this peculiarity to the ancient law of treason, which distinguished "high" treason, which was disloyalty against some superior, from "petit" treason, which was disloyalty to an equal or an inferior.[11] According to Arthur Bestor, "[t]his element of injury to the commonwealth—that is, to the state and to its constitution—was historically the criterion for distinguishing a 'high' crime or misdemeanor from an ordinary one."[12] In summary, the English practice involved

> a difference of degree, not a difference of kind, separat[ing] 'high' treason from other 'high' crimes and misdemeanors[,and] [t]he common element in [English impeachment proceedings] was [the] injury done to the state and its constitution, whereas among the particular offenses producing such injury some might rank as treasons, some as felonies and some as misdemeanors, among which might be included various offenses that in other contexts would fall short of actual criminality.[13]

Third, the framers and ratifiers seemed to have shared a common understanding of impeachment as a political proceeding and impeachable offenses as political crimes.[14] The delegates at the constitutional convention were intimately familiar with impeachment in colonial America, which, like impeachment in England, had basically been a political proceeding. Although those delegates primarily focused on the offenses for which the president could be impeached and removed, they generally agreed that the president could be impeached only for so-called "great" offenses.[15] Drawing in part upon their understanding of the kinds of offenses for which people may be impeached in England, various delegates gave examples of the types of conduct that they felt justified impeachment. For instance, George Mason objected to limiting impeachment to treason and bribery, because he thought impeachment should reach "attempts to subvert the Constitution."[16] He recommended that the delegates include "maladministration" as an impeachable offense.[17] Mason referred approvingly to the contemporary impeachment of Warren Hastings—formerly the governor-general of India—as based not on treason but an attempt to "subvert the Constitution."[18] James Madison responded that "maladministration" was "so vague a term [as to] be equivalent to tenure during the pleasure of the Senate[.]"[19] Madison preferred the phrase "high crimes and misdemeanors" as an alternative that would encompass attempts to subvert the Constitution.[20] In short, the debates at the constitutional convention show at least that impeachable offenses were not limited to indictable offenses, but included abuses against the state.

Moreover, the ratification debates support the conclusion that, despite the apparent goals of narrowing the conditions for the removal of impeachable officials, "other high Crimes and Misdemeanors" were not limited to indictable offenses, but rather included great offenses against the federal government. For example, delegates to state ratification conventions often referred to impeachable offenses as "great" offenses, and they frequently spoke of how impeachment should apply if the official "'deviates from his duty'"[21] or if he "'dare to abuse the powers vested in him by the people.'"[22]

Alexander Hamilton echoed such sentiments, observing that "[t]he subject [of the Senate's] jurisdiction [in an impeachment trial] are those offenses which proceed from the misconduct of public men, or, in other words, from the abuse or violation of some public trust. They are of a nature which may with peculiar propriety be denominated POLITICAL, as they relate chiefly to injuries done immediately to the society itself."[23] Hamilton commented further that the impeachment court could not be "tied down" by strict rules, "either in the delineation of the offense by the prosecutors [the House of Representatives] or in the construction of it by the judges [the Senate]."[24] In short, Hamilton too believed that impeachable offenses comprised a unique set of transgressions that defied neat delineation.

Both Justices James Wilson and Joseph Story expressed agreement with Hamilton's understanding of impeachment as a political proceeding and impeachable offenses as political crimes. In a series of lectures on the new Constitution given immediately after his appointment to the Supreme Court, Justice Wilson referred to impeachments as involving, *inter alia*, "political crimes and misdemeanors."[25] Justice Wilson understood the term *high* describing "Crimes and Misdemeanors" to mean "political" almost certainly in the same sense as Hamilton had. Similarly, Justice Joseph Story recognized the unique political nature of impeachable offenses: "The jurisdiction is to be exercised over offences, which are committed by public men in violation of their public trust and duties. Those . . . duties are, in many cases, political. . . . Strictly speaking, then, the power partakes of a political character, as it respects injuries to the society in its political character."[26] Justice Story also viewed the penalties of removal and disqualification as "limiting the punishment to such modes of redress, as are peculiarly fit for a political tribunal to administer, and as will secure the public against political injuries."[27] Justice Story understood "political injuries" to be "[s]uch kind of misdeeds . . . as peculiarly injure the commonwealth by the abuse of high offices of trust."[28]

In much the same manner as Hamilton, Justice Story believed that the framers crafted the federal impeachment process as if there would be a federal common law on crimes from which future Congresses could draw the specific or particular offenses for which certain federal officials could be impeached. Justice Story explained that "no previous statute is necessary to authorize an impeachment for any official misconduct."[29] Nor, in Justice Story's view, could such a statute ever be drafted because "political offenses are of so various and complex a character, so utterly incapable of being defined, or classified, that the task of positive legislation would be impracticable, if it were not almost absurd to attempt it."[30] The implicit understanding shared by Hamilton and Justice Story was that subsequent generations would have to define on a case-by-case basis the political crimes comprising impeachable offenses to replace the federal common law of crimes that never developed.

The remaining problem is how to identify the nonindictable offenses for which certain high-level government officials may be impeached. This task is critical for providing notice to impeachable officials as to the conditions of, and for narrowing in some meaningful fashion, the grounds for their removal. The challenge is to find contemporary analogues to the abuses against the state that authorities such as Hamilton and Justices Wilson and Story viewed as suitable grounds for impeachment. On the one hand, these abuses may be reflected in certain statutory crimes. At least one federal criminal statute—the bribery statute[31]—codifies an impeachable offense because bribery is expressly designated as such in the Constitution. Violations of other federal criminal statutes may also reflect abuses against the state sufficient to subject the perpetrator to impeachment, insofar as the offenses involved demonstrate serious lack of judgment or disdain for the law and their commission lowers respect for the office. In other words, there are certain statutory crimes that, if committed by public officials, reflect, in Congress's estimation, such lapses of judgment, breaches of the public trust, and disregard for the public welfare, the law, and the integrity or reputation of the office held, that the occupant may be impeached.

On the other hand, not all statutory crimes demonstrate unfitness for office. For example, a president's technical violation of a law making jaywalking or speeding a crime "obviously would not be an adequate basis for presidential impeachment and removal."[32] Moreover, it is equally obvious that some noncriminal activities, such as "[a] deliberate presidential decision to emasculate our national defenses or to conduct a private war in circumvention of the Constitution," may constitute nonindictable, impeachable offenses.[33] The full range of such political crimes defies specification because it rests on the circumstances under which the offenses have occurred (including the actor, the forum, and the offensive act) and on the collective *political* judgment of Congress.

For example, the different duties or circumstances of impeachable officials might justify different bases for their respective impeachments. In the case of federal judges, the good behavior clause meant to guarantee not that they may be impeached on the basis of a looser standard than the president or other impeachable officials, but rather that they may be impeached on a basis that takes into account their special duties or functions. Thus, a federal judge might be impeached for a particularly controversial law review article or speech, because these actions undermine confidence in the judge's neutrality and impugn the integrity of the judicial process. In contrast, an executive official who has done the same thing may not be impeached, because neutrality is not necessarily important to his or her job, especially if the person has been charged with advancing a controversial policy agenda. Moreover, as a practical matter, an executive official's decisions can be ratified or countermanded (and not just censured) by his superiors, and he may be further disciplined by the president (who may fire him) or the head of his department (if he is not the head of a department), or he may be impeached, which is a likely last resort. The differences in the political climate at the time the offense is committed and in the officials' responsibilities, tenure, political accountability, and actions, explain how something might be an impeachable offense in one context but not in another or might be an impeachable offense in more than one context but only treated as such in one setting.

The peculiar nature of political crimes, particularly the ways in which they need to be defined on an ongoing basis, is further illustrated through two common hypotheticals posed to and by impeachment scholars. The first is whether an official may be impeached for conduct in office that does not relate to his or her formal responsibilities. Resolving this dilemma requires understanding why political crimes or abuses against the state are impeachable offenses at all. The answer is that someone who holds office also holds the public's trust, and an officeholder who violates that trust effectively loses the confidence of the people and, consequently, must forfeit the privilege of holding at least his or her present office.[34] In this context, conduct that may plainly be unrelated to the responsibilities of a particular office may still relate to an official's capacity to fulfill the functions of that office and to hold the people's trust. Hence, the Congress understood that Harry Claiborne's commissions of income tax fraud may not have been directly related to, nor even influenced his performance on, the district court bench, but nevertheless justified his impeachment and removal because his misconduct showed disdain for federal law and serious lapses of judgment and were offenses against the federal government. In contrast, Congress concluded that William O. Douglas's eccentricities, including his promiscuity, were not impeachable offenses, even though they offended many people. The offense in question was not pertinent to Justice Douglas's competence or integrity in discharging the duties of his office. Yet, it is easy to imagine that a president who murdered someone in a jealous rage committed an impeachable offense. Even if such a crime were unrelated to the president's constitutional duties, his criminal act considerably cheapens the presidency, destroys his credibility with the other branches (and other nations, for that matter), and shows such lack of respect for human life and disdain for the law (which he is sworn to enforce faithfully) that Congress could reasonably conclude that he had seriously breached his trust and no longer deserved to hold office.

The second hypothetical is more difficult. It involves wrongdoing committed before one assumes office. As a general matter, it is noteworthy that no one has ever been impeached, much less removed from office, for something he or she did prior to assuming an impeachable position in the federal government. No doubt, anyone impeached on such a basis could argue that Congress' consistent failure ever to bring an impeachment on this ground clearly indicates that Congress has never considered misconduct prior to entering federal office to constitute an impeachable offense. One could further argue that this failure, combined with the consistent congressional practice of bringing impeachments only against officials for their wrongful acts in office, establishes the principle that federal impeachments are limited to the wrongful conduct of impeachable officials committed while they were in office. Moreover, impeaching someone for something they did in their private life prior to entering public office conceivably frustrates the framers' plan to preclude the impeachments of private citizens.

A counterargument is that the fact that no one has ever been impeached on this basis is irrelevant. Congress's failure to impeach someone for something they did prior to entering federal office is not surprising, especially when one considers that this situation is likely to be quite rare and that, even when it arises, Congress is bound to have great difficulty in marshaling sufficient political support to proceed with an impeachment. Indeed, if Congress's failure to bring certain kinds of impeachments permanently precludes their initiation, then Congress could never impeach someone on grounds that any reasonable person would accept as legitimate, such as an impeachable official's commission of a murder while in office. Moreover, the dividing line between the nonimpeachable offenses of private citizens and the impeachable offenses of certain federal officials is not so neat: the first chapter in this part discussed the propriety of impeaching people who had resigned from or left office, and it is easy to imagine instances in which impeachable offenses could be based on present misconduct consisting of fraudulent suppression or misrepresentation of prior misconduct. Particularly in cases in which an elected or confirmed official has lied or committed a serious act of wrongdoing to get into their present position, the misconduct that was committed prior to entering office clearly bears on the integrity of the way in which the present officeholder entered office and the integrity of that official to remain in office.

The problem is further complicated, however, by the fact that it may manifest itself in two different ways, each requiring a separate analysis for determining whether an impeachable offense is involved. First, the public could elect, or the Senate could confirm, an official, even though it knew that he or she had done something wrong. The only reason for trying to impeach someone in this circumstance is the perceived need for Congress to express its independent judgment that the official in question is not fit for office and should be punished.

The difficulty is that it is unclear how the nation has been injured or the public trust has been violated when the electorate or the Senate was fully informed of the misconduct and still elected or confirmed the person. If the impeachment process aims to remove people to protect the public trust, that goal seems to have become moot when the public has passed on (or even ratified) the conduct involved. No matter how serious the offense involved, it is hard to see how an impeachment could be successfully pursued in a case in which Congress is trying to impeach someone for an act that the Senate knew about at the time it confirmed the person. If the conduct made known to the electorate or the Senate was committed in an elected or confirmed official's private capacity prior to his or her election or confirmation, it is even less clear how the interests protected by the impeachment process are implicated. In the latter circumstance, all that can be safely said is that, as a matter of common sense and good policy, Congress may wish to take into consideration the information made public during the election or confirmation and the nature of the alleged offense involved during its deliberations on impeachment, because a successful impeachment ultimately depends on the credibility of Congress's claim that it is acting in the best interests of the people, who may have ratified or at least expressed no disapproval of the prior (mis)conduct. Thus, it is conceivable that one ground for not re-impeaching Alcee Hastings was that his election to Congress arguably ratified his misconduct.

The other problematic circumstance is when the public or the Senate did not know about the misconduct of an official prior to his or her election or confirmation. In this situation, Congress could claim that something akin to voter fraud occurred, that the integrity of the electoral or confirmation process is involved, and that it has a fiduciary obligation to remedy the situation by conducting an impeachment to put into effect what it or voters likely would have done had either been fully advised or to determine the official's continued fitness to serve in light of the new data. The kinds of factors Congress might consider in determining the existence of an impeachable offense are the seriousness of the misconduct, its timing, the relevence of the offense to the election or confirmation, the link between a misdeed and an offiice, and the proximity of the next relevant election (Congress might prefer to let the voters decide, if possible).

For example, if the public elected a president and the media later found out that prior to the election he had been a Ku Klux Klan member who had committed numerous civil rights violations, Congress could in good faith find that the suppression of this data would have materially altered the election for the presidency. The fact that Congress refused to impeach Justice Hugo Black under similar circumstances is irrelevant. To be sure, the initial newspaper report that he had been a member of the KKK as a young lawyer occurred in the midst of his confirmation hearings. In his only public statement on the issue, Justice Black gave a short radio address in which he admitted that he had been a member only for a short while during his youth and that he did not intend ever again to talk about the issue publicly. Even though there were threats of impeachment leveled against Justice Black, nothing came of them.[35] It is clear, however, from subsequent events, including the civil rights movement and the more widespread disdain today for the KKK or its agenda, that reports of membership or affiliation with the Klan or similar groups would, in the future, defeat anyone nominated to the federal bench or prompt an impeachment investigation against any impeachable officials.

In any event, constitutional safeguards apply to the impeachment process and should circumscribe congressional efforts to define political crimes. The Constitution includes several guarantees to ensure that Congress will deliberate carefully prior to making any judgments in an impeachment proceeding: (1) when the Senate sits as a court of impeachment, "they shall be on Oath or Affirmation";[36] (2) at least two-thirds of the Senators present must favor conviction in order for the impeachment to be successful;[37] and (3) in the special case of presidential removal, the chief justice must preside so that the vice-president, who otherwise normally presides, is spared from having to oversee the impeachment trial of the one person who stands between him and the presidency.[38]

Three other safeguards derive from the nature or structure of the federal political process. First, members of Congress seeking reelection have a political incentive to avoid any abuse of the impeachment power. The knowledge that they may have to account to their constituency may lead them to deliberate cautiously on impeachment questions. Second, the cumbersome nature of the impeachment process makes it difficult for a faction guided by base personal or partisan motives to impeach and remove someone from office. Third, as with any other decision it must make in an impeachment, Congress must be sure that its judgments are acceptable to, or will be respected by, key leaders or decision makers in the other branches or face the prospect or onset of a constitutional crisis. Thus, these structural and political safeguards help to ensure that, at least as a practical matter, "[s]ome type of wrongdoing must exist in order for an impeachment to lie—there can be no impeachment for mere policy difference. . . ."[39]

Chapter Ten

THE PROPER PROCEDURE FOR IMPEACHMENT PROCEEDINGS

THE FOUR MOST controversial procedural questions raised in impeachment proceedings have been (1) whether an impeachment trial is more like a criminal or civil proceeding for purposes of determining the appropriate burden of proof; (2) whether any presidential privilege applies to impeachment proceedings; (3) what rules of evidence, if any, should be applied in impeachment hearings, particularly in Senate impeachment trials; and (4) the propriety of the Senate's using a special trial committee to take testimony and receive evidence. Clarifying each of these issues is important either to give needed guidance to the participants, including the much-maligned Senate, or to show that impeachment trials are defective for reasons that cannot be resolved without radically revising the process.

THE APPLICABLE BURDEN OF PROOF

The degree to which an impeachment proceeding is analogous to a criminal or civil trial is important for determining the applicable burden of proof. If impeachment is more like a criminal trial, then the appropriate burden for establishing the guilt of the impeached official would be beyond a reasonable doubt, whereas, if impeachment more closely resembles a civil trial, then the proper burden of proof is a preponderance of the evidence.

Both the language and the structure of the Constitution suggest, however, that an impeachment trial is neither a criminal nor a civil proceeding. On the one hand, the Constitution expressly limits the punishments for impeachment to removal and disqualification from office, punishments that are unavailable in any other proceeding in our legal system.[1] In addition, the Constitution does not entitle the target of an impeachment the right to a jury[2] or to counsel; the president may not pardon a person convicted by impeachment (whereas he is able to pardon any other convicted criminal);[3] the federal rules of evidence do not apply in an impeachment trial; and a conviction does not require unanimous agreement among the senators sitting in judgment.[4] On the other hand, the impeachment clauses include at least two serious crimes—treason and bribery—as impeachable offenses.[5] Also, impeachment is lumped together with criminal proceedings in other sections of the Constitution.[6]

If an impeachment trial is, as the relevant provisions suggest, an unusual hybrid proceeding, then the burden of proof required for a conviction should be fashioned accordingly and, thus, need not be the same as the criminal or civil burden of proof. Indeed, a hybrid of the criminal and civil burdens of proof may be desirable, because neither a "preponderance of the evidence" standard nor a "beyond a reasonable doubt" standard neatly fits the impeachment setting. Too lenient a proof standard would allow the Senate to impose the serious punishments for impeachment "even though substantial doubt of guilt remained."[7] Too rigid a standard might allow an official to remain in office even though the entire Senate was convinced he or she had committed an impeachable offense.[8]

The solution to this dilemma is to balance these concerns. Charles Black has recommended that

> [t]he essential thing is that no part whatever be played by the natural human tendency to think the worst of a person of whom one generally disapproves, and the verbalization of a high standard of proof may serve as a constant reminder of this. Weighing the factors, I would be sure that one ought not to be satisfied, or anything near satisfied, with the mere "preponderance" of an ordinary civil trial, but perhaps must be satisfied with something a little less than the "beyond reasonable doubt" standard of the ordinary criminal trial. . . . "Overwhelming preponderance of the evidence" comes perhaps as close as present legal language can to denoting the desired legal standard.[9]

In short, the standard of proof in an impeachment trial should be a hybrid of the standards of proof in civil and criminal trials to accommodate the hybrid nature of impeachment trials.

Even if the Senate could reach some consensus on which burden to apply, there is the additional difficulty of figuring out how to enforce the chosen burden on each senator. The intractability of this problem has led the Senate to take the position that each senator should follow whatever burden of proof he or she thinks is best.[10] This practice can often work, however, to the disadvantage of all of the participants in an impeachment trial by precluding them from knowing in advance what standard the Senate will actually apply.

THE APPLICABILITY OF EXECUTIVE PRIVILEGES IN IMPEACHMENT PROCEEDINGS

The debate over whether the president should be allowed to invoke any special privileges in an impeachment proceeding typically turns on whether one wants a strong or weak president. For example, Charles

Black suggests that the president should generally enjoy an absolute "privilege of withholding from other branches of government the tenor and content of his own conversations with his close advisors in the White House."[11] Black explains that, even in the impeachment context, "upholding [an absolute executive privilege] [is] essential to the efficacious and dignified conduct of the presidency and to the free flow of candid advice to the president."[12] He suggests further that such a privilege would also allow the president to protect himself from overreaching by either of the other two branches.

Yet, both constitutional history and structure suggest that an impeachment proceeding is precisely the context in which the president should not be able to assert superiority over Congress. The framers never evidenced any desire that the president should have the authority or means by which to thwart an impeachment proceeding. Indeed, meaningful separation of powers suggests that "[t]he political efficacy of presidential assertions of executive privilege is perhaps most limited in the context of . . . impeachment proceedings."[13] John Quincy Adams recognized that it would be a "mockery . . . to say that the House should have the power of impeachment extending even to the president . . . and yet to say that the House had not the power to obtain the evidence and proofs on which [his] impeachment was based."[14] The same should hold true for the Senate's power to try impeachments. In addition, the House Select Committee's approval of the third article of impeachment against Richard Nixon[15] could be construed as confirming congressional authority to make assertions of executive privilege that thwart impeachment proceedings the grounds for an impeachment article.

The relative strength of an executive privilege depends, however, on the context in which and the bases on which it is asserted. For example, in *United States v. Nixon*,[16] the Supreme Court held that in a criminal trial a president's claim of executive privilege is qualified by the basis on which he asserts it *and* by the need of the other party for the evidence subpoenaed.[17] Yet, in a presidential impeachment, the grounds for the assertion is virtually irrelevant, given that the whole point of the proceeding is to determine his fitness to remain in office, which would obviously encompass testing the soundness of his asserted reasons for his alleged misconduct. The resolution of this central issue may require the president to share with the House, the Senate, or the chief justice highly sensitive information regarding executive branch operations, or to face the consequences for not doing so. The president's concerns about national security and excessive congressional oversight may be alleviated by requiring Congress to show relevance prior to forcing the president to divulge certain information. If the president declines to share the information after one or both chambers of Congress show its relevance, he risks being impeached for refusing to comply with a lawful congressional request or subpoena. If the president lacks confidence in Congress's procedures for maintaining the confidentiality of certain material, he can ask Congress to use a different procedure. But the president's lack of confidence in Congress's ability to preserve confidential information is not a sufficient reason for withholding information Congress is entitled to consider in discharging its constitutional duties to investigate and conduct hearings into his wrongdoing.

By its very nature, the impeachment process is reserved for Congress to demand an accounting from the president regarding alleged abuses of his power. The framers explicitly rejected the British practice of insulating the king from impeachment. Instead, they made the president impeachable in part to ensure that he would not be above the law.[18] Allowing the president to withhold information from Congress on the basis of an assertion of privilege undercuts that goal, because he then could hinder the only constitutionally authorized process by which Congress may hold him accountable for his misconduct.

THE APPROPRIATE RULES OF EVIDENCE FOR IMPEACHMENT TRIALS

It is unnecessary to make any particular rules of evidence applicable to impeachment proceedings. Both state and federal courts require special rules of evidence to make trials more efficient and fair or to keep certain evidence away from a jury, whose members might not understand or appreciate its reliability, credibility, or potentially prejudicial effect.[19] The concerns leading to the use of special rules of evidence in state and federal courts do not, however, apply to impeachment trials. An impeachment trial is not the usual kind of trial, nor does it involve a typical jury. Rather, impeachments are extraordinary hearings administered by a sophisticated and politically savy body—the Congress of the United States.

As Charles Black suggests, "the House and the Senate ought to hear and consider *all* evidence which seems relevant, without regard to technical rules."[20] In the House, the need for a thorough investigation is paramount, and the risk of error is minimal, because the House has no punitive authority. Once the matter gets to the Senate, which does have the power to impose special punishments, the risk of error may be greater, but, as Black argues further, "Senators are in any case continually exposed to 'hearsay' evidence; they cannot be sequestered and kept away from newspapers, like a jury. If they cannot be trusted to weigh evidence, appropriately discounting for all the factors of unreliability that have led to our keeping some evidence away from juries, then they are not in any way up to the job, and 'rules of evidence' will not help."[21]

The Constitutionality of the Senate's Use of Trial Committees

Given the likelihood of the Senate's continued reliance on trial committees in the aftermath of the Supreme Court's decision in *Walter Nixon v. United States*,[22] the question of the constitutionality of impeachment trial committees still merits consideration. Judge Nixon set forth the basic argument against their constitutionality in his lawsuit challenging his removal from office by the Senate. He contended that, in granting to the Senate "the sole Power to try impeachments,"[23] the Constitution mandated the full Senate to conduct impeachment trials.[24] Moreover, impeachment trials before the full Senate under specified conditions guarantee judicial independence to the fullest extent possible.[25] The Senate's practice to conduct impeachment trials before the entire body up until the Claiborne, Hastings, and Nixon impeachment trials "confirms that impeachment trials must be conducted before the full Senate."[26] By not conducting Judge Nixon's impeachment trial before the full body, the Senate deprived him of the kind of fair impeachment trial conducted previously by the Senate. In Nixon's view, the need for the full Senate to see and hear the live testimony of all witnesses was especially important in his impeachment trial because the perjury charges against him turned on credibility issues, particularly given his claim that the chief witness against him in his criminal trial had perjured himself.[27] The fact that the trial committee members were far more "receptive" to Nixon's claim than the full body seems to underscore the dangers of leaving seven-eighths of the Senate unexposed to the live testimony in the case.[28] In Nixon's opinion, eighty-eight senators were uninformed in whole or in part about the merits of his defense.

In spite of the appeal of some of these arguments, there is little reason to doubt rule XI's constitutionality. First, the relevant constitutional text suggests that the Senate's use of rule XI trial committees is permissible. The Constitution specifies only a few details of what is required for an impeachment trial, including (1) the senators voting on the impeachment must be on oath or affirmation,[29] (2) two-thirds of the senators present must concur in order for there to be a conviction,[30] (3) the only permissible punishments that may be imposed upon a conviction on impeachment are removal from office and future disqualification,[31] and (4) the chief justice of the United States should preside when the president is tried.[32] The gap that is left about the rest of the specifics of an impeachment trial is to be filled according to the discretion of the Senate, as provided in Article I, section 5 that "[e]ach House may determine the Rules of its Proceedings."[33] Second, Thomas Jefferson's *Manual of Parliamentary Practice*,[34] *The Federalist Papers*,[35] and the states' practices prior to the drafting and ratification of the Constitution[36] reflect that, in designing the American impeachment process, the framers used the British procedure as a model[37] and were aware of but did not reject the practice of the House of Lords in the seventeenth century to use committees to gather evidence for impeachment trials.[38] Third, Nixon had a fair trial before the full Senate. The whole Senate reviewed de novo the committee's limited findings of fact, two-thirds of the Senate voted to convict Nixon on two articles of impeachment, and the full Senate exercised its judgment in Nixon's impeachment (as it can in any impeachment trial) not to call witnesses other than the judge to testify before the entire body.

Moreover, if the Senate's use of trial committees were unconstitutional, a serious question would arise as to the constitutionality of each of the branches' internal delegations. Like any other branch of the federal government, the Senate has the inherent or implied authority to make delegations to assist its discharge of its constitutional responsibilities. For example, the Senate routinely delegates fact-finding authority to committees to assist it in rendering judgment on various matters over which it has exclusive control, such as treaty ratifications and judicial nominations; the Supreme Court has relied on special masters in cases of original jurisdiction;[39] the federal district courts have delegated fact-finding responsibilities to special masters and others "[f]rom the commencement of our Government";[40] and the House and the Senate have long used committees to gather evidence when acting as "the Judge of the Elections, Returns and Qualifications of its own Members"[41]—a role in which the House or Senate is clearly acting as "a judicial tribunal."[42] If the Court ever were to hold rule XI unconstitutional because it violated an express limitation that only the full Senate could conduct any aspect of an impeachment trial, then the constitutionality of these (and many) other delegations is doubtful because they might conflict similarly with explicit grants of arguably nondelegable authority to the full membership of a branch to perform an important function.

Chapter Eleven

JUDICIAL REVIEW OF IMPEACHMENTS

T HE SUPREME COURT'S dismissal of Judge Walter Nixon's challenge to his removal from office is significant for two major reasons. First, the decision[1] breathed life back into the much-maligned political question doctrine—the Court's practice of claiming textual authority, separation of powers concerns, or prudential reasons for not deciding the merits of certain constitutional questions.[2] In doing so, the Court took a position on an issue—the justiciability of impeachment challenges—that had long divided constitutional scholars[3] and is basic for understanding the limits of judicial review. Second, *Nixon* recognized that in the area of impeachment, Congress may make constitutional law—that is, make judgments about the scope and meaning of its constitutionally authorized impeachment function—subject to change or overturning only if Congress later changes its mind or by a constitutional amendment. Thus, *Nixon* raised an issue about Congress's ability, in the absence of judicial review, to make reasonably principled constitutional decisions.

In an effort to provide some insight into the latter issue, this chapter explores *Nixon*'s ramifications on the relationship between the political-question doctrine and the impeachment process.[4] After reviewing *Nixon*, the chapter examines the decision's constitutional underpinnings, considers the prospects for post-*Nixon* judicial review of an impeachment challenge, and explores the implications for these prospects raised by the most serious kinds of impeachment challenges likely to arise in the aftermath of *Nixon*.

THE *NIXON* OPINION

Judge Nixon's challenge to his removal from office by the Senate required the Supreme Court to consider for the first time the propriety of judicial review of impeachment proceedings. Six justices held Nixon's claim to be a nonjusticiable political question. They found that the word *try* did not represent an "implied limitation on the method by which the Senate might proceed in trying impeachments."[5] Instead, they determined, based on their application of some of the factors for determining a political question set forth in *Baker v. Carr*,[6] that the word *try* "lack[ed] sufficient precision to constitute a judicially manageable standard of review of the Senate's actions,"[7] especially when contrasted with the three "precise" limitations set out in the Impeachment Trial Clause[8]—that Senate members shall "be on Oath or Affirmation," that the chief justice shall preside at a presidential impeachment trial, and that conviction requires a vote of at least two-thirds of the members present. Moreover, other language in the same clause—giving the Senate the "sole" powers to try impeachments—constituted a "textual commitment" to a coordinate branch. Finally, the Court emphasized that judicial review was inappropriate for several reasons: it would upset the framers' decision to allocate to different fora the powers to try impeachments and to try crimes; it would disturb the system of checks and balances, under which impeachment is the only legislative check on the judiciary; and it would create a "lack of finality and [a] difficulty [in] fashioning relief."[9]

The Court distinguished *Powell v. McCormack*[10] on the basis that it involved a constitutional provision authorizing that "each House shall be the Judge of the Elections, Returns and Qualifications of its own Members,"[11] which was limited by Article I, section 2. The latter provision "specified three requirements for membership in the House: The candidate must be at least 25 years of age, a citizen of the United States for no less than seven years, and an inhabitant of the State he is chosen to represent."[12] Hence, "[t]he decision as to whether a member satisfied these qualifications *was* placed in the House, but the decision as to what [they] consisted of was not."[13] In contrast, the Impeachment Trial Clause contained no separate provision that "could be defeated by allowing the Senate final authority to determine the meaning of the word 'try'."[14]

Concurring in the judgment, Justice White, joined by Justice Blackmun, thought the case presented a justiciable question, though in his view of the merits the Senate had "very wide discretion in specifying impeachment trial procedures,"[15] so that as a practical matter a successful judicial challenge was unlikely. Still, Justice White believed that proper checks and balances were best preserved when Senate impeachment trials helped control the largely unaccountable judiciary, "even as judicial review would ensure that the Senate adhered to a minimal set of procedural safeguards in conducting impeachment trials."[16] The requirement that the Senate "try" impeachments created judicially manageable standards, which would be violated "[w]ere the Senate, for example, to adopt the practice of automatically entering a judgment of conviction whenever articles of impeachment were delivered from the House."[17]

Concurring separately in the judgment, Justice Souter agreed that the case presented a nonjusticiable political question, but he thought that this determination should be made on a case-by-case basis. If the Senate were to convict upon a coin toss, or (borrowing an example from Justice White) upon a summary determination that the official was a "bad guy," Justice Souter thought that, "judicial interference might well be appropriate."[18]

Nixon's Constitutional Underpinnings

In the most serious challenge to *Nixon* raised to date, Rebecca Brown argues that separation of powers exists to protect individual rights, that judicial review is an integral part of separation of powers, and that the *Nixon* Court should therefore have "permit[ted] judicial review of the exercise of the impeachment power" to ensure that no individual right was being violated.[19] The individual right at risk in an impeachment trial is a federal judge's potential loss of position, including the independence he or she is guaranteed by Article III.

Nixon may also be problematic because the Court did not reconcile the apparent irony of its reviewing the contours of an area of political decision making for the sake of preserving it from judicial review in the name of nonjusticiablity with its refusal to acknowledge that its deference may have turned on an implicit judgment that the Constitution simply granted the political actor broad discretion. In addition, the Court's reliance on constitutional and prudential factors in dismissing Nixon's claim as a political question may have cast doubt on the legitimacy of the Court's inquiry. The concern is that the political question doctrine may have enlarged the judiciary's role in deciding constitutional questions because it has allowed courts to use disingenuous analysis to reach the results it wants to reach or to ground constitutional decisions on a nonconstitutional basis.[20]

There are three reasons why these problems are not as serious as they might first seem. First, the Court referred to a finding of "nonjusticiab[ility]"—a constitutionally compelled conclusion barring judgment on a dispute's merits—as the functional equivalent of discovering "a political question."[21] This reference may reflect a strategic decision to preserve a majority committed to avoiding the merits of the case despite widespread criticism of the political question doctrine. Some justices might not have minded that the latter doctrine was judicially created or has allowed consideration of the consequences of judicial review, whereas other justices might have felt more comfortable viewing their inquiry as being guided solely by the Constitution's limits on justiciability. Even so, *Nixon* relied heavily on the textual, historical, and structural arguments supporting the Court's finding of nonjusticiability.[22]

The Court found further that prolonged battles in the courts over an impeachment would create uncertainty about its finality and "what relief a court may give other than simply setting aside the judgment of the conviction. Could it order the reinstatement of a convicted federal judge, or order the Congress to create an additional judgeship if the seat had been filled in the interim?"[23] Hence, the Court's opinion in *Nixon* also relied on prudential concerns related to the possible consequences of certain constitutional decisions. In short, *Nixon* does not bury the political question doctrine; rather, *Nixon* resuscitates it by clarifying its derivation from the Constitution *and* its sensitivity to the need for constitutional stability.

Second, the idea that a federal court may have to exercise some degree of judicial review in order to determine the existence of a political question is hardly a reason to jettison the entire enterprise as disingenuous or too easily manipulated. For example, in explaining his willingness to reach the merits of Nixon's claim in the D.C. Circuit, Judge Harry Edwards suggested that " '[t]he lesson of *Powell* is that the Supreme Court may use judicial review to determine whether Congress followed the proper procedures for making the political decision committed to it by the Constitution. *Powell* does not allow overly intrusive judicial review, but rather allows review solely to ensure that Congress made the particular kind of political decision entrusted to it by the Constitution.' "[24] Judge Edwards proceeded to find that Nixon's challenge required the appellate court to determine the scope of the term *try* and, therefore, to reach a ruling on the merits of the lawsuit's contentions.[25] Yet, his characterization of *Powell* is a direct quote from an earlier article of mine, which, admittedly not as clear as it should have been, was meant to support a different conclusion. It recognized that, in determining whether a case poses a political question, a court may look to see if Congress is in fact exercising the power it claims to be using and is not trying to achieve an end it could have only achieved legitimately through the exercise of some other power.[26] If Congress were using an inappropriate means to achieve a legitimate objective, then further judicial intervention would be permissible.

Moreover, in a political question case, a court does not just look at the contours of a particular area of political decision making and decide that it will defer to any decision made within that sphere because it is constitutional; rather, a court exercises judicial review to determine the scope or boundaries of an area about whose subject matter it should not express any opinion. Hence, as a practical matter, *Nixon* reveals something significant about the political question doctrine in the impeach-ment context: it allows the Court to stand by mutely while the Senate exercises very poor judgment, whereas a holding deferring to the Senate's actions as long as they were reasonable would have allowed judicial re-view of all impeachments to ensure that the Senate never acted foolishly or recklessly.

Viewed in this manner, the determination of a political question re-quires a court to make the kind of decision it must routinely make in adjudicating preliminary issues about the ripeness or mootness of a law-suit, personal jurisdiction, standing, and advisory opinions. The obvious consequence of a decision finding absent at least one of the essential crite-ria for a lawsuit to qualify as a case or controversy is that a court dis-misses the case without a decision on the merits, even though, in reaching such a conclusion, it must appreciate the nature of a particular dispute and speculate on the applicability of a wide variety of constitutional and prudential concerns. The kind of inquiry required to determine a political question is no less appropriate than any other preliminary inquiry under-taken in a federal case to determine the propriety of adjudicating its merits.[27]

To be sure, there is a subtle distinction between reaching the merits of a dispute because it falls within an area over which a court decides some political actor has extensive constitutional authority and not reviewing the substantive merits of a political actor's decision because it is within a sphere about which a court may not express any opinion. Nevertheless, a finding of nonjusticiability is different from a court's deciding that a wide realm of governmental behavior is constitutional, in that a determination of nonjusticiability forecloses a range of potential litigation and signals once and for all that there is no judicial remedy available for any official misconduct occurring within a certain area.

Of course, a federal court needs constitutional authority to dismiss a constitutional case permanently without a ruling on its merits. Accord-ingly, the third argument favoring Nixon's resuscitation of the political-question doctrine is that no other outcome is as compatible with the Constitution. If the national government in fact is one of "enumerated powers," as Chief Justice Marshall observed in *McCulloch v. Maryland*,[28] then it should follow that the federal judiciary is, like the other branches, subject to certain constraints, even self-imposed ones. Yet, many of the critics of the political question doctrine seem uncomfortable with having any branch other than the judiciary declare what the Constitution means; they would prefer that federal judges have the final say on the constitu-tional limitations for each and every governmental action. No decision more clearly indicates, however, the fallacy of this notion than *Nixon*. It recognizes that the Constitution limits even federal judicial power. It suggests that the special duty of federal courts is to "say what the law is," but that sometimes the law might be that a federal court should not decide the merits of a particular constitutional issue.

Nor does the Constitution necessarily support the notion that it only has meaning as long as the judiciary is empowered to enforce *all* of its guarantees or limits. Judicial review may be necessary to make the enforcement and vindication of various federal rights and limitations possible, but that acknowledgment does not establish a constitutional basis for judicial review over every case or controversy implicating the Constitution.

As the *Nixon* Court acknowledged, judicial review over impeachment procedures frustrates the original constitutional scheme in which the framers foresaw impeachment as the only political check on the judiciary. The Court observed further that the parties had not offered "evidence of a single word in the history of the Constitutional Convention or in contemporary commentary that even alludes to the possibility of judicial review in the context of the impeachment powers."[29] The Court found this "silence" revealing, because it was at odds with "the several explicit references to the availability of judicial review as a check on the Legislature's power with respect to bills of attainder, *ex post facto* laws, and statutes."[30]

Moreover, the Court acknowledged the framers' reasons for excluding any role for federal judges, including Supreme Court justices, as impeachment authorities. The framers wanted the body empowered to try impeachments to be sufficiently "numerous" and to have sufficient fortitude and public accountability to make the necessary policy choices in an impeachment.[31] The framers also designed the impeachment process to protect impeachable officials from being tried more than once in the same forum for the same offense by preventing judges from being able to oversee an individual's impeachment and criminal trials. Moreover, the framers sought to preclude the "eviscerat[ion]" of impeachment as a critical " 'constitutional check' placed on the Judiciary by placing the final reviewing authority with respect to impeachments [in] the hands of the same body that the impeachment process is meant to regulate;"[32] and to fashion explicit constitutional safeguards "to keep the Senate in check."[33] The framers believed that these protections, including dividing impeachment authority between the House and the Senate and the two-thirds supermajority vote requirement for a conviction, would be sufficient to prevent the Senate from "usurp[ing] judicial power."[34] The critical problem is that allowing any level of judicial review of this unique mechanism is incompatible with both the judicial function and the framers' objectives in designing the judicial impeachment process.

THE PROSPECTS FOR JUDICIAL REVIEW OF POST-*NIXON* IMPEACHMENT CHALLENGES

After *Nixon*, three possibilities exist for judicial review of impeachment challenges. The first is that the only justiciable challenges to impeachments are for violations of explicit constitutional constraints, while the second is that judicial review of any impeachment challenge is never permissible. A third prospect is a compromise between the other two positions that would allow for judicial review of only the most extreme abuses of the impeachment power. The following section examines the arguments for and against each prospect.

Treating Violations of Explicit Constraints as Justiciable

The principal argument supporting judicial review of certain impeachment challenges after *Nixon* is based on analogizing a case involving the House's or the Senate's deviation from an explicit constitutional constraint to *Powell v. McCormack*. In *Nixon*, the Court explained that it exercised judicial review in *Powell* to overturn the House's decision not to seat Adam Clayton Powell as a representative based on certain alleged financial improprieties, because the House's claim that

> its power to be [the Judge of its members' qualifications] was a textual commitment of unreviewable authority [that] was defeated by the existence of [a] separate provision specifying the only qualifications which might be imposed for House membership. The decision as to whether a member satisfied these qualifications was placed with the House, but the decision as to what these qualifications consisted of was not.[35]

The *Nixon* Court held, however, that a separate constitutional provision did not defeat the Senate's power to "try" impeachments as it saw fit. The Court identified four other explicit constitutional constraints on the impeachment power: the division of impeachment authority between the House and the Senate, a two-thirds vote in the Senate for a conviction, the members of the Senate must be under oath, and the chief justice shall preside in a presidential impeachment trial.[36] A court looking for the impeachment analogue to the judicially enforced provision in *Powell* may find justiciable the failure to comply with any of these explicit constraints on the impeachment power, because they each conceivably confine the discretion the House or the Senate is otherwise constitutionally authorized to exercise in discharging its respective impeachment functions.

Such limited judicial review is based on the general need for federal courts to "say what the law is" as an indispensable guarantee of congressional compliance with the Constitution's express limits. Such judicial review also identifies bright-line or unambiguous rules that will both constrain the discretion of Congress and avoid manipulating results or sidestepping tough issues through the political question doctrine.

If violations of explicit impeachment restraints are justiciable, the next step is to identify them. Sometimes this is easy, as with the division of impeachment authority between the House and the Senate and the requirements that the senators must be under oath in an impeachment trial, that at least two-thirds of the Senate must concur on a conviction, and that the chief justice must preside at presidential impeachments.

Although ignored by the *Nixon* Court, there are other such explicit constraints. One example is the need for the House to have a majority to impeach. Moreover, the clause limiting the Senate's choice of punishments only after a conviction to removal and disqualification[37] clearly restrains it from imposing any other sanction, such as imprisonment or death. In addition, Congress's impeachment authority is to be exercised only against the president, the vice-president, and "all Civil officers of the United States,"[38] obviously precluding the House or Senate from exercising its respective impeachment power over a private citizen who has never worked a day in government service.

The Conceivable Nonjusticiability of Any Impeachment Challenge

A second prospect after *Nixon* is that *any* challenge to the impeachment process is nonjusticiable. This position requires distinguishing *Powell*, which suggests,[39] as the *Nixon* Court noted,[40] that where a constitutional provision plainly restricts the discretion of a political branch, then a court may intervene to enforce compliance.

One could distinguish *Powell* on the basis of the uniqueness of impeachment as a constitutional matter. The point is that judicial review, even in a case involving the violation of an explicit constitutional constraint, would undermine impeachment's effectiveness as a check on executive and especially judicial abuse of power. After all, *Powell* did not involve what the *Nixon* Court recognized as "a situation in which judicial review would remove the only check placed on the Judicial Branch by the Framers."[41] Obviously, judicial review of presidential impeachments does not pose a similar conflict, because the judiciary at least has little or no vested interest, at least as an institution, in his remaining in office. Nevertheless, some judges may feel loyal to the president, because he appointed them. In short, *Powell* conceivably did not deal with the propriety of judicial review of a power the framers chose not to give to the judiciary because they felt judges could not be trusted with it.

This position is supported by many of the same separation of powers concerns that led the *Nixon* Court to treat procedural challenges to the Senate's trial process as nonjusticiable. For example, the *Nixon* Court thrice stressed that the unique function served by the impeachment process as the *only* legislative check on the judiciary would be "eviscerate[d]" by judicial review.[42] This threat does not dissipate or diminish even if an explicit constraint is involved.

One arguably serious problem with this position is that it is based, as Rebecca Brown argues, on the erroneous presumption that "judicial review of [impeachment] procedures is equivalent to judicial determination of outcome."[43] A critical difficulty with this critique, however, is that it merely assumes that impeachment's effectiveness as the only political check on judicial abuse of power is not weakened if it can be reviewed by the judiciary. Yet, judicial review of the impeachment process would give judges the last word on the propriety of the procedures for their own removals and, thus, the chance to make their own or their colleagues' removals virtually impossible by ensuring that Congress could achieve such outcomes only through the most complex, time-consuming ways. Nor is it inconceivable that judges might have a vested interest in making their removals as difficult as possible. The risk of self-interested judicial review of judicial impeachments is irrelevant only if, like Brown, one trusts the judiciary more than Congress not to abuse its respective authority over impeachments.[44]

The problem with such faith is that the framers did not share it. The delegates' decision to preclude the Supreme Court or any other federal judges from trying or hearing impeachments was based on their distrust of the judiciary to be impartial on such matters. The framers were well aware of several states, including Maryland, New York, North Carolina, and Virginia, that had explicitly provided for judges to participate in some fashion in those states' respective impeachment processes. Nevertheless, Gouverneur Morris remarked that "no other tribunal other than the Senate could be trusted. The Supreme Court were too few in number and might be warped or corrupted."[45] Similarly, Roger Sherman took the position that Supreme Court participation in impeachment trials would be "improper . . . because the judges would be appointed by" the president and, therefore, partial to him.[46] In *The Federalist Papers*, Hamilton explained that the framers believed that the special constraints on the impeachment power's exercise, such as the political accountability of members of Congress and the division of impeachment authority between the House and the Senate, were meant to be a "complete security" against its abuse.[47]

In addition, it is not clear that the conflicts of interest the framers sought to avoid by precluding judges, including Supreme Court justices, from serving as the trial authorities for judicial removal and by providing for separate criminal and impeachment proceedings would have diminished significantly or disappeared if judicial review over a judicial impeachment were allowed. The framers also substituted the chief justice for the vice-president in the impeachment trial of a president to preclude the former from presiding over the impeachment trial of the one official standing between him and succession to the presidency.[48] Given the framers' efforts to avoid conflicts of interest in the administration of impeachment, it seems implausible that, if they had accepted or assumed the possibility of judicial review of impeachments, no one would have commented on the obvious conflict posed by allowing the chief justice to participate in the subsequent review of his decisions as the presiding officer of a presidential impeachment trial. Given the strong objections to the proposed impeachment process in the constitutional and state ratifying conventions,[49] it is likely that, if anyone had expected judicial review of impeachments, that person would have objected to or commented on potential conflicts with the chief justice's role.

Moreover, it would have been unusual or novel for judges to have reviewed (as opposed to having participated as parts of the trial bodies in) impeachment actions, because judicial review of impeachment proceedings simply had not occurred prior to the Constitution's drafting and ratification either in the states or in England. To be sure, the framers did not discuss judicial review much at all, but this was so because they were familiar with judicial review of written documents, including state constitutions and legislation, and, thus, expected there would be judicial review of statutory questions or constitutional challenges to legislation. Given that judicial review of impeachments would have been unprecedented for the framers, however, it is reasonable to believe that if they had wanted this to have become part of the constitutional design they would have had to make explicit provision for it or at least to have acknowledged or discussed the possibility explicitly.

Indeed, it is possible to read the constitutional convention's debates of August 27, 1787, as settling any question about the framers' intentions to extend any kind of judicial authority, including judicial review, to impeachments. In the midst of debating the Supreme Court's jurisdiction on August 27, 1787, the constitutional convention delegates "dropped 'impeachment' altogether from the list which later became, by stylistic revision, the list defining the Article III 'judicial power.'"[50] After initially agreeing to postpone considering whether to extend Supreme Court jurisdiction to "the trial of impeachments of officers of the United States,"[51] the delegates considered the appropriate phrase or clause for accurately describing or designating the scope of the Supreme Court's jurisdiction. Madison "doubted whether it was going too far to extend the jurisdiction of the Court generally to cases arising under the Constitution, and whether it ought not to be limited to cases of a Judiciary nature."[52] After Dr. Johnson suggested "that the jurisdiction given [in the former phrase] was constructively limited to cases of a Judiciary nature,"[53] the delegates agreed to drop consideration of extending the Court's jursdiction "in cases of impeachment."[54]

The critical aspect of this debate is that it occurred in the midst of the delegates' consideration of which cases, for whatever reason, would fall within the jurisdiction of the Supreme Court. The framers took great pains to set forth as precisely as possible the kinds of cases they anticipated would fall properly within the Court's jurisdiction—those "of a Judiciary nature," as both Madison and Dr. Johnson put it. Not surprisingly, given that the framers never regarded impeachments as constituting such cases, they balked at the prospect of including either "the trial of impeachments of officers of the United States" or "cases of impeachment" within the original or appellate matters that would fall with the jurisdiction of the Supreme Court.

The fact that the framers understood that they would have had to make special mention of impeachments as falling within federal court jurisdiction in any manner makes complete sense, given that judicial participation in the impeachment process had always been explicitly provided for in other jurisdictions with which they were familiar and that judicial review of impeachments would have deviated from the prevailing practice of their times. That the framers declined to make the extension is consistent with the common understanding that, unless there were an explicit statement in the Constitution to the contrary, impeachments would remain, as they had always been up until then, cases of a unique nature not subject to judicial review.

In addition, the prudential concerns—particularly the lack of finality and the trouble with devising appropriate relief—that led the Court to find nonjusticiability in *Nixon* apply equally to cases involving alleged violations of explicit impeachment constraints. Significantly, the *Nixon* Court used examples from presidential and judicial impeachments to explain how these prudential factors supported a finding of nonjusticiability.[55]

Given the unsettling prospect for many modern readers of an explicit constitutional violation without a judicial remedy, it may be helpful to examine more closely the degree to which the factors used for identifying a political question could support precluding any judicial review of an impeachment. Of special concern may be the extent to which judicial review is inappropriate in a presidential impeachment in which a conflict between the judiciary and the political process constitutionally authorized for its regulation is either not present or reduced.

In fact, Article I states that the House "shall have the sole Power of Impeachment"[56] and that the Senate "shall have the sole Power to Try all Impeachments."[57] In addition, the speech or debate clause,[58] has been interpreted as precluding judicial review of the legitimate activities of legislators acting within their official duties, including impeachment.[59] However, these provisions do not necessarily preclude judicial review because there may be other judicially enforceable limitations, such as the explicit constraints, on the impeachment power. Nor is the textual support for nonjusticiability settled by the provision in Article I, section 5, that "[e]ach House may determine the Rules of its Proceedings."[60] As the Court has explained, "[E]ach house . . . may not by its rules ignore constitutional restraints or violate fundamental rights, and there should be a reasonable relation between the mode or method of proceeding established by the rule and the result which is sought to be attained."[61] Thus, it is conceivable that, as previously suggested, violations of explicit constraints could be justiciable on the basis that those provisions, unlike the term *try*, spell out the terms or conditions of their enforcement.

Other aspects of the Constitution counsel even more strongly against the justiciability of explicit constitutional violations in the impeachment context. First, impeachment is the only nonjudicial power that the framers expressly considered but declined to give to any part of the federal judiciary. As Justice Story explained, the framers viewed Congress as better equipped than the judiciary to deal with the difficult political issues raised in impeachments. He noted that the framers rejected giving the impeachment power to the judiciary because they believed that impeachment required "a very large discretion [that] must unavoidably be vested in the court of impeachment."[62] Justice Story explained further that the framers understood the power of impeachment as inherently political and vested the power solely with the House of Representatives, "where it should be, in the possession and power of the immediate representatives of the people."[63] He also regarded the sanctions available to the Senate in impeachment trials as "peculiarly fit[ting] for a political tribunal to administer, and as will secure the public against political injuries."[64] In other words, impeachments require skills incompatible with the judicial function.

Second, impeachments are laced with issues incompatible with, and not easily narrowed for, judicial review. For example, it is difficult to settle on judicially manageable standards for reviewing the House's or the Senate's judgments on the scope of impeachable offenses. Such judgments depend in each case on the House's or the Senate's political judgment, the natures of the impeachable official's duties and of the offense involved, and the circumstances under which the alleged misconduct was committed. Indeed, these difficulties led the Court of Claims in *Ritter v.*

United States[65] to dismiss as nonjusticiable Judge Ritter's claim—the first judicial challenge ever made against a federal impeachment—that the Senate had improperly convicted him for nonimpeachable offenses. Nor is there a clear standard amenable to judicial review that federal courts could use to evaluate the propriety of the House's or the Senate's finding that certain misconduct actually constituted an impeachable political crime.[66]

Third, as the *Nixon* Court acknowledged,[67] judicial review of impeachments undermines their finality. Judicial review of impeachments might also lead to embarrassing conflicts between the Congress and the federal judiciary. No doubt, given contemporary concerns about avoiding the appearance of impropriety or conflicts of interest in judicial hearings, allowing the chief justice to participate in the judicial review of a president's impeachment trial over which the chief justice had presided would be awkward, if not unseemly. More importantly, it would be confusing and humiliating and risk serious political instability at home and abroad if the Senate voted to remove the president and then a federal court countermanded that judgment.

Yet another basis on which to distinguish *Powell*, either apart from or in addition to the uniqueness of impeachment, is that *Powell* has not been properly understood. One could argue that the real problem for the House in *Powell* was that none of its existing powers for disciplining current or prospective members fit Powell's alleged financial improprieties. The House's expulsion authority required a representative to have been seated and the concurrence of at least two-thirds of its members;[68] however, many members were not sure that an expulsion could be based on misconduct committed during a prior Congress, as would have been the case for Powell's infractions, and, even if the House had such power, they were not sure they had the requisite number of votes.[69] The other alternative—the one chosen by the House—was to exclude Powell, but this authority turned on Powell's not having met the three standing qualifications for House membership. Although more than two-thirds of the House voted to exclude Powell, they did so only pursuant to a vote on exclusion. The Court refused to assume that the vote would have been the same if it had been on the question of expulsion, which the Court noted was not a "fungible proceeding[]" with exclusion.[70] Because the House chose to exercise its exclusion rather than its expulsion power, the Court declined to express any "view on what limitations may exist on Congress' power to expel or otherwise punish a member once he has been seated."[71] In his concurrence, Justice Douglas speculated that "if this were an expulsion case I would think that no justiciable controversy would be presented, the vote of the House being two-thirds or more. But it is not an expulsion case. Whether it could have been won as an expulsion case, no one knows. . . . It well might be easier to bar admission than to expel one already seated."[72] In short, the House faced a no-win situation in trying to punish Powell because his alleged misconduct fell outside of the existing House disciplinary mechanisms.

This understanding of *Powell* could lead one to argue, as I have previously, that the Court there

> could [probably] not have interfered with the decision by [the House] to expel Representative Powell if [it] had followed the constitutional standards for expulsion; however, the Court could step in where Congress used a procedure to accomplish impermissible ends. *Powell* indicates that while [the House] has full, complete, and sole power to exclude, it does not have the power to change expulsion into exclusion—to turn one constitutional procedure for another.[73]

Given this understanding of *Powell*, judicial review of impeachments would be limited to determining whether the House or the Senate used impeachment to do something that it could only do under some other power, such as exclusion or expulsion.

One could go further and argue that the Court in *Powell* was mistaken in its conclusion that "the qualifications for members of Congress had been fixed in the Constitution."[74] One could contend that these qualifications are not fixed, that they constitute instead an irreducible minimum to which the House could make an addition, if it chose to do so.[75] This argument would be similar to the popular one leveled against chief justice John Marshall's opinion in *Marbury v. Madison*,[76] that he misread the allocation of original jurisdiction in Article III as being fixed rather than as being an irreducible minimum to which Congress could make additions through its authority to regulate federal jurisdiction. This argument is also similar to the contention being made by some of the proponents of state-enacted limits on the numbers of terms a person can serve in either chamber of Congress—that while the Constitution precludes Congress from adding to or changing the qualifications for a member of the House, it leaves each state the discretion to fix others. The relevance of these other arguments to judicial review of an impeachment challenge is that they conceivably demonstrate *Powell*'s erroneous reasoning and, thus, help to remove the case as an obstacle to barring judicial review of impeachments altogether.

One problem with even the latter reading of *Powell*, though, is that it does not preclude judicial review of an impeachment altogether. To be sure, it preserves judicial review for what would be extremely unlikely abuses of the impeachment power, but it implicitly accepts that all congressional powers have judicially enforceable limits, at least at the point at which one power is being improperly substituted for, or being exercised in the place of, another. *Powell* arguably followed this line of reasoning by suggesting that exclusion and expulsion could be used by the

House for different purposes and that the bases for the House's exclusion of Powell did not fit within the scope of that particular power.

For many, an even more serious problem with the position that the Constitution precludes judicial review altogether is that it seems unlikely that the Court would ever abdicate an entire area of constitutional law to another branch. This is especially true with respect to checks and balances; in almost every other situation in which the Constitution allows one branch to check another's excesses or abuses, the Court has taken the position as a mediator, albeit sometimes with very limited authority. For example, the Court has never characterized congressional control of federal jurisdiction as involving a political question. Moreover, some of the areas in which the Court has found a political question, such as determining the appropriate time period for ratification of a constitutional amendment[77] or whether a state government is republican in form,[78] are not subject (at least as clearly) as the impeachment power to defeat by other plainly applicable clauses, such as the requirement of a supermajority vote for a conviction. Even in other areas often treated by scholars as comprising or involving nonjusticiable political questions, such as foreign affairs, the Constitution either provides no clear standard by which to measure the propriety of a branch's political judgment (such as whether the situation declared to be a war by Congress was one) or explicitly provides for the involvement of more than one branch, which has in the past given rise to confusion among the political branches as to whose authority should govern and the need for the Court to act as arbiter.[79]

There are two tenable responses to the reluctance to abandon any judicial review of impeachments. First, the Court has yet to find an impeachment challenge to be justiciable. Regardless of what one thinks is the need for judicial review of impeachment challenges, the Court has never sanctioned it. Thus, as a practical matter, the Court has left the federal impeachment process for over two centuries to the complete, unreviewable discretion of the Congress.

Second, the most worrisome kinds of impeachment abuses have yet to occur. Even if one were inclined to find the need for judicial review of impeachment challenges in extreme cases, the likelihood of such controversies ever arising is, for all practical purposes, nonexistent. If one were truly interested in knowing what Congress is likely to do with its impeachment authority in the absence of judicial review, one need look no further than the pages of history. The latter do not contain any of the nightmarish episodes imagined by proponents of judicial review of the impeachment process. Moreover, many of the constitutional restraints on Congress's impeachment authority are self-defining, such as the supermajority vote for conviction in the Senate, making it easy for the Senate to know what it must do at a minimum in order to convict an impeached official and to avoid obvious controversy. In addition, in many areas of constitutional law, particularly those that involve or are likely to involve political questions, informal accommodations are frequently reached that obviate the need for judicial review. The point is that oftentimes a political branch, if it senses opposition or resistance from the other or the possibility of meddlesome judicial review, will only proceed if it thinks it will win in the long run or exigent circumstances or principle give it no other choice. Otherwise, it takes a less provocative course of action. As the next section suggests, this is true for the federal impeachment power.

The Propriety of Judicial Review for the Most Extreme Abuses of the Impeachment Power

To some, all of the difficulties with judicial review of impeachment might argue in favor of allowing it only in the most extreme cases—that is, only the most minimal judicial review, around the edges of the process, makes sense. Otherwise, the Court needs to be prepared even in the case of a deviation from an explicit constraint to balance the need for judicial review against its consequences on constitutional stability.

Despite the fact that this position attempts to preserve a relatively modest role for the Court in interpreting the impeachment clauses, it is not clear how the Court would distinguish extreme abuses of the impeachment power from violations of explicit constitutional constraints. If the Court did not confine itself to enforcing the latter, it is unclear precisely on what basis it would be acting and which limitations it would be enforcing.

One serious counterargument to this position is that it premises judicial review on an unrealistic basis. Nor is this an inappropriate attitude to adopt in determining the propriety of judicial intervention.[80] The history of the federal impeachment power shows, for example, that, even when attendance and preparation for an impeachment trial in the Senate have been poor (as with Judges Ritter and Louderback), most senators have taken seriously (at least at the time they cast their final votes) the consequences of a conviction and never considered failing to comply with—much less taken any steps toward violating—any of the explicit constitutional constraints on their power to try impeachments. The fact that senators have never conducted an impeachment proceeding in violation of these clear restraints shows the degree to which the latter have achieved their desired effect. Moreover, the advent of media coverage in the twentieth century and the omnipresent need to ensure that the president and the federal judiciary accept Congress's impeachment judgments to avoid lingering conflicts or uncertainty over their acceptability help to ensure even further that Congress complies with the explicit constitutional restraints on its impeachment authority.

The real problem for proponents of judicial review of impeachment proceedings, particularly for serious abuses, is that they might be looking in the wrong direction. As a practical matter, the likelier cases for abuses are those involving low-profile impeachments or more ambiguous or obtuse constitutional constraints. The reason for this is that in higher-profile impeachments, the public pressure and scrutiny on Congress is more intense and Congress knows that if it at least follows the obvious or clear constitutional constraints, its impeachment judgments are less suspect and are likelier to stand the test of time. In other words, the obsession with congressional compliance with the clear constitutional constraints, such as the supermajority vote for a conviction, is misplaced, because that concerns the easy case.

Consequently, it is not surprising to find that the few judicial challenges that have been made to the federal impeachment process have not involved questions about whether the House or the Senate have complied with one or more of the clear or unambiguous constitutional constraints. Rather, those challenges have involved issues about the reach or meaning of the more open-ended or ambiguous constitutional limitations on the federal impeachment power. Judge Ritter challenged his removal on the basis that the impeachment article on which he was convicted did not set forth misconduct that qualified or constituted impeachable offenses, Judges Nixon's and Hastings' lawsuits dealt with whether the Senate's power to "try" impeachments imposed on it a duty to provide a certain kind of hearing before the full body, and Judge Claiborne's lawsuit raised a question about the proper sequence of criminal and impeachment proceedings. Moreover, the hypotheticals of concern to Justices White, Blackmun, and Souter in their concurrences in *Nixon*—those involving the Senate's tossing of a coin[81] or summarily determining that an impeachable official was "a bad guy"[82]—test the limits even further of the Senate's discretion in exercising its authority to "try" impeachments.

These lawsuits, if not the hypotheticals as well, have invited the federal courts to review less extreme abuses of the impeachment power. The problem for the plaintiffs is that their cases have focused on particular policy judgments of the Senate about whose propriety reasonable people could disagree. The plaintiffs' difficulty is that as one moves away from congressional deviations from the explicit constraints on the federal impeachment power, one moves closer to the heart of the federal impeachment process itself, which involves, among other things, the Senate's making of policy judgments on the appropriate procedures to use or the particular political crimes involved in certain impeachment trials. These judgments, like all of those made by the Senate in impeachment trials, turn on the Senate's balancing of competing concerns, including but not limited to the political climate of the impeachment and the relative needs to vindicate the public interest, punish or redress official misconduct, and provide an impeached official the opportunity to state his or her case. For example, at the end of the Ritter impeachment trial, senators reached a compromise as to the nature of the political offenses committed by Judge Ritter; even though they might have had some differences of opinion over the gravity or perhaps even the existence of Judge Ritter's financial improprieties, at least two-thirds of the senators present did agree that there was enough evidence of such misconduct to cast a fatal taint on his impartiality and on the integrity of the federal judiciary. Part of the Senate's policy-making function in an impeachment trial is to define the nature of the political crime(s) involved in a particular impeachment trial. Moreover, in much the same manner that it decides (pursuant to constitutional authorization) on the rules or conditions for various hearings to assist it in making decisions on various legislative matters, the Senate balanced various considerations, including efficiency and fairness, in determining the special procedures for gathering evidence for each of the judicial impeachment trials in the 1980s.

The impeachment trials of Judges Ritter, Claiborne, Hastings, and Nixon also raise concern about whether senators behave differently, depending on the visibility or popularity of the impeached official involved in the trial before them. In the impeachment trial of a low-profile figure, in which there is less public and partisan pressure and media scrutiny, senators seem generally to be freer either to devote greater attention than usual to the real merits of or to ignore almost entirely the substantive issues involved. Consequently, it is not surprising to find, particularly in the twentieth century, that some senators treat the impeachment process as a unique chance to perform a sacred constitutional duty to address official misconduct and others view it as disruptive and distracting. In contrast, in the impeachments of higher-profile officials, such as a president or Supreme Court justice, it seems practically impossible for senators to take either of these extreme attitudes. Moreover, these latter impeachment trials are rare, so that senators need not fear they will be constant thorns in their sides. Yet, these proceedings also will obviously involve matters that will be of concern to constituents and the public interest.

Given these differences in senators' attitudes about different kinds of impeachment trials, the question is whether judicial review is especially appropriate for one type or another of these proceedings. As it turns out, these proceedings do not necessarily differ with respect to senators' relative levels of interest and preparation. For example, in the nineteenth century, Congress never succeeded in removing any official for purely partisan reasons. That lesson has carried over into the twentieth century. The impeachment threats against both Chief Justice Warren and William O. Douglas never came close to being realized. To be sure, 74 percent of the Democrats in the Senate voted guilty on the one impeachment article on

which Judge Ritter—a Republican—was convicted "in a strongly Democratic era [in which] the Court and the executive and legislative departments" were deadlocked over the constitutionality of the New Deal.[83]
Yet, Judge Ritter was not a strongly partisan jurist. Moreover, the
charges against him had dogged him at least since 1933—four years prior
to his impeachment—when the House of Representatives previously investigated him. Under these circumstances, the best guess remains that
"[s]enators voting guilty on the cumulative article must have decided that
multiple accusations, even if not accepted as separately proved by the
requisite [super]majority, somehow created a pattern of misconduct mer-
iting conviction."[84]

In addition, even though partisanship was fervent in Congress
throughout most of the 1980s, Judges Hastings and Nixon were each
convicted by a Democratically controlled Senate. While Harry Claiborne—a Democrat—was convicted by a Republican-controlled Senate
in 1986, his convictions were based on strongly bipartisan votes on three
of the four articles of impeachment against him.

Thus far in the 1990s, with partisanship seemingly becoming even
more intense, the only two impeachments to which the Congress (Democratically controlled until January 1995) has given any thought to initiating are against federal district judges Robert Collins and Robert Aguilar—both of whom are Democrats. The House's failure thus far to initiate
an impeachment action against either of these judges is not attributable to
partisanship. Instead it can be blamed either on bad timing—the need to
consider impeaching Judge Collins coincided with busy legislative sessions in 1993 and 1994 and an election year in 1994 in which many, if
not most, incumbent representatives faced stiff reelection bids—or on the
fact that Judge Aguilar's impeachment would impose a tough burden on
the House to figure out whether, in spite of the finding of the ninth circuit
sitting en banc that neither of the offenses for which he was prosecuted
and convicted actually constituted indictable crimes, he still might have
engaged in misconduct constituting a political crime and, hence, an impeachable offense. The House's difficulty in making a judgment call (if
not also authorizing some additional investigation) in Judge Aguilar's
case is further complicated by the fact that at least by the time of the
fall elections of 1994 the Judicial Conference of the United States had
not certified a request for the House to inquire into the propriety of his
impeachment.

The demise of partisanship in impeachment proceedings has put pressure on presidents or members of Congress to use other means for political reprisals against unpopular impeachable officials. Whereas the threat
of impeachment might have meant (at least a little) something to Chief

Justice Marshall, it did not faze or intimidate Chief Justice Warren or Justice Douglas in the least. The grumblings among Democrats about possibly trying to impeach President Reagan after some of the early revelations about the Iran-Contra affair quickly turned into awareness of his weakened position and helped to fuel the partisanship that played a part in the Senate's rejection of Robert Bork's nomination to replace Justice Lewis Powell on the Supreme Court and Judge Douglas Ginsburg's forced withdrawal from his nomination to fill the same seat. Not surprisingly, the confirmation process provides a more hospitable forum for partisan bickering, because the House is not required to act at all and the Senate needs only a majority vote for a decision.

The issue boils down to how judicial review of these impeachment judgments would contribute either to the constraints on the impeachment power already in place or to the proper functioning of the impeachment process itself. Ironically, judicial review of the federal impeachment process would almost certainly achieve one of two outcomes: either a constitutional amendment (or at least an attempted one) that would insulate the federal impeachment process from judicial review (or at least set forth its conditions) or would delegate the federal impeachment authority (at least for judicial impeachments) to some other body (because the House or the Senate or both could reasonably conclude the system is more trouble than it is worth) *or* the virtual abandonment of the federal impeachment process (because many members of the House and the Senate would probably not be prepared or willing to trust that the judiciary could engage in disinterested review of judicial impeachment proceedings).

In the final analysis, though, the extent to which the political accountability of senators actually checks their judgment, particularly in low profile impeachments, is beyond the scope of this book. Nevertheless, the absence of judicial review ensures that senators involved in impeachment trials will feel a peculiar mix of freedom (from being second-guessed by a federal court) and responsibility (to make the best decision possible given that they are the sole and final arbiters of the impeached official's guilt or innocence) that they experience only on a few other occasions— namely, confirmation and treaty ratifications. The critical difference between impeachments and these latter proceedings is that senators might find themselves subjected to fewer external pressures, such as lobbyists, the media, interest groups, and constituents, in dealing with the former, at least with respect to low-profile impeached officials. Under such circumstances, the odds are that senators will still be somewhat concerned about about how their impeachment decisions will be regarded by subsequent senates or the court of history and how those judgments will affect the Constitution.

Nor is it likely that, given the various pressures on them from their colleagues or their sense of history and media coverage, senators will ever resort to flipping coins in order to make impeachment decisions. Even so, such a hypothetical case merely supposes that the Senate is still exercising some judgment—albeit, very poor—in an impeachment proceeding. It would be hard to distinguish on some principled basis a senator's choosing to decide guilt in an impeachment trial on the basis of a coin toss rather than on the basis—implicitly accepted as nonreviewable by *Nixon*—of guessing as to guilt or innocence because he or she had not read the record. The unpredictability or uncertainty of defining the basis for judicial interference in this context compounds the *Nixon* Court's concerns about preserving the "finality" of impeachment decisions and "fashioning" appropriate "relief."[85]

Because they are so unlike anything actually ever tried in an impeachment, hypotheses about tossing coins or voting on the basis of an impeached official's hair color ultimately do not supply reasonable bases for building reliable understandings of the justiciability of impeachment challenges. As Judge Stephen Williams observed in his opinion for the D.C. Circuit in *Nixon*,

> If the Senate should ever be ready to abdicate its responsibilities to school-children, or, moved by Caligula's appointment of his horse as senator, to an elephant from the National Zoo, the republic will have sunk to depths from which no court could rescue it. And if the senators try to ignore the clear requirement of a two-thirds vote for conviction, they will have to contend with public outrage that will ultimately impose its sanction at the ballot box. Absent judicial review, the Senate takes sole responsibility for its impeachment procedures as a full-fledged constitutional actor, just as the framers intended.[86]

Putting aside Judge Williams's hyperbole, it is still not insignificant that even the worst situations he imagines simply would not occur in this country. Given media scrutiny on Congress, party divisions within both the House and the Senate, and peer pressure in Congress (as well as the voters' basic interest in having representatives and senators of whom they can be proud at least in some minimal way), it is difficult to conceive how Congress would ever get away with violating an explicit constraint on the impeachment power, especially in an event as closely watched as a presidential impeachment. The unlikely prospect that Congress would ever violate an explicit constraint on or extremely abuse its impeachment power conveys something important about the continued effectiveness of current restraints and the similarly remote possibility that judicial review of the violation of an explicit constraint on impeachment would remedy the level of corruption or malfeasance that could have caused such a breach.

The Range of Nonjusticiable Impeachment Challenges after *Nixon*

The Justiciability of Impeachment Challenges Based on Arguable Violations of the Fifth Amendment Due Process Clause

Those taking the position that the only justiciable challenges to the impeachment process are for violations of explicit constraints might disagree over the applicability of the Fifth Amendment due process clause to impeachment but might concur that, if the clause is properly applied, then its violation would be justiciable.[87] Those reading *Nixon* as indicating that no (or virtually no) impeachment challenge is justiciable would argue that, even if the due process clause applied to impeachments, any violation of it would not be justiciable. The latter argument is bolstered by the Court's observation in *Nixon* that "opening the door of judicial review to the procedures used by the Senate in trying impeachments would 'expose the political life of the country to months, or perhaps years, of chaos.' "[88] Even so, the central question remains about the applicability and justiciability of the Fifth Amendment due process clause in the impeachment context.

Although the Fifth Amendment due process clause could plainly be read to apply to a situation in which an impeachable officer has been deprived of his or her "property" interest in a governmental position, it is far from certain that this provision applies to impeachments. For one thing, the clause's language does not necessarily support such a result. The clause explicitly provides that no "person" shall be deprived of life, liberty, or property without due process of law, whereas the impeachment process expressly concerns only the president, the vice-president, and "officers of the United States." The primary purpose of the Fifth Amendment due process clause was to guarantee procedural protections for private citizens against coercive, arbitrary governmental action.[89] In contrast, the impeachment process is not directed at its subjects in their private capacities.

Although the Supreme Court has held that the clause requires certain procedural protections in limited circumstances against the arbitrary dismissal of low-level governmental employees,[90] impeachment is directed at a different class of higher-level governmental officials. An impeachment proceeding is a unique forum in which Congress may demand a public accounting of the misbehavior of one of an elite set of officials. The question in an impeachment is whether an impeachable officer is fit to preserve the public trust and, therefore, to remain in office. The specific procedural protections given to the subjects of an impeachment are spelled out in a special section of the Constitution. Treating impeachments as *sui generis* is consistent with the absence of any evidence that the Fifth Amendment, including the due process clause, was ever intended to apply to impeachments or to countermand the incompatibility between judicial review of impeachment challenges and the impeachment process that the constitutional design otherwise seems to contemplate.

This understanding is supported by the only judicial decision ever rendered on this issue. After initially overturning Judge Hastings' impeachment trial in part because it lacked fundamental fairness and therefore violated the Fifth Amendment due process clause,[91] U.S. District Judge Stanley Sporkin begrudgingly agreed on remand of the case subsequent to the Court's decision in *Nixon* to dismiss Hastings' case as nonjusticiable,[92] notwithstanding the former judge's Fifth Amendment claim.

The argument against applying the Fifth Amendment due process clause to impeachment proceedings, however, seems forced. By its plain terms, the clause forbids Congress from depriving a "person" of "life, liberty, or property without due process of law;" and it is not a stretch to think that the impeachment process seeks to deprive someone of their current and perhaps future office, which could easily constitute a form of property. Moreover, the fact that the Fifth Amendment postdates the impeachment clauses makes irrelevant any of the framers' or ratifiers' original desires regarding the federal impeachment process. The point of an amendment is to change what came before and that could logically cover the impeachment process no matter how special it was conceived to be.

Even if the Fifth Amendment due process clause applied to the impeachment context, though, it is not likely that it would mandate any different procedures from those already applicable. The argument supporting application of the due process clause to the impeachment process maintains in part that an impeachable official has a property interest in his or her position. Yet, a property interest for purposes of the due process clause is defined as an entitlement or expectation based on state or federal law.[93] For example, the president assumes office under the conditions for impeachment as spelled out in the Constitution. He serves for four years and may run for a second term if he so chooses; however, he is also subject to removal from office through impeachment with the special procedures spelled out in the text. This is true for every impeachable official, whose interest in his or her office is subject to his or her impeachment. Consequently, the Fifth Amendment due process and the impeachment clauses conceivably fit together to the extent that the latter provision arguably defines all the process that is due—that is, constitutionally required at a minimum—in an impeachment trial. This construction of the impeachment and the Fifth Amendment due process clauses would mean that the extent to which impeachment challenges could be justiciable would coincide with deviations from the aspects of an impeachment proceeding required by due process—the latter aspects consisting of violations of the explicit constraints on the federal impeachment authority.

If the Fifth Amendment due process clause were construed to require an impeachment trial to follow at least the explicit constraints spelled out in the Constitution, it would not be likely that the former would restrain the Senate's discretion to conduct impeachment trials any more than does the term *try*. The *Nixon* Court observed, for example, that the fact that the framers set out specific limitations applicable only to impeachments confirms "that the Framers did not intend to impose additional limitations on the form of the Senate proceedings by the use of the word 'try.'"[94] The point is that where the framers wanted to ensure specific constraints on the procedure used by the Senate for trying impeachments, they spelled them out in the Constitution. The process that is due in an impeachment trial conceivably consists of the explicit constitutional requirements set forth in the document. Otherwise, the Senate has nonreviewable discretion to conduct its hearings as it prefers. There is no evidence to suggest that at the time the Constitution was amended to include the Bill of Rights, the goal included revising the specific safeguards explicitly set forth in the text for impeachments *or* to add any other procedural requirements on impeachments to those listed in the Constitution. The significance of this silence is reinforced by the fact that none of the records of federal impeachment proceedings have contained any arguments about the applicability of Fifth Amendment due process until the 1980s. (Various officials have complained about the fairness of their impeachment proceedings, but it was not until the 1980s that these claims were linked to the due process clause.) In other words, even after the latter clause went into effect, the general understanding of members of Congress (even in the First Congress) of the uniqueness of the impeachment process never changed. That singularity is undercut by efforts to model impeachments on judicial proceedings or to limit congressional autonomy at least within the confines of explicit constraints in the name of due process.

The Justiciability of Challenges to the Senate's Failure to Follow Rules of Evidence or a Uniform Burden of Proof

Another difficulty left unanswered by *Nixon* is whether the Senate's adoption of, and subsequent failure to comply with, specific rules of evidence or a uniform burden of proof for impeachment trials is justiciable. This problem raises two, interrelated questions: (1) does the Senate have the power to tie its hands in this manner, and, if so, (2) does such conduct on the part of the Senate amount to a waiver of the insulation or immunity from judicial review its procedural decisions otherwise enjoy to the extent recognized in *Nixon*. Each of these issues in turn raises special concerns.

Apart from the prior discussion in part II concerning the practical problems with the Senate's ability to bind each individual senator in an impeachment trial to follow certain procedural rules,[95] one critical constitutional concern is whether the adoption of such rules would constitute a waiver of the Senate's immunity from judicial review as recognized in *Nixon*. The settlement of this issue depends on whether the Senate has the power to waive its constitutional immunity from judicial review.

On the one hand, several factors argue against the existence of such power. These include the framers' distrust of and consequent decision—changeable only by constitutional amendment—to exclude judges as decision makers in the impeachment process and to exclude impeachment cases from those subject to the judicial power set forth in Article III; the weakening of impeachment as a check against executive and especially judicial abuse of power; the conflicts of interest judges would have in overseeing the only constitutionally recognized process for their removal; and the difficulties judicial review would pose for finality and fashioning appropriate relief.

On the other hand, in the context of administrative law, the Supreme Court has declared that "judicial review of a final agency action by an aggrieved person will not be cut off unless there is persuasive reason to believe that such was the purpose of Congress."[96] In other words, if a lawmaking body or administrative agency were really interested in barring judicial review of certain actions or proceedings, it may do so only if it issues a "clear statement" of that wish.[97] Under these circumstances, courts ask for a "clear statement" because they want to be sure about precisely how much of its power Congress has delegated to some politically unaccountable body. If the Senate's adoption of evidentiary or burden of proof rules were to be construed as the functional equivalent of a legislative or administrative act undertaken for the purpose of giving up some of the Senate's discretion in impeachment trials, then waiving nonjusticiability in the impeachment context might be possible only if there were a "clear statement" to that effect.

At least one advantage of allowing the Senate to waive nonjusticiability (or to presume nonjusticiability unless there is some clear statement to the contrary) is to make it easier for it to use evidentiary rules or a uniform burden of proof by not treating either as legally binding or by treating its noncompliance as justifying legal sanctions. Such deference seems particularly appropriate in the impeachment context, because of the longstanding tradition of courts not to interfere in this area and because the adoption of set procedures for impeachment trials is likely to work to the advantage of all of the participants by providing them predictable and consistent practices or standards.[98] Moreover, judicial deference makes sense in light of the omnipresent concerns in an impeachment with the likelihood that judicial review of an impeachment is likely to produce uncertainty as to the finality of impeachment decisions and potentially intractable problems of devising an appropriate remedy.

Obviously, a lot turns on which presumption of judicial review is appropriate in this context. One view is that, because judicial review of impeachment trials might normally he thought not to be permissible, it should be presumed impermissible unless the Senate issues a clear statement of its intent to subject its compliance with certain procedural rules to judicial review. Another view is that impeachment proceedings are usually nonjusticiable, unless they violate express constitutional limits. In other words, if violations of express constraints were justiciable, the question is whether set evidentiary rules or a uniform burden of proof constitute such limits and, if so, are similarly justiciable. One simple way to resolve this conundrum is for the Senate, at the appropriate time, to clearly state its intent to retain or to preclude judicial review—whichever it prefers—of its compliance with set evidentiary rules or a uniform burden of proof.

The Nonjusticiability of Challenges to Deficiencies in Presidential Impeachments

A presidential impeachment trial poses many of the same problems encountered in judicial impeachments and also offers a more dramatic illustration of the dilemmas involved with judicial review of the federal impeachment process. I explore below the problems with judicial review of any aspect of a presidential impeachment trial.

THE DIFFICULTY OF DEVISING PROPER JUDICIAL REMEDIES

Sometimes it is difficult to devise a judicial remedy for a violation of an explicit constraint. For example, the Constitution provides that "[w]hen the President of the United States is tried, the chief justice shall preside."[99] At first glance, the chief justice's failure to preside over a president's impeachment trial is a constitutional violation, which arguably may justify judicial review in a way similar to the Court's intervention in *Powell* to ensure that an explicit textual constraint has not been ignored.

Yet, the situation is more complex than it seems. Imagine further that before the president's impeachment trial is about to begin, the chief justice dies or claims a conflict of interest precluding his participation; or, after the trial begins, the chief justice refuses to participate further because he does not want to be a party to what he perceives as the Senate's use of an unconstitutional procedure. It is unlikely that the Senate would delay the president's impeachment trial, so that it could hold confirmation hearings on the person he has nominated as chief justice, who would then preside over his impeachment trial. Thus, it is quite probable there would be no chief justice to preside over the presidential impeachment trial.

Under such circumstances, one could argue that the provision mandating the chief justice to preside over a presidential impeachment trial has been violated but that judicial review of its violation would be pointless if, for example, the justices were to designate an acting chief justice or the most senior associate justice were to preside instead. Judicial review would also probably compound the problem, because it would lead to outrageous results, including further delays in the impeachment trial, causing substantial domestic and foreign confusion over who should be the president of the United States. For example, the courts might order the Senate to schedule a confirmation hearing on a matter it believes it has the constitutional prerogative to schedule as it sees fit, or might order the president to appoint a chief justice that the Senate sooner or later would have to confirm (if it wanted to move forward) when it might be in the president's interest to delay the appointment as long as possible. These judicial orders involve the courts in making or directing policy choices committed by the Constitution to political actors, and they are not as likely to preserve constitutional stability as letting Congress and the president work out a mutually satisfactory settlement.

THE OMNIPRESENT NEED FOR FINALITY, ESPECIALLY IN PRESIDENTIAL IMPEACHMENTS

If the Senate were to use a special committee to do fact-finding for a presidential impeachment trial, there are two conceivable arguments supporting justiciability. The first is that the president is entitled to a trial before the full Senate because of the clause mandating that the chief justice "shall preside" at his impeachment trial. This is a dubious basis to justify justiciability, however, given *Nixon*'s holding that the Senate is the final arbiter of impeachment trial procedures.

The second argument is that the president has a special constitutional status that entitles him to a particular kind of impeachment trial. This argument is supported by the mandate that the chief justice preside over a presidential impeachment trial. Nevertheless, the need for finality and the difficulty of fashioning relief counsel against justiciability. As the Court observed in *Nixon*, there would be considerable domestic and foreign strife "if the president were impeached. The legitimacy of any successor, and hence his effectiveness, would be severely impaired, not merely while the judicial process was running its course, but during any retrial that a differently constituted Senate might conduct if its first judgment of conviction were invalidated."[100] The briefest uncertainty about who is properly the president of the United States puts national security at risk.

The reason for the uncertainty is that, for all the reasons previously set forth against judicial review of impeachments, there is no legitimate basis for a federal court to claim jurisdiction over a president's impeachment trial. One obvious reason is the strong indication that this prospect is incompatible with the constitutional design, reflected, for example, by the framers' decision not to include impeachment among the cases to which the Article III judicial power extended.[101] Moreover, the Supreme Court could claim authority over a presidential impeachment trial only if it had original or appellate jurisdiction over impeachments. The Court does not, however, have original jurisdiction over any kind of suit seeking to overturn a senatorial directive pronounced in a presidential impeachment trial.[102]

It is also implausible that the Court has appellate jurisdiction over an impeachment. The likeliest portion of Article III granting the Supreme Court appellate jurisdiction over an impeachment is the part that covers "all cases, in law and equity, arising under the Constitution."[103] The words *Law* and *Equity* are terms of art, referring to the two kinds of regular judicial courts existing, in England and the United States, at the time the Constitution was ratified;[104] however, impeachments are not technically in "Law" or "Equity." This understanding is consistent with Article III's primary focus, which has to do with the regular judicial business of ordinary courts of law, except for a passage clarifying that jury trial was to play no part in impeachment.[105] This latter provision was left in Article III when the framers shifted responsibility for impeachment trials from the Supreme Court to the Senate, and therefore to Article I, dealing with the legislative branch.[106] The framers left this provision in place because its main purpose was to provide a general rule of trial by jury, which logically fit in the judiciary article, and they left in the reservation on impeachments to avoid any confusion.

Another argument barring judicial review of impeachments under Article III is that Congress has the power to provide for "exceptions" to the Supreme Court's appellate jurisdiction[107] and thus may have excepted it from appellate review by not providing for it in any statutes governing appeals to the Court. The major problem with this argument is that it gives too much away: if Congress's power over appellate jurisdiction enables it to provide for appellate jurisdiction over an impeachment, it would have been absurd for the framers to have given Congress the powers to impeach and to make exceptions to appellate jurisdiction over impeachments, because Congress would then have been able to undo the framers' decision to move impeachment trials out of the Supreme Court and into the Senate. It makes no sense for the framers to have gone to all this trouble, without mentioning that Congress could reconsider or overturn the framers' decision at any time. In short, the mentioning of impeachment in Article III does not provide any basis for judicial review of impeachments. To the contrary, the framers' decision not to include "cases of impeachment" among those specifically mentioned as under Article III judicial power—a position that would be consistent with the prevailing practice of their time to have judges hear only "cases of a Judiciary nature," which did not include impeachment—or to sit in judgment on impeachments only if expressly authorized to do so but not to be engaged in reviewing impeachments, as well as their deliberate exclusion of federal judges from having a role in the federal impeachment process should resolve any reasonable doubt as to whether judicial review of impeachments is ever permissible.

PART IV

IMPEACHMENT REFORMS

PROPOSALS for modifying the impeachment process, particularly for federal judges, have been around as long as the Constitution itself. One of the first such measures was the Bribery Act of 1790, which has been previously discussed.[1] In 1791, the first proposed constitutional amendment for changing the system for judicial removal was introduced.[2] Between 1807 and 1812, various members of Congress, disgruntled over the failed attempt to remove Justice Chase, proposed nine other constitutional amendments for altering the procedure for removing Article III judges, but none of those proposals ever was enacted.[3] Just after the Civil War, there were several unsuccessful attempts to provide for the mandatory retirement of federal judges.[4]

In the twentieth century, proposals for reforming the impeachment process have also largely focused on judicial misconduct. Many of these have tried to change the nature or length of judicial tenure to deal with concerns about the lack of accountability of the federal judges or the impeachment process itself to remedy its perceived inability to deal effectively with the increasing need for judicial discipline and removal.[5] Each of the impeachments conducted in this century have provoked proposals either to amend the constitutional system for judicial removal or to establish statutory means for disciplining or removing federal judges.[6]

Focusing on a few of the more significant efforts to improve the judicial removal system provides a sense of the kinds of problems many reform proposals have tried to solve and of the most common difficulties with the proposals themselves. Consequently, chapter 12 considers the major proposals for changing the House's and especially the Senate's procedural rules for their respective impeachment proceedings. Chapter 13 examines statutory proposals and constitutional amendments either for modifying the status of federal judges or for substituting a different body for the Senate to try impeachments.

Chapter Twelve

PROPOSED PROCEDURAL REFORMS FOR
JUDICIAL IMPEACHMENTS

GIVEN RELATIVELY widespread consensus that House proceedings need nothing more than some fine tuning and that the Senate's proceedings require potentially more radical revision, this chapter will add a few comments to what the book already has said about the necessity for procedural reform in the House of Representatives, and will primarily focus on the problems involved with the more significant reform proposals for Senate impeachment trials.

PROPOSED PROCEDURAL REFORMS FOR IMPEACHMENT PROCEEDINGS IN THE HOUSE OF REPRESENTATIVES

The proposals for reforming impeachment proceedings in the House of Representatives are much smaller in number and less ambitious in scope than those for revising the Senate's role in the impeachment process. The major focus of the suggestions for reforming the House's impeachment role is on streamlining or reducing delays in initiating the House's impeachment proceedings.

As a general matter, the House has investigative powers ancillary to its "sole power of impeachment."[1] Nevertheless, in order to better discharge the House's constitutional duty to conduct an inquiry into impeachable conduct, the House Judiciary Committee could benefit from prompt access to investigative data, including any relevant grand jury materials and wiretap information. At present, the sources of much of this data are not under any statutory obligations to make expedited disclosure to the House of Representatives of information relating to the possible commission of impeachable offenses. Consequently, Congress could make special exceptions for granting the House expedited review of impeachment-related information contained in such disparate sources as grand jury evidence that is otherwise protected by rule 6(e) of the *Federal Rules of Criminal Procedure*; electronic surveillance materials, the disclosure of which is regulated by statute;[2] and the investigative files of a judicial council investigation undertaken pursuant to the Judicial Disability Act of 1980.[3] As long as these changes do not result in automatically trigger-

ing impeachment proceedings or in the disruption of any of the investigative processes covered, no conceivable problem with them exists.[4]

Another, more problematic proposal for expediting impeachments in
the House, previously described in part II,[5] is the formalization of more
timely communications between the House and the Justice Department,
or, in an appropriate case, an independent counsel. This practice could
lead to an early removal from office (through resignation) or at least prevent the House from delaying its initiation of or preparation for impeachment proceedings until the Justice Department's work was completed and
a mutually satisfactory transfer of information could be worked out between the Justice Department and it. Indeed, present law authorizes an
independent counsel to inform the House of the possible need for an impeachment—a procedure that is consistent with separation of powers as
long as the final authority to initiate impeachment proceedings rests with
the House.[6] Although one potential problem with this proposal is that
neither the House nor the executive branch may want the other to have a
say in how it performs its affairs any more than is absolutely necessary,
the underlying difficulty could be solved if the Justice Department were to
give timely notice to the House of its intentions, including, for example,
its plan to pursue an indictment or convene a grand jury.

Once an impeachment inquiry has been formally initiated, the House
has several options for streamlining it. These include the House's adapta-
tion for its unique purposes and setting some of the same methods the
Senate might use to expedite impeachment trials, including (1) issue preclusion; (2) hiring outside counsel with expertise in impeachment matters
to assist the House Judiciary Committee, relevant subcommittee, or
house managers; (3) having members with relevant experience routinely
sit on impeachment panels (assuming, of course, they are interested in
continuing to handle such affairs). The next section evaluates the efficacy
of each of these proposed procedural reforms in Senate impeachment trials, with the understanding that any or all of them could be tailored for
the House to use as it sees fit.

PROPOSED PROCEDURAL REFORMS FOR SENATE
IMPEACHMENT TRIALS

Four factors should be kept in mind as background to any discussion of
reforming the procedures for Senate impeachment trials. First, although
the Senate has rejected many proposals for modifying impeachment trial
procedures, it may change its mind. For example, a differently constituted
Senate in the future might reach a different conclusion regarding the via-
bility of issue preclusion or other procedural reforms (such as set rules of

evidence or a uniform burden of proof) it has previously rejected. Second, rejecting set procedural rules arguably makes it easier for senators in impeachment trials to debate substantive as opposed to procedural questions. A helpful analogy may be that impeachments more closely resemble administrative proceedings, which tend to favor the elimination of formal procedural barriers or evidentiary restrictions, than judicial trials, in which the primary focus is on process. While the absence of uniform procedural rules creates some uncertainty and unpredictability for the participants in impeachment trials, it might also enable senators to cut through procedural nuances to get to the substance of the hearings.

Third, adopting uniform procedural rules would not necessarily streamline impeachment trials to the Senate's satisfaction. Efforts to use the same procedural rules of civil or criminal trials in impeachment trials can (1) burden those proceedings with substantial debate on the meaning or scope of particular procedural rules; (2) require the senators to deal with procedural matters they may not have the expertise, interest, or time to handle; (3) encourage counsel for impeached officials to devote as much of their time to debating procedural questions as to the substantive issues involved in an impeachment trial; and (4) divert senators' time and energy away from the substance of the allegations against the impeached official.

Lastly, the efficacy of each proposal for reforming Senate impeachment trial procedures depends on one's attitude about the general need to salvage or retain the Senate's role in the impeachment process. The more one tends to think that the system is not broken, the likelier one is to accept only minor suggestions for change. Yet, if it can be shown that internal reforms cannot remedy basic problems with the Senate's performance in impeachment trials, then more radical reform, such as excluding the Senate altogether from the removal process, may be in order.

Issue Preclusion

Given the likelihood of a criminal conviction prior to the inception of impeachment proceedings, a common proposal is for the Senate to use some form of issue preclusion to expedite its impeachment trials. Proposals for issue preclusion in the Senate have varied, including the House's third article of impeachment against Judge Claiborne claiming the fact of his conviction (upheld on appeal) as a basis for his removal[7] and Stephen Burbank's proposal for "granting substantial preclusive effect to the findings of fact necessarily grounding a guilty verdict, at least when the judgment of the conviction has been affirmed on appeal and so long as those involved in the impeachment process consider claims of error regarding the antecedent fact-finding process that have not previously been rejected by the courts."[8] Each of these proposals allows impeached officials to argue that, even though they have exhausted their appeals, there is a compelling reason, such as new evidence, that should preclude the Senate from relying on their convictions.

The earlier discussion of issue preclusion in this book[9] should have made clear that that device, properly understood and used, could increase the efficiency of removal proceedings.[10] As long as the Senate finds that a criminal conviction has been obtained in a fair proceeding that has fully complied with due process and contains no disturbing irregularities, then the Senate could reasonably accept the conviction as settling any factual disputes regarding the commission of the misconduct in question. As the house managers explained in the Claiborne impeachment trial,

> Collateral estoppel [is] based on the premise that where a party has been able to litigate certain issues in dispute before a regular and appropriate forum, one that provides procedural and substantive safeguards, as the jury system provides, that finding of fact by that tribunal is final insofar as those issues [are concerned. We] [suggest] that it is appropriate to take from a coordinate branch of government a finding of fact that has already been determined by the triers of fact beyond a reasonable doubt and found to be true. [The] rationale is obviously to avoid repetition, to avoid an inconsistent result, and to set a proper precedent for cases in the future. And . . . it is important that we set a proper precedent for any cases to follow since this is a case of first impression.[11]

Moreover, the procedural protections provided in criminal trials, including the rights to counsel and to confront witnesses and the requirement of proof beyond a reasonable doubt, tend to ensure that the records for those proceedings are reliable for adjudicating or finding facts. Issue preclusion also does not prevent the Senate from deciding on its own if the misconduct constitutes an impeachable offense.[12]

The primary reason the Senate might forgo using issue preclusion is its concern that it would deprive civil officers of what Alexander Hamilton referred to as the "double security intended . . . by a double trial."[13] For many senators, the Senate's acceptance of the findings of a judicial proceeding (even from a criminal trial) defeats much of, if not the whole, purpose underlying the framers' separation of impeachment and criminal proceedings. Even if the Senate's reliance on issue preclusion allows the federal courts to build a reasonably dependable record for an impeachment trial, it also increases the authority of federal judges to control the outcomes of impeachment proceedings. Some senators view this development as an abdication to the judiciary of the Senate's "sole power" to try impeachments.[14]

Delegations by the Senate to Other Bodies to Conduct Various Responsibilities

The Senate may delegate certain duties for impeachment trials to a sub-group within it or to some other separate body. I consider the feasibility of each such delegation.

IMPROVING RULE XI

There is little doubt that a trial committee saves the Senate a considerable amount of time and provides a more efficient (and informed) forum than the full body could furnish for taking testimony and receiving evidence. Even so, a critical question is whether the Senate can improve the operations of a rule XI trial committee.

One option might be for the Senate to diminish the size of trial committees in order to reduce the numbers of senators having to deal with the resulting scheduling conflicts of trial committee membership. Indeed, the number of senators serving on a trial committee was not a factor in the *Nixon* Court's finding challenges to rule XI to be nonjusticiable.[15] Nor is there anything in *Nixon* to suggest that the decision would have been any different if there were even just one senator on the trial committee. Nevertheless, the problem with a smaller trial committee is that it may not give the full Senate adequate "assurance that decisions as to the conduct of those proceedings were made by a group large enough to approximate differences in the Senate as a whole."[16]

The Senate might also consider clarifying the matters it should hear prior to the formation of a rule XI trial committee.[17] The Senate could develop "a subset of rules applicable in, and only in, proceedings before a committee of less than the whole."[18] Rule XI trial committees could adopt a formal rule to allow the house managers or the impeached judge to raise interlocutory questions for the full Senate's consideration prior to the start of rule XI removal proceedings. This change would notify each participant in an impeachment trial of the preferred timing for particular motions and would allow the Senate to make a decision that otherwise might have preempted rule XI trial proceedings. One such possible rule is "motions for summary judgment or the application of issue preclusion should be made before the full Senate even before a trial committee takes form." The rationale underlying this rule is that such motions have the potential, if granted, of obviating the need for a trial or rule XI trial committees. Such a policy also allows the Senate to expedite matters, particularly when prior adjudication of the underlying facts has already occurred in reliable, fair circumstances. It is obviously inconvenient for the members of a trial committee to go through hearings only to have the Senate later decide it was unnecessary for them to do so.

The disadvantage of this rule is that it can deprive an impeached official of the chance to have the Senate reach independent judgments about the occurrence and significance of the facts underlying his impeachment. Moreover, such a rule effectively delegates to the executive branch the responsibilities of uncovering judicial misconduct and gathering evidence and to the judicial branch the job of fact-finding. Thus, the rule's reliability ultimately depends on whether judicial independence and integrity could be adequately protected if the Senate were to relieve itself of a significant portion of the fact-finding it (or at least the House) otherwise would have to conduct on its own in an impeachment trial.

The Senate might also consider creating a rule XI trial committee in waiting or asking those senators most familiar with impeachment trials to serve on rule XI trial committees or to help expedite the process by overseeing the discovery or pretrial phase. This reform might help the Senate to overcome the difficulties it has had in the past of having senators serve on impeachment panels, even though they did not have any training or experience in dealing knowledgeably or effectively with impeachment matters. The more experienced senators would not have to re-invent the wheel for each impeachment; they would likely be sufficiently familiar with relevant precedents and procedural traditions to provide a relatively streamlined, efficient hearing.

The disadvantage of this proposal is that it may be difficult to find senators who would be so interested in serving on impeachment trial committees that they would be willing to forgo other important legislative business likely to be more relevant to their reelection. This complication is compounded by the fact that impeachment trials do not occur on a routine basis and, therefore, can arise at especially inconvenient times, as with the impeachment of Judge Ritter in the midst of legislative debates over the New Deal.[19] Moreover, turnover in the Senate may deplete the numbers of available senators with relevant experience.

DELEGATIONS BY THE SENATE TO A BODY OF EXPERTS

Another popular suggestion is for the Senate, acting under its own authority, to delegate certain duties (such as fact-finding) to a body or group separate from the Senate. Such delegations would allow the Senate to empower suitable experts to deal with certain preliminary aspects of an impeachment trial, such as discovery, that most senators have neither the time nor the bent to handle.

It is quite likely that the same reasoning that led the Court in *Nixon* to find challenges to rule XI to be nonjusticiable would support finding challenges to a broader delegation of the sort described above to be similarly nonjusticiable. The likeliest textual challenge to this practice would arise under the clause empowering the Senate "to try all impeachments;"[20] however, the Court made clear in *Nixon* that that language, the relevant history and structure of the Constitution, separation of powers concerns, and the need for "finality and the difficulty of fashioning relief" counsel against justiciability.[21] To be sure, the argument against this practice would be, as Nixon's counsel argued, that a delegation of impeachment power to a body or persons outside of the Senate removes the Senate altogether from the process, and, therefore, violates the relevant clause that seems to be premised on the Senate's actual involvement in impeachment trials.[22] However, as long as the Senate retains the authority to review anew any findings or recommendations made by outside experts, it is functionally not in any worse position than it was in *Nixon*, in which the Court recognized that its enforcement of any "limitations" on the Senate's discretion in using trial committees "would be inconsistent with the construction of the [Impeachment] Clause as a whole, which . . . sets out three explicit limitations in separate sentences."[23] Since delegating limited duties to experts outside of the Senate is not violative of any of the explicit limitations on impeachment trials, challenges to such delegations, like those to trial committees, are entitled to be treated as nonjusticiable after *Nixon*.

Moreover, even if the Senate's delegation of some impeachment authority to an outside group were justiciable, it is plainly constitutional. The same historical arguments that convinced Justices White, Blackmun, and Souter,[24] as well as Judge Harry Edwards,[25] that rule XI was a constitutionally permissible delegation argue in favor of finding that delegating even more limited authority to an outside body, such as a special master, is constitutional. In particular, the support for this practice comes from the considerable discretion in each chamber to determine its methods for obtaining evidence necessary to carry out its constitutionally defined tasks and

> an 1851 statute prescribing a procedure for taking testimony in House election contests that is very similar to the procedure followed when using a master. [Moreover,] the Senate's power to use masters to gather testimony and collate evidence in an impeachment trial may correspond to a court's power to use masters for similar purposes. Since both the Supreme Court, as a court of original jurisdiction, and the federal district courts have the inherent power to appoint masters in certain cases, there is no reason to suppose that the Senate, when acting as a judicial body in an impeachment trial, would lack similar authority to appoint a master to facilitate the hearing of evidence.[26]

The National Commission on Judicial Discipline and Removal similarly concluded, "the full Senate has discretion to delegate responsibility for the handling of discovery and other pretrial motions. The Senate could . . . delegat[e] pretrial matters to a component of a rule XI trial committee, such as professional staff or specially hired masters (former Senators or outside counsel)."[27]

If the Senate were to delegate discreet matters to permanent staff or specially hired experts, then it should consider the standard of review the committee or the full body should have over such delegations. The fairest standard is de novo review. Even though de novo review might lead to dilatory or abusive antics from obstructive defense counsel, it enables the trial committee to rehear any questions it believes should receive a full and fair hearing by the Senate and to retain full authority to deal with all substantive matters and live testimony.

LEGISLATIVE OVERSIGHT

There are at least three areas over which the House or the Senate could exercise oversight to improve the federal impeachment process. First, oversight of the activities under the Judicial Disability Act of 1980 would help to ensure that judicial self-regulation does not result in any abuses. Indeed, the House Judiciary Committee, acting through the Judicial Administration Subcommittee, already has a proven track record overseeing the Judicial Disability Act of 1980. Requested and promised during the floor debate on that enactment, such oversight has been welcomed by the judiciary and responsible for more effective implementation of the act as well as minor adjustments to it in 1990.[28] Moreover, the House's Administrative Law Subcommittee has monitored developments in judicial ethics. Although judges routinely examine applicable ethical standards, such oversight, along with the monitoring of activities under the Judicial Disability Act, secures better congressional understanding of the relationship between judicial discipline and ethics. Nor is it unreasonable to ask the House Judiciary Committee or the committee(s) responsible for governmental affairs or the House itself to create a special committee to oversee the general ethical behavior of all impeachable officials. In other words, the link between discipline and ethics is not unique to the federal judiciary; it is a connection that justifies and is important to the oversight of any impeachable officials. Nevertheless, the Senate Judiciary Committee has never conducted oversight of the Judicial Disability Act of 1980, in spite of the fact that senators who sponsored the act have spoken of the need to do so.[29] In light of the explosive growth of the federal judiciary and the fact that the House and the Senate only share oversight findings unless joint hearings—an admittedly rare occurrence—are held, Senate oversight seems equally appropriate.

Second, several senators have asked for, but not yet received, hearings to explore the merits of the charges made by each of the five federal judges prosecuted by the Justice Department since 1980 of investigative and prosecutorial misconduct.[30] In the meantime, one forum has already found merit to such claims made by Harry Claiborne. On May 18, 1988, the Nevada Supreme Court ruled that Claiborne, who by then had completed his term, could resume practicing law in the state.[31] After reviewing the criminal and impeachment trial records, the court concluded that "questionable investigative and prosecutorial motivations, as well as anomalous and arguably unfair practices and procedures pervade the record of this matter from its inception. . . . In light of the above we decline to impose additional punishment upon respondent Claiborne."[32] Given the seriousness and implications of each of these official's allegations of prosecutorial misconduct, the Senate should consider postimpeachment oversight as a useful way, consistent with separation of powers, to monitor enforcement of relevant laws and measure the impact of a prosecution and subsequent impeachment on judicial independence.

Another area about which many people are curious is the relationshp between the confirmation and impeachment processes. Given that the Senate has the constitutional authority to confirm or reject presidential nominees for federal judgeships and certain other impeachable offices,[33] and to remove or even disqualify those same officials for committing impeachable offenses, it is reasonable to doubt (as did some of the opponents to the Constitution in ratifying conventions) the Senate's willingness to second-guess its initial judgments about the integrity of the individual involved. Administrations are likely to be even less willing to open their selection processes to allow second-guessing of their judgments on their nominees' fitness for office.

That a connection exists between the appointment process and the integrity or quality of confirmable officials seems indisputable. If, for example, only the most qualified and honest judges were appointed, the need for disciplinary action would probably be greatly reduced. The same, of course, could be said for any official elected to or selected for an office whose occupant is subject to impeachment. The obvious problem, however, is that predicting the likelihood of impeachment for certain impeachable officials at the times of their elections or confirmations is much easier said than done. Even if one could have made such predictions for Richard Nixon (because of his penchant for hard-ball politics), Robert Archbald (who had engaged in shady business transactions prior to becoming a federal judge), Harry Claiborne (because of suspicions he might have lacked judicial temperament and because he had been a colorful trial lawyer who had enjoyed a substantially higher income in private practice than what he would get as a federal district judge), Halsted Ritter (whose nomination had been opposed by the Republican and Democratic state party organizations in Florida because he was considered deficient in training and experience), or perhaps Alcee Hastings (based on the questionable character of some of his friends prior to his becoming a federal district judge), no one could have predicted Judge Pickering's demise, nor has anyone raised similar questions about Walter Nixon's integrity prior to becoming a federal district judge. Moreover, just as it is impossible for the president to predict infallibly which factors are likely to undo which of his nominees in the confirmation process, it is not reasonable to assume or believe the president or the Senate could agree on a standard for sifting through prospective nominees to choose the ones likeliest to fall prey to the impeachment process at some point in the future. Just as importantly, the president and the Senate each might have good reasons to fight for or against certain nominees in spite of whatever hypoethical prospects they might have for impeachment, especially when the latter is relatively rare and the nominees themselves will be accountable to a respected superior authority. Nevertheless, in spite of all of these potential dilemmas, the impeachment process, like the rest of government, might be best served if dubious candidates for office were scrutinized with better care prior to assuming office. In other words, the best reform of the impeachment process might well consist of more careful consideration by a president of his nominees and more thorough confirmation hearings.

Chapter Thirteen

PROPOSED STATUTORY CHANGES AND CONSTITUTIONAL AMENDMENTS TO THE IMPEACHMENT PROCESS

THIS CHAPTER considers the merits of the most significant proposed statutes and constitutional amendments for reforming the federal impeachment process. All of these proposals seek to eliminate or severely restrict the Senate's role in that system, and each proposal is premised on the existence of an alternative forum superior to the Senate.

PROPOSED STATUTORY MODIFICATIONS TO THE IMPEACHMENT PROCESS

Over the past two hundred years, Congress has shown serious interest in two major kinds of proposed statutes for reforming the federal impeachment process. Some statutory proposals have tried to provide for the automatic suspension, removal, or disqualification of federal judges who have been convicted of a felony. Other statutes have tried to delegate either the entire removal power or at least the fact-finding responsibilities to a body other than the Senate, such as a specialized court or even the Supreme Court. I consider below the constitutionality of each of these kinds of statutory proposals.

The Constitutionality of Proposed Statutory Suspensions of Judicial Tenure and Compensation

There are two prominent types of proposed statutes for suspending or automatically removing or disqualifying federal judges. The most prominent example of the first type is the Bribery Act of 1790, enacted by the First Congress to provide that upon conviction for bribery in federal court, a federal judge shall be "forever disqualified to hold any office."[1] Senator Strom Thurmond has introduced an example of the second kind, which would provide "that a justice or judge convicted of a felony shall be suspended from office without pay pending the disposition of impeachment proceedings."[2] Since I have explored the constitutionality of this first statute in part III, I consider below the constitutionality of a statute of the sort proposed by Senator Thurmond.

The argument in favor of the constitutionality of the latter statute is that it does not provide for the actual reduction of a federal judge's salary or for the formal removal or disqualification of a federal judge in the absence of a Senate impeachment trial. In other words, this statute conceivably does not pose a threat to the federal judiciary, because it is directed only at a small number of federal judges who have already jeopardized their status by virtue of having been convicted of felonies and who will be compensated for their loss once the Senate decides not to remove them from office.

The fatal problem with this proposed statute, however, is that it violates Article III's literal guarantee of undiminished compensation for each federal judge. The fact that the Thurmond statute tries to return later the income it has confiscated does not cure or erase the initial violation. Moreover, Senator Thurmond's statute deprives a federal judge of the chance to demonstrate the reasons he or she should not be impeached in spite of a felony conviction. In other words, the statute deprives certain federal judges of the "double security" guaranteed to them through a "double trial."[3] This unfairness is compounded by the fact that not all felonies are equally grave. If a federal judge were convicted, for example, of a state felony forbidding the poisoning of a cat or a federal felony prohibiting damaging a mail box, it is far from clear that the targeted judge deserves to have his or her salary temporarily suspended, much less to be removed from office. If the motive for this statute is to avoid the unseemly scenario of a convicted federal judge's sitting in jail but continuing to receive his or her salary, then a less extreme, constitutional alternative is for Congress to enact suitable amendments to title 18 to allow the postponement of sentences in federal criminal cases involving a convicted federal judge until the judge is impeached and removed from office.[4]

The Constitutionality and Desirability of a Statutory Proposal for Reducing the Senate's Role in Judicial Removals

Interestingly, the Senate has seriously considered only one statute that has tried to eliminate the Senate's role in the federal impeachment process. In the late 1930s and early 1940s, Congressman Hatton W. Sumners, then-Chairman of the House Judiciary Committee (and a house manager for the Louderback and Ritter impeachment trials), proposed several versions of a statute that would have removed the Senate, but not the House, from the impeachment process. In 1937, he initially proposed H.R. 2271, which directed that judicial removal would be handled by a special court consisting of three judges of the circuit courts of appeal designated by the chief justice. The House of Representatives would initiate charges by directing a resolution to the chief justice, stating that "in the opinion of the House there is reasonable ground for believing that the behavior of a judge [has] been other than good behavior within the meaning of that term" in the Constitution. If the court determined that the behavior was not "good behavior" within the meaning of the Constitution, the judge would be removed from office, although no other penalty could be imposed. Such judgement could not be appealed. This proposal applied only to federal district judges.

On October 22, 1941, the House passed H.R. 146, which was quite similar to the earlier H.R. 2271. Again, the House was to initiate proceedings by directing a resolution to the chief justice, and the chief justice had the authority to convene a special court. However, this legislation applied to all judges of the United States, except Supreme Court justices, and the chief justice had less discretion in choosing those who would sit on the court. The targeted judge would have had a right to object to the judges selected by the chief justice to serve on the special court, subject to the chief justice's review. If the chief justice found the reasons for the judge's objections to have been adequate, he was to select a different designee. The attorney general represented the United States in the removal proceedings. If the special court determined that the judge did not meet the "good behavior" standard in the Constitution, it would order removal of the judge. The defendant would then have a right of appeal to the Supreme Court.

A month after the House passed H.R. 146 in October 1941, a subcommittee of the Senate Judiciary Committee held hearings on the bill. Congressman Sumners presented his proposal, and a number of prominent individuals testified in support of the bill, including Supreme Court justice (and former Attorney General) Robert H. Jackson and Attorney General Francis Biddle.[5] In addition, the Judicial Conference, composed of the chief justice of the United States and the senior circuit judges, "approve[d] in principle the provisions embodied in" the proposed legislation.[6] Moreover, the American Bar Association (ABA) supported the bill on the ground that "[e]xperience has demonstrated that no sufficient number of members of the Senate will listen to, or even read, the testimony in removal proceedings initiated by the House of Representatives as to Federal judges other than justices of the Supreme Court. [The] testimony as to misbehavior should be taken, and the appropriate findings made, in a judicial atmosphere and by experienced, impartial triers of fact."[7]

There are several plausible arguments in support of the bill's constitutionality. First, it arguably represents Congress's effort to combine its necessary and proper and impeachment powers to devise a solution to the Senate's current problems, including lack of time, interest, and expertise, in handling impeachment trials. As the House report observed, "there is nothing more ridiculous than the picture of the whole Senate sitting for ten days to determine whether or not a district judge ought to be removed."[8] The ABA's then-president, Arthur Vanderbilt, wrote to the subcommittee that the bill would

> strengthen the administration of justice in the Federal courts, [help] preserve a high standard among the personnel of the judiciary, and [enable] Senators to devote the time to their legislative duties and free them of the [charge that] their other duties prevent them from sitting as the triers of the matter in the way that ordinary judges are required to listen to all of the evidence before pronouncing judgment.[9]

Second, the bill could be construed as Congress's exercise of its inherent powers under the "good behavior" clause of Article III to pass legislation to deal with judicial misconduct. Third, the bill did not necessarily aggrandize another branch at the expense of the judiciary or Congress. Under the statute, the attorney general was empowered to bring complaints against federal judges, but this authority would have been checked by the other statutory provision empowering judges to serve as the members of the special court and the Supreme Court to review the removal proceedings. Fourth, the proposed statute conceivably protected judicial independence and integrity because it would have placed the power to make and review removal decisions within the judiciary, which plainly has a vested interest in ensuring the integrity and reputation of its members. Fifth, the judges sitting on the special tribunal and the Supreme Court are competent to do the necessary fact-finding, handle the motions, make evidentiary rulings, and generally protect the individual rights of impeached judges. Lastly, as Congressman Sumners explained, the bill sought to avoid the possibility that the Senate's failure to conduct timely impeachment trials might tempt the executive into trying to oust federal judges on its own.[10] Sumners was concerned (as many people still are) that the cumbersome nature of the impeachment process tended to pressure the House into avoiding impeachments and preferring instead to have the Justice Department fill the vacuum by prosecuting federal judges prior to their impeachments. Other supporters of the bill argued that it would relieve the Senate from having to deal with the likely rise in the numbers of impeachment trials that would correspond with the expected increase in the size of the federal judiciary.[11]

In all probability, the proposed statute was, however, unconstitutional for four reasons. First, it tried to bypass two explicit requirements recognized by the Court in *Nixon v. United States*[12] as applying to all impeachment trials: that "the members [of the Senate] must be under oath [and] a two-thirds vote [of the Senate] is required to convict[.]"[13] These requirements could only be avoided if the act somehow could be justified as dealing only with judicial discpline for misconduct falling short of impeachable offenses; otherwise, as long as the proposed mechanism provided for the imposition of the special punishments usually available in an impeachment proceeding by some body other than the Senate, it seems to conflict directly with the special constitutional requirements for certain Senate action prior to imposing appropriate sanctions.

Second, the bill's empowerment of the attorney general to issue complaints against federal judges arguably would have enabled him or her to harass federal judges who disagreed with the Justice Department's policies. The problem would have been that the act would have added to the kinds of actions the attorney general was otherwise authorized or allowed to bring against federal judges, such that it would have created a problematic imbalance of power by enabling the attorney general to persecute federal judges by initiating various kinds of proceedings, including civil, criminal, and impeachment, against them. Nor is it hard to imagine that the act might have made federal judges think twice before issuing rulings against the government that had the potential to provoke retaliation by the attorney general.

Third, permitting specialized tribunals consisting of judges to make removal decisions that are also appealable to the Supreme Court creates an imbalance of power in another direction—by giving the federal judiciary too much of a final say over the disciplining and removal of federal judges. The question is whether the judiciary can reasonably be trusted to exercise this power fairly when the proposal makes it even less accountable to the public and political forces than it is under the present system.[14] The problem is that, whereas the Judicial Disability Act of 1980 requires trusting judges to discipline each other for nonimpeachable misconduct, this proposed statute requires abandoning altogether the framers' distrust of the federal judiciary's ability to be a neutral or competent arbiter of the impeachable misconduct of individual federal judges.

There is also a practical problem with the proposed statute: it is unrealistic to expect the Senate ever to agree to removing itself from the process of judicial impeachments while retaining the House's role in the same system. The proposed statute raised concerns among many senators about the arrogance underlying and accuracy of the House's apparent claim that the Senate was not as competent as the House to handle judicial impeachments. Even if it were empirically true that the House is more competent than the Senate in impeachment matters, a majority of the Senate still needs to be persuaded of that fact. The subsequent failure to enact the statute, given the extraorinary support at the time of some of the most prominent judges and lawyers in the country, suggests the unlikelihood of the Senate's ever being convinced of this latter prospect.

PROPOSED CONSTITUTIONAL AMENDMENTS

In recent years, five different kinds of constitutional amendments have been proposed in the Senate.[15] I consider the merits of each of these in turn.

Elimination of Life Tenure for Federal Judges

One of the most common subjects of proposed amendments to the federal impeachment process is the elimination of life tenure for federal judges.[16] The major argument in favor of such amendments is that they will help to eradicate the so-called "countermajoritarian difficulty"[17]—the problem of unprincipled or self-interested interference by unelected federal judges with the decisions of the people's duly elected representatives—by making federal judges politically accountable by subjecting them to limited terms of office, popular election, reconfirmation, or reappointment. If one regards the countermajoritarian difficulty as intractable, then the only practical way to curb unprincipled judicial decision making is to deprive federal judges of life tenure and to make them less immune to political reprisals. A contrary view is, however, that the framers' decision to grant federal judges life tenure to ensure judicial independence from partisan influences or factional retaliation for principled exercises of judicial review has not been shown to be so fundamentally mistaken as to justify the abolition of life tenure for federal judges.[18]

In any event, changing the tenure of federal judges to eliminate the "countermajoritarian difficulty" has almost nothing to do with remedying the kinds of judicial misconduct that seem to overwhelm the impeachment process. Other than Justice Chase, no federal judge has ever been impeached because of his or her decisions on the bench; and no federal judge has ever been convicted by the Senate for his or her judicial philosophy. Moreover, changing judicial tenure is not likely to remove the need for a disciplinary process to deal with the lapses in judicial integrity that have given rise to the need for disciplinary action under the Judicial Disability Act of 1980 or in Congress through the initiation of impeachment proceedings.

Automatic Judicial Removal Based on Felony Convictions

Constitutional amendments have been proposed that would automatically remove a federal judge who has been convicted of certain crimes, such as any felony.[19] For example, on January 25, 1989, Senator Thurmond introduced the following resolution, S.J. Res. 11, providing in pertinent part that "any officer of the United States appointed by the President with the advice and consent of the Senate, upon conviction of a felony, shall forfeit office and all prerogatives, benefits, or compensation thereof."[20]

Such a proposed amendment has a number of potential merits. First, the class of governmental officials to whom it applies is clear, thereby eliminating the problem with the present system's lack of clarity over who are "officers of the United States." Second, it provides ample notice to its subjects that *any* felony conviction will result in the automatic forfeiture of their positions. Third, it would relieve Congress of the duty of conducting a number of time-consuming impeachments and eliminate the problem of federal judges receiving compensation while they sit in jail waiting to be impeached and removed. Lastly, a constitutional amendment is an appropriate way to provide for the automatic removal of certain governmental officials, given that the Constitution requires that for judicial removal senators must be on oath or affirmation and at least two-thirds of them must concur for a conviction.

Yet, this proposed amendment poses several serious constitutional concerns. First, it is unfair to provide automatic forfeiture upon a felony conviction without allowing the convicted official the chance to reverse that conviction through an appeal as of right, especially given that convictions are often reversed for sound legal reasons. By separating criminal and impeachment trials, the framers hoped to prevent people from being tried for the same offense twice in the same forum and to allow an impeached official a chance to argue his or her cause on its own merits before the House and the Senate. Moreover, courts often do not impose punishment on a criminal defendant until the latter at least has had a chance to exhaust his or her criminal appeals. Fundamental fairness requires that the targeted officials should at least be given a chance to do the latter, especially prior to being subject to the permanent, nonreversible punishment of removal.

Second, the Thurmond amendment provides no check against partisanship in guiding criminal investigations and prosecutions. The political motivations or abuse of power underlying a criminal prosecution may not be uncovered until after a conviction is secured, at which point it may be too late because the prosecutor's desired effect—the removal, for example, of a federal judge—would have already occurred. Because criminal and impeachment trials are separate proceedings by constitutional design, the impeachment process at present can serve as an independent check against prosecutorial misconduct.

Third, all felony convictions are not equal for purposes of justifying automatic forfeiture of office. The amendment does not distinguish, for example, between different kinds of state and federal felonies, many of which do not constitute reasonable bases for automatic removal of impeachable officials. Nor does the amendment allow members of Congress the chance to debate or exchange views on which felonies, if committed, should constitute reasonable bases for automatic forfeiture of office.

Fourth, the Thurmond amendment tends to gloss over the historic and formal distinctions between removal and disqualification. By its plain language, the amendment seems to effect the automatic removal of certain impeachable officials from their current positions. The amendment leaves open the question of whether the impeachment process may still be used to impose the punishment of disqualification on these officers.[21]

The Creation of a New, Constitutionally Authorized Body for Handling Judicial Removals

Following the approach of some states, a few proposed amendments seek to establish a new body in the constitutional system that would have the authority to discipline and remove federal judges.[22] For example, Senator Howell Heflin has repeatedly urged the adoption of his preferred amendment that would establish a Judicial Inquiry Commission and a Court of the Judiciary.[23] The commission would receive complaints and investigate allegations of judicial wrongdoing or incompetency. Subsequently, the Court would adjudicate all cases brought before it and have the power to discipline and remove federal judges. This proposed amendment also would prohibit federal judges convicted of a felony from thereafter receiving their salaries otherwise due for services as judges.[24]

There are four major problems with the Heflin amendment. First, it can possibly produce both the appearance of, and serious potential for, conflicts of interest in judicial impeachments. It allows judges to hear impeachment charges against other judges with whom they have often sat or built personal relationships or allegiances. The amendment also grants the Supreme Court virtually absolute power to monitor and discipline the judiciary, including the justices themselves: the Court would have the powers to appoint some of the members of the special commission empowered to initiate and investigate complaints; to devise a "canon of ethics" "binding" upon all the federal judges, including themselves; to "adopt rules to govern the procedures of the Commission"; to appoint three of the members of the special impeachment court; to "adopt" the "rules to govern the procedures of the [special] Court"; and to review the impeachment proceedings covered by the amendment, including any brought against a fellow justice. In short, it could be argued that Senator Heflin's amendment would effectively make the federal judiciary even less accountable than it now is, because the only political check against judicial misconduct it leaves intact is Congress's traditional impeachment power over Supreme Court justices.

Second, such a proposed amendment conceivably compounds the potential conflicts of interest it might produce by delegating impeachment power over the judiciary to a special commission and special court whose respective members are not politically accountable. The framers put the impeachment trial authority in the hands of a politically accountable body. As Senator Lieberman warned, the problem with this proposal is that "a small court, especially one that is unelected with a majority of political appointees could easily become the target of charges of political or other bias and impropriety."[25] In contrast, the constitutional requirements for Senate impeachment trials, including the participation of the senators themselves, "confer[] a greater inherent legitimacy on the removal process, and that is critical if we are taking the extraordinary step of pulling somebody off the federal judiciary."[26]

Third, the proposed amendment could possibly threaten judicial independence by making judicial removal easier than it is now and perhaps easier than it ever ought to be. In the hearings on Senator Heflin's proposed amendment, Judge Walter Stapleton argued that it made political retaliation possible against federal judges who have made unpopular decisions. He recognized that Congress must "strike a balance between judicial accountability and independence, but we say that balance has got to involve the least threat to judicial independence that is consistent with maintaining the public confidence in the system."[27] He further argued that

> [b]ecause judicial disciplinary sanctions, and indeed even disciplinary proceedings, provide opportunities for retaliation, any judicial disciplinary system must strike a balance between the twin goals of insuring the integrity of the judicial system and preserving judicial independence. The ideal balance is one that involves the least possible threat to judicial independence consistent with maintaining public confidence in the system. The Conference believes that the Congress and the judiciary, building on the foundations provided in our Constitution, struck just such a balance in 1980, and that this balance should not be disturbed.[28]

The Heflin amendment would make political reprisals against federal judges possible because the standards for removals it sets forth (such as "misconduct in office," "failure to perform duties," and "violation of any canon of judicial ethics") are arguably so vague as to be easily manipulable and might subject judges to the kind of political reprisals against which life tenure was designed to protect them.[29] In other words, the Heflin amendment would risk blurring the line between judicial review of the merits of lower court decisions and of the competency, integrity, and independence of the lower court judges making those decisions. Moreover, his proposed amendment would discount the importance of collegiality to judicial independence: it would create situations in which federal judges could charge or try to remove other judges, who, if they were acquitted, must still sit with or have their decisions reviewed by their accusers. Such circumstances compromise rather than enhance the independence of individual federal judges.

Lastly, an amendment proposing the establishment of a new, constitutionally authorized body to handle judicial impeachments might lead to the creation of an independent bureaucracy, whose sole reason for existence would be to identify and prosecute judicial misconduct. In other words, this type of bureaucracy might feel the need to make work for itself by substantially increasing disciplinary investigations and proceedings. Such developments would seriously threaten judicial independence.

To be sure, many senators seem to believe that the impeachment process does not work because Congress simply does not have the time, resources, or training to conduct fair and efficient judicial impeachments.[30] For senators convinced of the inadequacies of the current system, this kind of suggested amendment may be attractive because it relieves the Senate of the burden of conducting removal trials.

Yet, there are two potential problems with this justification. On the one hand, a number of senators have found that the current removal process adequately safeguards judicial independence and integrity.[31] On the other hand, it is not entirely clear that burdening an already busy Supreme Court or creating a special commission or tribunal will solve the distractions preventing Congress from conducting effective impeachment proceedings.

A second possible justification for the Heflin amendment is the commission's and Supreme Court's presumed superiority over Congress in defining or resolving the complex procedural issues involved in impeachment trials. In addition, the decision makers authorized by the Heflin amendment, most of whom are judges, will have greater appreciation for the kinds of procedures that ought to be provided impeached judges to guarantee that their removal proceedings are fundamentally fair and respect judicial independence and integrity. Hence, the amendment possibly enhances judicial independence. Its proponents argue that Congress has more of an abstract than a real interest in maintaining the independence of the judiciary and that the judiciary itself has the greatest interest in preserving its own autonomy and integrity and will consequently police itself rigorously for the sake of maintaining the respect that its independence requires.

Another troublesome legal issue that Senator Heflin's proposed amendment addresses concerns the permissibility of allowing prosecution, indictment, or imprisonment of federal judges prior to impeachment and removal. The statute provides a clear answer to the problem of convicted judges being incarcerated, receiving their salaries, and waiting for impeachment and removal proceedings.

Authorizing Congress to Determine Procedures and Practices for Judicial Removal

Yet another proposal would give Congress authority to determine the practice and procedures to be used in removing federal judges for misconduct or disability.[32] For example, the proposed amendment, S.J. Res. 233, provides that

> the Congress shall have the power to provide practices and procedures for the removal from office and to provide lesser sanctions for justices, judges, and other federal judicial officers found to be guilty of misconduct in office, failure to perform the duties of office, inability to physically or mentally perform the duties of office, and for violating judicial ethics cannons; and to provide for the suspension of such judicial officer from their duties, with or without pay, when convicted on a felony or under indictment or information charging such judicial officer with a felony.[33]

This proposal preserves the power in Congress already granted by the Constitution to prescribe procedural rules for impeachments. It empowers Congress to make delegations of the sort embodied in rule XI or in the statute discussed in the previous section. In addition, it clarifies the kinds of offenses for which judges may be removed (essentially it lists the offenses for which judicial officers may be either removed or disciplined, short of removal depending upon the judgment of Congress) *and* resolves the problem of an incarcerated judge receiving his salary until such time as Congress impeaches and removes him. Lastly, this proposed amendment may be preferable to the Thurmond proposal because the former grants to Congress the discretion to stop compensation for judicial officers "when convicted of a felony or under indictment or information charging such judicial officer with a felony"; to allow appeals as of right; and to treat on an individual basis the merits of charges against federal judges.

There are three potential problems with this suggested amendment. First, it could expand the bases on which federal judges may be removed from office. The current understanding is that the Constitution permits disciplining (short of removal) of judges by other judges on matters that do not rise to the level of impeachable offenses. Yet, the proposed amendment seems to eliminate any such distinction, thereby making it easier for Congress to remove federal judges on the basis of misconduct that has never previously been considered to constitute an impeachable offense. According to Judge Stapleton, "it gives Congress carte blanche to prescribe by whom and how a judicial officer could be removed from office and acquire the withholding of the pay of a judicial officer upon conviction of a felony before rights of appeal have been exhausted and without regard to any seriousness of the offense."[34]

A second problem that seems to be posed by this proposed amendment is that it may not be necessary. Article I, section 5 makes clear that the House and the Senate have sole authority over the rules they each may adopt for the proceedings they are empowered by the Constitution to conduct.[35] This authority apparently includes within it the power to construct impeachment proceedings against federal judges in any manner each chamber of Congress determines is appropriate, with the only constitutionally required guidelines being the Constitution's division of impeachment authority between the House and the Senate and the explicit constraints set forth for impeachment trials.

The amendment's provision "for the suspension of such judicial officers from their duties, with or without pay, when convicted of felony or under indictment or information charging such judicial officer without a felony" also may be unnecessary. It is already within the power of the Congress to make suitable amendments to title 18 allowing postponing of sentences in cases involving impeached judges until they are impeached and removed. In addition, prosecution before impeachment can produce a record that may be used to expedite an impeachment. Moreover, the judicial councils already have the power to reassign caseloads for judges, regardless of the reasons for their disabilities.

Lastly, one could argue that it is unclear whether this kind of amendment permits judicial review of Congress's impeachment rules or delegations or of the delegatees' actions (to ensure they comply with congressional guidelines). The proposed amendment might waive or supersede the nonjusticiability of impeachment challenges as recognized in *Nixon*.

Involving the Supreme Court in Judicial Removal and Discipline

There have also been three proposals that would involve the Supreme Court in judicial removal.[36] For example, Senator Warren Rudman proposed a constitutional amendment[37] that

> grants power to the Supreme Court to remove an Article III judge from office (other tha[n] a justice of the Supreme Court), by a two-thirds vote of the justices, for treason, bribery, or other high crimes or misdemeanors. The Supreme Court, and the Congress by law, are granted authority to adopt rules to carry out the impeachment process. If removal from office is ordered by the Supreme Court, the judge has the right to appeal the order to the Senate, under such rules and regulations as the Senate prescribes. A vote of two-thirds of the Senate is necessary to sustain the order of the Supreme Court. If the House of Representatives votes an article of impeachment with respect to the judge, then the proceedings before the Supreme Court would be terminated. Finally, the amendment specifies that [] nothing in its language shall be construed to limit the powers of the House of Representatives and the Senate to impeach and convict a judge, Supreme Court justice, or other officer of the United States.[38]

According to Senator Rudman, this proposed amendment is desirable because it "addresses many of the concerns expressed by critics of the Senate process."[39] He explained that "[i]n the hands of the Supreme Court, the removal process offers the judiciary the assurance that impartial judges will rule on their cases. The Senate retains oversight authority by means of the appeals process. The amendment does not limit the ability of the Congress to initiate impeachment proceedings; the Supreme Court process ends if the House of Representatives takes action to impeach."[40]

The Rudman amendment, however, has three potential problems. First, it adds an unnecessary layer to the impeachment process. It is likely that impeached judges will take their cases through every level of review they can get. It is also conceivable that many senators may feel that an impeached judge is entitled to separate proceedings in the Senate despite conviction by the Court, under which circumstances the Senate is put back in its present position (with perhaps the not insignificant addition of the Senate's having the Supreme Court's findings as a potentially reliable record on which the Senate could base its own conclusions).

Second, for those proceedings initiated in the House, the Senate is essentially left in its present position with the same kinds of responsibilities and problems it currently has. Nor is an amendment requiring the Supreme Court to oversee judicial removals likely to clarify many of the procedural issues remaining in question (such as the burden of proof) in the Senate's removal proceedings.

Third, by empowering the Supreme Court to conduct judicial impeachments, the proposed amendment raises the conflict-of-interest problems the framers had hoped to avoid in federal impeachments. The amendment's provision for appeals from the Supreme Court to the Senate reduces but does not eliminate the risk of the Court's acting on a self-interested basis in conducting judicial impeachments. Even if appeals to the Senate provided a check on self-interested decision making by the Supreme Court, the Senate must still find the time and dedicate the necessary resources to review impeachment matters.[41]

Postscript

THE FUTURE OF THE IMPEACHMENT PROCESS

FOR MOST of American history, impeachment has been Congress's weapon of last resort to deal with judicial or presidential misconduct. Yet, its effectiveness even in this latter capacity is being widely questioned today. Impeachment seems more antiquated than useful, as reflected, for example, by the House's failure thus far to commence impeachment proceedings against Judge Robert Collins, even though he exhausted his appeals from his federal felony convictions in 1993 and is sitting in prison receiving his salary as a federal judge, and by the doubts of many senators about whether they have the time or the skill to handle impeachment proceedings even as seemingly uncomplicated as the one for Collins promises to be. Moreover, the facts that a ninth circuit panel overturned all but one of Judge Robert Aguilar's federal felony convictions, and the ninth circuit en banc reversed his remaining criminal conviction, and that the Judicial Conference of the United States has not yet asked the House to investigate his impeachment have paralyzed the initiation of impeachment proceedings against Judge Aguilar. In one sense, the basis for proceeding with Judge Aguilar's impeachment seems sounder than that which existed for the impeachment of Alcee Hastings, because Judge Aguilar was at least convicted in federal district court, but in another sense the impeachment of Judge Aguilar seems more problematic than that of Hastings, given that the ninth circuit overturned Judge Aguilar's convictions in part on technical grounds and that the Judicial Conference called for Hastings' but not as of yet for Judge Aguilar's impeachment.[1]

Threatening impeachment or investigation for possible presidential misconduct seems, however, to carry some weight, because it seems to signal or perhaps precipitate the loss of a president's popularity. Hence, as the prospect of President Nixon's impeachment became increasingly realistic, his power waned, and he ultimately resigned. Though President Reagan might never have taken seriously the threats of some members of Congress to initiate an impeachment inquiry against him for his involvement in or responsibility for the so-called Iran-Contra affair, those threats reflected the loss of his popularity and precipitated the forced resignations of several high-level White House aides. More recently, media hype fueled by Republicans' growing concern about the nature and consequences of the investments of Bill and Hillary Clinton in an

Arkansas land deal (referred to as "Whitewater") at the time President Clinton was the governor of Arkansas, eventually led to two congressional inquiries, the initial fallout from which included the forced resignations of President Clinton's Deputy Treasury Secretary Roger Altman (who was an old friend of the president's) and General Counsel to the Treasury Department Jean Hanson. In addition, Chief White House Counsel Bernard Nussbaum resigned after it was revealed that he had met with federal regulators to learn about the progress of their investigation of the collapse of a savings and loan owned by the Clintons' partner in the land deal.

The future of the impeachment process depends, nonetheless, on whether Congress is at least as good at conducting impeachment proceedings as it is at legislating or conducting other legislative business. The best available evidence indicates that neither the House nor the Senate is any worse at conducting impeachment proceedings than either is at making legislation. For example, senators are relatively adept at making delegations to committees or masters and relying on the delegatees' findings in making legislative judgments. In addition, the attendance of senators at the final arguments for each of the three impeachment trials in the 1980s was at least as good, if not better, than the attendance for its other legislative activities. Perhaps most importantly, the Senate is ideally suited for balancing the tasks of making policy and finding facts (as required in impeachment trials) with political accountability. Moreover, empowering federal judges to deal exclusively with judicial misconduct would run the risk of allowing a politically unaccountable branch to monitor its own misconduct. While there have not been any abuses yet under the Judicial Disability Act of 1980, it is clear that the disciplinary authorities operating under it walk a fine line. They have vested interests in maintaining judicial independence and integrity and in making judicial discipline as difficult as possible.

As a general matter, the impeachment process has also not produced the abuses imagined by its critics. No federal official has ever been impeached and removed in American history for purely partisan reasons. Nor have the worst nightmares of the critics—ranging from determining guilt on the basis of a coin toss or by the color of the targeted official's skin—ever been realized. Even in the 1980s impeachments, each of the respondent judges had the chance to personally argue his case before the entire Senate, which, with almost every member present, heard and saw the live testimony of the judge and could have, if it chose, recalled any witnesses or have had any other evidence resubmitted. Subsequently, in accordance with the explicit commands of the Constitution, the Senate convicted all three judges in the 1980s for misconduct that could reasonably constitute impeachable offenses.

Put slightly differently, the awkwardness of impeachments might be a fatal problem if there were a history of corrupt officials remaining in office as a result of the practical unavailability of the constitutional mechanism to oust them. The real dilemma with impeachment is not that it fails to get around to punishing officials who have engaged in misconduct in office but rather that it neglects to punish them quickly enough or in a sufficiently informed fashion. Yet, up until the 1980s, the realistic threat of impeachment often prompted corrupt officials to leave office. In addition, the fact that there have only been fourteen impeachment trials in American history is conceivably one of the most encouraging aspects of federal impeachment; it shows, even in the absence of judicial review, that Congress feels enough pressure from the division of the impeachment authority between the House and the Senate, the requirement of at least a two-thirds majority in the Senate for a conviction, and the political accountability of its members, to avoid overusing or abusing its impeachment power. In other words, critics cannot have it both ways in arguing that the federal impeachment process is cumbersome; the unwieldy or awkward nature of impeachment hinders its exercise and, thus, reflects at least the effectiveness of the constitutional restraints already in place.

Moreover, the quality, speed, and level of informed judgment in the impeachment process may be improved in at least five ways without radical revision or constitutional amendment. First, both the House and the Senate could streamline fact-finding for impeachment hearings and impeachment trials.[2] For example, the House and the Senate might agree that automatic removal upon conviction of a federal felony (or at least a prescribed range of them) may be constitutional but not desirable for political reasons. They could give certain convictions preclusive effect in impeachment hearings by providing that once there has been a criminal conviction for a certain offense, both chambers could defer to the factual findings already resolved under the high standard of proof required for criminal convictions. The convicted official would then have the chance to attack his conviction collaterally during an impeachment proceeding, as he or she would on a typical criminal appeal, or through the introduction of certain limited evidence not introduced for good reason at trial, but he or she could not argue for de novo review or claim a right to a new trial.[3] By relying on prior convictions as effectively creating rebuttable presumptions, Congress could reduce the time and personnel necessary for its thorough deliberations on the impeachment questions and avoid the risk of a prolonged hearing that would involve a convicted, incarcerated official still receiving his or her salary.

Second, Congress could, as it does now, create committees to receive and distill information.[4] Nothing in the Constitution precludes the House from relying on information gathered outside the impeachment process to initiate an impeachment proceeding, as long as the noncongressional investigation does not bind the House's view of the facts or compel the investigating entities to go beyond their own particular constitutional limitations. No doubt, Congress would stand on firmer constitutional ground if it at least initially directed some outside agency to investigate the alleged commissions of particular impeachable offenses in certain limited circumstances. The Senate has already demonstrated in the impeachment trials of Harry Claiborne, Alcee Hastings, and Walter Nixon that it is possible to streamline receipt of evidence regarding removal through special trial committees that provide the full Senate with tapes of hearings and neutral summaries of submitted evidence. Especially after the decision of the Supreme Court in *Walter Nixon v. United States*[5] to hold challenges to the legitimacy or the Senate's use of trial committees as nonjusticiable, it is clear that the Senate is the ultimate arbiter of the kind and quality of fact-finding and hearing it provides in an impeachment trial. Because *Nixon* and constitutional and pragmatic concerns about finality and redressability likely preclude judicial review of the procedural aspects of any challenge to an impeachment proceeding, the most meaningful constraint on the Congress's interpretation and application of its impeachment authority is probably the political accountability of its members, including the latter's vulnerability to public and media scrutiny (and peer pressure).

Third, a manual of precedents would provide useful background material for many senators (and their staffs) struggling to deal with the procedural nuances of impeachment trials. It would also help to improve the level of informed decision making in the House and the Senate and argumentation on behalf of the parties involved in impeachment proceedings. A manual on precedent establishes something that does not fully exist at this time: an institutional memory with respect to such proceedings.

Fourth, given that the House has inconsistently identified the form of relief the Senate should impose on a convicted impeachable official, the House should consider, at the time it votes on impeachment articles, whether to ask for both removal and disqualification in an impeachment trial. This practice would help the House to clarify its prosecutorial objectives. Moreover, the Senate should become accustomed to voting on disqualification in all cases, regardless of whether the House asks for it or not, so that no punishment issues fall between the cracks.

Fifth, Congress should also consider how to mitigate the threat to judicial independence and the specter of imprisoned federal judges continuing to receive their salaries posed by the criminal prosecutions of federal judges prior to their impeachments. For example, Congress could design a procedure under which prosecutorial decision making regarding sitting judges is vested largely in judicially appointed special prosecutors beyond the policy control of the president. In *Morrison v. Olson*,[6] the Supreme Court rejected contentions that depriving the president of plenary policy control over the decision making of judicially appointed prosecutors disabled the president from discharging his constitutional functions.[7] Permitting the judiciary to select prosecutors in cases involving judges, and removing those prosecutors from routine policy oversight by the executive, could significantly reduce any risk that criminal procedure poses of subjugating the judiciary to executive domination. Moreover, suitable amendments to title 18 would allow postponing sentences in cases involving convicted judges until such time as they were impeached.[8] In addition, prosecution before impeachment can produce a record that may be used to expedite an impeachment.

The study and reform of the federal impeachment process also points to three important lessons regarding constitutional interpretation, particularly the construction of the impeachment clauses. First, no attempt to explain the Constitution in terms of a single unifying concept answers all of the problems regarding the meaning of each and every constitutional provision. At best, a single theoretical approach to constitutional interpretation may clarify some but not answer all of the important questions raised by ambiguous constitutional language or gaps in the Constitution. For example, many of the terms and concepts in the impeachment clauses are not self-defining, nor are their limitations self-evident. The most sensible approach to clarifying such constitutional provisions is to identify their ambiguities and special problems and to use as many legitimate sources of decision, such as history or precedent, to guide their analysis.

Second, constitutional provisions grant each branch special power. This authority includes the responsibility to use creativity and common sense to exercise the power-granting provision in the contemporary world. Moreover, the judiciary is not the only branch empowered to interpret the Constitution and is not necessarily any more capable or better situated than the other branches to give the Constitution meaning. For example, Congress has long exercised the sole responsibility for applying the impeachment clauses, and there is nothing in the history of federal impeachment to suggest that the judiciary has any role to play in ensuring that Congress discharge its impeachment authority in different ways than it already has.

Third, constitutional law explicates what is permissible, but politics dictates what should be done. We should recognize that simply because some course of action is constitutional does not necessarily mean that such an undertaking is either prudent or mandatory. Constitutional commentators spend so much time debating the outer limits of constitutionally permissible behavior by the different branches that they sometimes lose sight of the important issues included within those limits—issues that political actors must resolve by exercising their own prudent judgments.

The point is that constitutional interpretation sets the outermost boundaries on the exercise of federal power and a minimum standard or floor for states. For example, Congress may regard a measure such as the Bribery Act of 1790 as constitutional, but choose to forgo it out of a sense of fairness or to avoid any political difficulties its use might entail. It is important not to confuse these constitutional limits with prudent politics or perceptions about necessity, which sometimes may support stretching a particular branch's power to its outermost boundaries or perhaps even beyond. It is also important not to lose sight of the constitutional interpretations branches other than the judiciary must make. Commentators spend far too little time analyzing the constitutional interpretations other branches must make as a function of their own constitutional responsibilities. One purpose of this book is to indicate that the Congress must interpret the impeachment clauses as part of its impeachment power, that these interpretations are as much a part of constitutional law as the Supreme Court's decisions, and that much of the constitutional commentary on the meaning of the impeachment clauses is not so much constitutional interpretation as it is advice to Congress on how to resolve the *political* problems or policy questions endemic to each impeachment. Indeed, unless and until our notions of politics are elevated and our understanding of the distinction between constitutional law and politics is refined, constitutional commentators will continue to tell the different branches of government—as they have in the area of impeachment— what they *must* do as opposed to what they *may* do only after careful and thorough deliberation.

In the meantime, studying the impeachment process leaves us to ponder the wisdom of the framers' judgment not to trust any judicial involvement with the impeachment process. After two hundred years, it is far from clear who can be better trusted than Congress to do the right thing in this area. It has been the purpose of this book in part to suggest, paraphrasing Winston Churchill's comment on democracy and its critics,[9] that impeachment may be the worst imaginable system for disciplining and removing impeachable officials, except for all of the others.

NOTES

INTRODUCTION

1. The literature on judicial discipline and removal is voluminous. See, e.g., Federal Judicial History Office, Federal Judicial Center, "The History of Judicial Discipline and Removal in America: A Preliminary Working Bibliography" (June 1992), prepared for the National Commission on Judicial Discipline and Removal; Corr and Berkson, *Literature on Judicial Removal*; Kingsley, *The Federal Impeachment Process*.

2. 113 S.Ct. 732 (1993).

3. See, e.g., Fox, Note, "Impeachment," 1275; Luchsinger, Note, "Committee Impeachment Trials," 163; Auslander, Note, "Impeaching the Senate's Use of Trial Committees," 68; Stewart, "Commentary: Impeachment by Ignorance," 54.

4. See Brown, "When Political Questions Affect Individual Rights," 125.

CHAPTER ONE
THE IMPEACHMENT DEBATES IN THE CONSTITUTIONAL CONVENTION

1. See generally, Hoffer and Hull, *Impeachment in America*, 68–77.

2. See generally, Berger, *Impeachment*, 54, 87n.160, 143n.97, 170, 171n.217.

3. See, e.g., Hoffer and Hull, *Impeachment in America*; Berger, *Impeachment*; Bestor, "Impeachment," review of *Impeachment: The Constitutional Problems*, by Raoul Berger, 255; Feerick, "Impeaching Federal Judges," 1, 5–15.

4. For a discussion of many of these problems, see generally, Gerhardt, "The Constitutional Limitations to Impeachment," 19–32.

5. See Rotunda, "An Essay on the Constitutional Parameters," 707, 708–14.

6. Elliot, *Debates on the Adoption of the Federal Constitution*, 42–43. The delegates took this requirement quite seriously. See, e.g., *Annals of Congress* 5 (1796): 775–76 (statement of Representative James Madison, criticizing as a breach of the convention's rule of secrecy President George Washington's reference in his message to Congress on March 30, 1796, to the unpublished Journal of the Constitution); ibid., 734 (remarks of Representative Albert Gallatin on the same).

7. Ibid., 123.

8. Quoted in Farrand, *The Framing of the Constitution*, 58.

9. See ibid.

10. Rotunda, "Essay on the Constitutional Parameters," 710, 710n.13.

11. See generally, Hutson, "The Creation of the Constitution," 1, 24–27, 33–35.

12. Quoted in Warren, *The Making of the Constitution*, 794; see also letter from James Madison to S. H. Smith (February 21, 1827); letter from James Madison to Thomas Ritchie (September 15, 1821); letter from James Madison to M. L. Hulbert (May 1830), all cited in ibid., 800–801n.1.

13. There are five constitutional provisions commonly referred to as the impeachment clauses because they each relate in some way to the federal impeachment process:

The House of Representatives shall . . . have the sole Power of Impeachment. (U.S. Const., art. I, § 2, cl. 5.)

The Senate shall have the sole Power to try all Impeachments. When sitting for that Purpose, they shall be on Oath or Affirmation. When the President of the United States is tried, the Chief Justice shall preside: And no Person shall be convicted without the Concurrence of two thirds of the Members present. (Ibid., art. I, § 3, cl. 6.)

Judgment in Cases of Impeachment shall not extend further than to removal from Office, and disqualification to hold and enjoy any Office of honor, Trust or Profit under the United States: but the Party convicted shall nevertheless be liable and subject to Indictment, Trial, Judgment and Punishment, according to Law. (Ibid., art. I, § 3, cl. 7.)

The President and all civil Officers of the United States, shall be removed from Office on Impeachment for and Conviction of, Treason, Bribery, or other high Crimes and Misdemeanors. (Ibid., art. II, § 4.)

The Judges, both of the supreme and Inferior Courts, shall hold their Offices during good Behavior, and, shall, at stated Times, receive for their Services a Compensation, which shall not be diminished during their Continuance in Office. (Ibid., art. III, § 1.)

14. See, e.g., Hoffer and Hull, ibid., 96.

15. Ibid.

16. M. Ferrand, *Records of the Federal Convention of 1787*, 1:22 (hereafter *Records*).

17. *Records*, 3:595–609, app. D.

18. Although the original of Pinckney's plan has never been located, it has been reconstructed by certain scholars relying on references to it after the constitutional convention. See ibid., 604. The plan is believed to have provided for a tripartite system of government, to have lodged the power of impeachment in the lower house of the legislature and assigned the power to try impeachments to the federal judiciary, and to have referred to "Treason, Bribery, or Corruption" as the grounds for presidential impeachment. See Feerick, "Impeaching Federal Judges," 16, 16n.89. The reconstructed plan refers to "all Crimes . . . in their Offices" as the grounds for impeachment of officers of the United States. *Records*, 3:608.

19. *Records*, 1:244.

20. Ibid., 252.

21. Ibid., 292.

22. Ibid.

23. On July 26, the constitutional convention appointed the Committee on Detail, in George Washington's words, to "draw into method and form the several matters which had been agreed to by the Convention as a Constitution for

the United States." Bowen, *Miracle at Philadelphia*, 192. The committee put resol"[utions], suggestions, amendments, and propositions into workable arrangement." Ibid. The original members were Randolph of Virginia, Wilson of Pennsylvania, Gorham of Massachusetts, Ellsworth of Connecticut, and Rutledge of South Carolina.

24. *Records*, 2:136, 159.
25. Ibid., 178–79.
26. Ibid., 185–86.
27. Ibid., 186.
28. Ibid., 427.
29. Ibid., 428.
30. Ibid.
31. Ibid.
32. Ibid., 429.
33. Ibid.
34. Ibid., 493.
35. Ibid., 551–52.
36. Ibid.
37. Ibid.
38. Ibid.
39. Ibid.
40. Ibid.
41. Ibid., 552–53 (September 8, 1787). Both James McHenry and Luther Martin of Maryland recalled after the convention "that the Senate alone seemed to be the body likely to view impeachments in a cool and dispassionate manner." Hoffer and Hull, *Impeachment in America*, 99. However, James Madison could not reconcile himself to impeachment trials in the Senate and voted against the provision. Ibid., 100.
42. Ibid., 100.
43. *Records*, 2:64–65.
44. Ibid., 64.
45. Ibid., 65.
46. Ibid.
47. Ibid., 66.
48. Ibid., 67.
49. Ibid.
50. Ibid., 68–69.
51. Ibid., 61, 69.
52. Ibid., 116.
53. *Records*, 2:69.
54. Hoffer and Hull, *Impeachment in America*, 101.
55. Ibid., 101. See also *Records*, 2:64–69.
56. Ibid., 337.
57. Ibid., 493.
58. Ibid., 550.
59. Ibid.
60. Ibid., 545.

61. Ibid.
62. Ibid.
63. Ibid., 545.
64. Ibid., 550.
65. *Records*, 1:140.
66. Ibid.
67. Hoffer and Hull, *Impeachment in America*, 102–3.
68. Ibid., 104.
69. See generally, Amar, Note, "The Senate and the Constitution," 1111.
70. For a modern expression of this perspective, see Carter, *The Confirmation Mess*, 146. "The Senate, responsive to public will but also sharing some of the distance of the courts, has the ability, if it chooses, to give voice not simply to the passions of the moment but to the enduring and fundamental values that shape the specialness of the American people. The institutional design of bicameralism makes this balance possible: what the House votes in its haste, the Senate may reconsider at its leisure."
71. Hoffer and Hull, *Impeachment in America*, 106.
72. Ibid. See also Hamilton, *Federalist No. 65*, 331–35.
73. Hoffer and Hull, *Impeachment in America*, 102–3.
74. See ibid., 96.
75. See generally ibid., 96–97; Bestor, "Impeachment," 262–71.
76. Bestor, "Impeachment," 261.
77. Hamilton, *Federalist No. 69*, 445.

CHAPTER TWO
THE IMPEACHMENT DEBATES IN THE RATIFYING CONVENTIONS

1. See, e.g., *Cohens v. Virginia*, 19 U.S., 264, 418 (1821); *McCulloch v. Maryland*, 17 U.S., 372, 433 (1819). Luther Martin's argument to the Court included reading extracts from *The Federalist Papers* and the Virginia and New York ratifying conventions.
2. See Hutson, "The Creation of the Constitution," 1, 12–24.
3. See Rossiter, *The Federalist Papers*, viii.
4. See notes 27–31 below and accompanying text.
5. Hamilton, *Federalist No. 65*, 397.
6. Ibid., 398.
7. Ibid.
8. Ibid.
9. Ibid.
10. Ibid., 399.
11. Ibid.
12. Hamilton, *Federalist No. 66*, 402.
13. Ibid.
14. Ibid., 404.
15. Ibid.
16. Ibid., 406.

17. Ibid.
18. Ibid.
19. Ibid.
20. Ibid.
21. Ibid.
22. Ibid.
23. Ibid., 407.
24. U.S. Const. art. II, § 4.
25. Ibid., art. I, § 3, cl. 7.
26. Hamilton, *Federalist No. 69*, 416.
27. *Records*, 2:819 (see chap. 1, m.16).
28. Ibid., 624.
29. Ibid., 625.
30. Ibid.
31. Ibid., 612.
32. Hamilton, *Federalist No. 79*, 473.
33. Ibid.
34. Ibid., 474.
35. Ibid.
36. Ibid.
37. Hamilton, *Federalist No. 81*, 483.
38. Ibid.
39. See Rotunda, "Original Intent," 507. Madison "urged us to look 'for the meaning of [the Constitution] beyond the face of the instrument . . . not in the General Convention which proposed, but in the State Conventions which accepted and ratified it'" (quoting from Warren, *Making of the Constitution*, 794, who was quoting Madison); Powell, "Original Understanding," 885, 937–38. "Madison thought it proper . . . to consult the direct expressions of state intention available in the resolutions of the ratifying conventions."
40. Elliot, *Debates*, 3:661 (Virginia) 4:246 (North Carolina) (see chap. 1, m.6).
41. Ibid., 2:168–69 (Massacusetts, statement of Mr. Stillman); 44–45 (statement of General Brooks).
42. Ibid., 460, 466 (Pennsylvania, statement of Mr. Smilie).
43. Ibid., 491 (statement of James Wilson). Interestingly, Wilson seems to have taken a similar stance in the constitutional convention. In response to the contention that the president's electoral accountability was not sufficient to preclude him from abusing power, Wilson remarked that "if the idea were to be pursued, the Senators who are to hold their places during the same term with the Executive, ought to be subject to impeachment & removal." *Records*, 2:68 (July 20, 1787). No one contested Wilson's inference that, at least as of that point in the Constitution's formation, senators were not impeachable.
44. Elliot, *Debates*, 492.
45. Ibid., 477.
46. Ibid., 492.
47. Ibid., 1:494 (Virginia, statement of George Mason objecting that "[t]he

President is tried by his counsellors. He is not removed from office during his trial. When he is arraigned for treason, he has the command of the army and navy, and may surround the Senate with thirty thousand people").

48. Ibid., 366 (statement of John Tyler expressing his fear "that the power of trying impeachments, added to that of making treaties, was something enormous, and rendered the Senate too dangerous").

49. Ibid., 221 (statement of John Monroe): "Two thirds of those who may happen to be present, may, with the President, make the treaties that shall sacrifice the dearest interests of the Southern States. . . . There is no check against this; there is no responsibility, or power to punish it".

50. Ibid., 516 (statement of James Madison).

51. Ibid.

52. Ibid., 4:113 (North Carolina, statement of James Iredell).

53. Ibid., 127.

54. Ibid.

55. Ibid.

56. Ibid., 126.

57. Ibid. (statement of General Johnston).

58. Ibid., 1:500 (statement of James Madison).

59. Berger, *Impeachment*, 89 (quoting Madison).

60. Elliot, *Debates*, 2:500 (Virginia, statement of Mr. Nicholas).

61. Ibid., 401 (statement of John Randolph).

62. Ibid.

63. Ibid., 401 (statement of Edmund Randolph).

64. *Annals of Congress* (1789): 498.

65. See above notes 58, 59, and accompanying text.

66. Act of April 30, 1790, ch. 9, § 21, Stat. 1:112 (1845).

67. See *Bowsher v. Synar*, 478 U.S. 714, 724n.3 (1986) (listing twenty members of the First Congress who were also delegates at the constitutional convention.

68. See Ervin, "Separation of Powers," 108, 118 and n.43.

69. For a fuller discussion of the nature of the different viewpoints on the constitutionality of the Bribery Act of 1790, see Shane, "Who May Discipline or Remove Federal Judges?" 209, 228–29. See also below chap. 8.

70. J. Wilson, "Considerations on the Nature and Extent of the Legislative Authority of the British Parliament," *James Wilson, Works*, 2:721.

71. See Farrand, *Framing of the Constitution*, 21. "Washington considered him to be one of the strongest men in the convention."; *Dictionary of American Biography*, 1st ed., s.v. "James Wilson." "With the possible exception of James Madison, . . . no member of the convention of 1787 was better versed in the study of political economy . . . and none was more far-sighted in his vision of the future greatness of the United States."

72. Wilson, "Considerations," 426.

73. Wilson, "Lectures on the Law, No. 11, Comparison of the Constitution of the United States with that of Great Britain, April 1792," in *The Works of James Wilson*, 1:408 (quoted in Hoffer and Hull, *Impeachment in America*, 101).

PART II
TRENDS AND PROBLEMS IN IMPEACHMENT PROCEEDINGS

1. Tocqueville, *Democracy in America*, 108.

2. See ibid., 109–11.

3. The fifteen officials and the years of their respective impeachment proceedings are as follows: William Blount, United States senator from Tennessee (1798–99); John Pickering, U.S. district judge for the District of New Hampshire (1803–4); Samuel Chase, associate justice of the United States Supreme Court (1804–5); James H. Peck, U.S. district judge for the District of Missouri (1826–31); West H. Humphreys, U.S. district judge for the District of Tennessee (1862); Andrew Johnson, president of the United States (1867–68); William W. Belknap, secretary of war (1876); Charles Swayne, U.S. district judge for the Northern District of Florida (1903–5); Robert W. Archbald, circuit judge, U. S. Court of Appeals for the Third Circuit, then serving as associate judge of the U.S. Commerce Court (1912–13); Judge George English, U.S. district judge for the Eastern District of Illinois (1926); Harold Louderback, U.S. district judge for the Northern District of California (1932–33); Halsted Ritter, U.S. district judge for the Southern District of Florida (1936); Harry Claiborne, U.S. district judge for the District of Nevada (1986); Alcee L. Hastings, U.S. district judge for the Southern District of Florida (1988–89); and Walter L. Nixon, Jr., U.S. district judge for the Southern District of Mississippi (1988–89).

4. All seven of those convicted in the Senate were federal judges, each of whom was removed from office: Judge Pickering (drunkenness and senility); Judge Humphreys (incitement to revolt and rebellion against the nation), Judge Archbald (bribery), Judge Ritter (kickbacks and tax evasion); Judge Claiborne (tax evasion); Judge Hastings (conspiracy to solicit a bribe); and Judge Nixon (false statements to a grand jury). Only Judge Humphreys and Judge Archbald also were disqualified from holding future office of honor or trust of the United States.

5. The federal officials acquitted by the Senate were Associate Justice Chase, Judge Peck, President Johnson, Judge Swayne, and Judge Louderback.

6. The Senate dismissed the impeachment articles against Senator Blount for several reasons, including lack of jurisdiction. See below, chap. 5, notes 1–7, and accompanying text. The Senate voted to acquit Secretary of War William Belknap, but for reasons largely unrelated to his innocence or guilt. See below, note 10 and accompanying text.

7. Judge George English resigned prior to the commencement of his impeachment trial. See below, note 11 and accompanying text.

8. National Commission on Judicial Discipline and Removal, *Report*, 30–31 (hereafter *Hearings*).

9. Ibid., 31. In the nineteenth century, the House did not vote on the articles of impeachment until after it had voted on impeachment and sent notice of its desire to have the representatives—otherwise known as house managers—designated to conduct the impeachment trial appear before the bar of the Senate to impeach the respondent. Hinds, *Hinds' Precedents*, 3: sects. 2413 (President Johnson), 2446 (Secretary Belknap).

10. Morgan, Eastman, Gale, and Areen, *Impeachment: An Historical Overview*, 689, 697. See also Brant, *Impeachment*, 155, 160.

11. *Cong. Rec.*, 69th Cong., 1st sess., 1926, 68, pt. 1:3.

CHAPTER THREE
IMPREACHMENT PROCEEDINGS IN THE HOUSE OF REPRESENTATIVES

1. Bryce, *American Commonwealth*, 1:212.

2. Grimes, *The Role of the U.S. House of Representatives in Proceedings to Impeach and Remove Federal Judges*, in Research Papers of the National Commission on Judicial Discipline and Removal, 1:67 (hereafter *Research Papers*).

3. U.S. Const. art. I, § 2, cl. 5.

4. See ibid., art. I, § 5: "Each House may determine the Rules of its Proceedings. . . ."

5. Jefferson's *Manual* and the *Rules and Practice of the House of Representatives* together control the House's procedure. Jefferson's *Manual* was prepared by Thomas Jefferson for his own use as president of the Senate during the years of his vice presidency (1797–1801). He based the *Manual* on English parliamentary practice. By a rule adopted in 1837, the House provided that the *Manual* should apply in cases in which it was suitable but not inconsistent with other governing rules of the House. Jefferson's *Manual* and the *Rules and Practice of the House* are regularly updated by the House parliamentarian to include annotations of rulings of the Speaker and presiding officers. Brown, *Constitution, Jefferson's Manual, and Rules of the House of Representatives*, 100th Cong., 2d sess., H.R. Doc. 279; 99th Cong., 2d sess., 1987, sect. 283: v, n.a (hereafter *House Rules*).

6. For a detailed description of House impeachment procedures, see Grimes, *Research Papers*, 49–57.

7. See generally, Dreschler, *Dreschler's Precedents*, 3: chap. 14, § 5.

8. *U.S. Code*, vol. 28, § 372 (1988).

9. Ibid., § 372 (c)(8).

10. See Grimes, *Research Papers*, 50.

11. *Ethics in Government Act*, U.S. Code, vol. 28, §§ 591–99 (1988). The act was first enacted in 1978 and has been reenacted twice, most recently in 1987. See *Independent Counsel Reauthorization Act of 1987*, P.L. 100–191, 101 Stat. 1293 (1987).

12. The enumerated officials include the president, the vice-president, the attorney general, assistant attorneys general, various people working in the executive office of the president, the director and deputy director of the Central Intelligence Agency, and the commissioner of Internal Revenue. See ibid., § 591(b).

13. *U.S. Code*, vol. 28, § 592 (1988).

14. See Dreschler's *Precedents*, 3: chap. 14, §§ 5, 5.10, 5.11.

15. The impeachment investigations were assigned to the Subcommittee on Courts, Civil Liberties, and the Administration of Justice (Claiborne); the Subcommittee on Criminal Justice (Hastings); and the Subcommittee on Civil and Constitutional Rights (Nixon).

16. Grimes, "Hundred-Ton-Gun Control," 1230.

17. Dreschler's *Precedents*, 3: chap. 14, § 7.1.

18. See *House Rules*, §§ 601–2.

19. Grimes, *Research Papers* 64.

20. Hinds, *Hinds' Precedents*, 3: §§ 2031 (Chase), 2323 (Pickering).

21. Ibid., § 2448 (Belknap).

22. Ibid., §§ 2388 (Humphreys), 2475 (Swayne).

23. *Proceedings of the U.S. Senate in the Impeachment Trial of Harry E. Claiborne*, 99th Cong., 2d sess., 1986, 1–2, setting forth H. Res. 501, designating nine house managers (hereafter "Claiborne Impeachment"); *Proceedings of the United States Senate in the Impeachment Trial of Alcee L. Hastings*, 101st Cong., 1st sess., 1989, S. Doc. 18, 3, setting forth H. Res. 511, designating six house managers (hereafter *Hastings Impeachment*); Proceedings of the United States Senate in the Impeachment Trial of Walter L. Nixon, Jr., 101st Cong., 1st sess., S. Doc. 22, 5, setting forth H. Res. 150, designating five house managers (hereafter *Nixon Impeachment*).

24. Grimes, "Hundred-Ton-Gun Control," 1215.

25. Ibid.

26. See generally, Bushnell, *Crimes, Follies, and Misfortunes*, 7.

27. See generally ibid., at 25–26, 44–45, 59; see also Hoffer and Hull, *Impeachment in America*, 146–63.

28. See U.S. House, *Special Subcommittee on H.R. Res. 920 of the House Committee on the Judiciary Final Report on Associate Justice William O. Douglas*, 91st Cong., 2d sess., 1970.

29. Grimes, *Research Papers*, 52–54.

30. See generally ibid., at 64–65.

31. *Cong. Rec.* 132, daily ed. (Sept. 16, 1986): S12597 (Claiborne replication); *Cong. Rec.* 134 daily ed. (Sept. 26, 1988): S13294 (Hastings replication); *Nixon Impeachment*, 21–22 (Nixon replication).

32. Borkin, *The Corrupt Judge*, 181–86.

33. Judge Kerner resigned following the exhaustion of his criminal appeals. See *Hearings*, 73.

34. Judge Fogel resigned in return for a commitment not to prosecute. See Grimes, "Hundred-Ton-Gun-Control," 1218 and n.53.

35. On June 13, 1989, the Justice Department filed an eight-count indictment against Judge Robert Aguilar of the Northern District of California. After a month-long trial, a federal jury cleared Judge Aguilar of one count of obstruction of justice, but deadlocked on seven other counts concerning false statements to the Federal Bureau of Investigation, informing an in-law of a federal wiretap, and seeking to influence other federal judges on behalf of certain acquaintances. In his retrial, Judge Aguilar was convicted in August 1990 of disclosing the existence of the wiretap to his in-law and lying to the FBI about the wiretap and his own involvement in another case. On appeal, the ninth circuit reversed all but one of Judge Aguilar's convictions. See generally, Peterson, *The Role of the Executive Branch in the Discipline and Removal of Federal Judges*, in *Research Papers*, 272–74. While he awaits retrial on that one count, Judge Aguilar continues to perform limited court duty in San Jose. Jim Doyle, "Judge's Conviction Upheld by

Court," *San Francisco Chronicle*, May 13, 1993, sec. A16. The fact that Judge Aguilar was wielding judicial power in spite of having been at that time a convicted felon spurred James Sensenbrenner (R.-Wis.) to introduce in May 1993 a resolution in the House to impeach Judge Aguilar. Jim Doyle, "Convicted Judge to Get a New Hearing," *San Francisco Chronicle*, Sept. 3, 1993, A18. On April 19, 1994, however, the ninth circuit sitting en banc reversed Judge Aguilar's remaining criminal conviction on the grounds that (1) disclosing information about a wiretap after the denial or expiration of its authorization is not a crime and (2) making false and misleading statements to the FBI is not "obstruction of justice." *United States v. Aguilar*, 21 F.3d 1475 (9th Cir. 1994, en banc).

36. The Justice Department indicted Judge Collins of the Eastern District of Louisiana on February 6, 1991, for taking bribery money from a drug dealer to reduce the dealer's sentence, conspiracy, and obstruction of justice. Collins was ultimately convicted on all three counts and has had his convictions upheld on appeal. See generally, Peterson, *Research Papers*, 274–75. Currently, he is incarcerated but still receiving his judicial salary. In June 1993, the Judicial Conference of the United States formally certified to the House its conclusion that "Judge Collins has engaged in conduct which might constitute one or more grounds for impeachment." "House Urged to Impeach Jailed Judge," *Chicago Tribune*, June 24, 1993, sec. N, p. 8.

37. See generally, Grimes, "Hundred-Ton-Gun-Control," 1233.

38. U.S. Senate, *Report of the Senate Impeachment Trial Committee on the Articles of Impeachment Against Judge Alcee L. Hastings, Hearings Before the Senate Impeachment Trial Commission*, 101st Cong., 1st sess., 1989, pt. 1:605–8, 740 (hereafter *Hastings Senate Report*).

39. See generally, Grimes, *Research Papers*, 66.

40. U.S. Senate, *Report of the Senate Impeachment Trial Committee on Articles of Impeachment Against Judge Harry E. Claiborne*, 99th Cong., 2d sess., 1986, pt. 1:687, 759, 803–4, 849.

41. *Hastings Senate Report*, 723 (statement of Senator Specter).

42. See Peterson, *Research Papers*, 322, 327, 330.

43. *Claiborne Impeachment*, 32, 40 (statement of Judge Charles Wiggins); ibid., 303 (statement of Sen. Jeff Bingamon); ibid., 339 (statement of Sen. George Mitchell); *Cong. Rec.* 132, daily ed. (July 22, 1986): H4712–13 (statement of Cong. Hamilton Fish).

44. 101st Cong., 1st sess., 124, 1989, H. Rep. 36, 15–16; 100th Cong., 2d sess. 1988, H. Rep. 810, 12–13; 99th Cong., 2d sess. 1986, H. Rep. 688, 6–7.

45. *Cong. Rec.* 135, daily ed. (May 10, 1989): H1811.

46. *Cong. Rec.* 132, daily ed. (July 22, 1986): H4721.

47. *Cong. Rec.* 134, daily ed. (August 3, 1988): H6193.

48. *Cong. Rec.* 48, 1912, 8933–34.

49. Judge Claiborne was acquitted of other misconduct charges at his first and second trials. None of these misconduct charges had, however, any relation to the income tax charges, which served as the sole basis of the House's impeachment articles.

50. On February 6, 1974, the House formally authorized the Judiciary Committee to begin impeachment hearings. On July 25, the Supreme Court handed

down its decision in *United States v. Nixon*, 418 U.S. 683 (1974) ordering President Nixon to turn over to a district court tapes of recorded conversations in the Oval Office to determine their relevance to the defense in an ongoing criminal prosecution. On July 27, the Judiciary Committee adopted the first article of impeachment, charging the president with obstruction of justice with respect to the Watergate break-in and other activities. On July 29, it adopted the second article of impeachment, involving abuse of power by misusing executive agencies and violating constitutional rights of the citizenry. On July 30, the committee adopted the third article, charging the president with willful disobedience of subpoenas issued by the Judiciary Committee. On August 6, Nixon decided to make the transcript of the tapes available to the public. Three days later, on August 9, he resigned.

51. See Grimes, *Research Papers*, 76.n.125 (suggesting that many House members equate their role in an impeachment with that of a grand jury and, thus, do not regard their vote on impeachment articles as a determination that an impeachable official should be removed from office). See also ibid., app. B, pt. I(K), 94 reporting that, when asked to choose the description that best described their role, most house managers responding to a survey conducted by Warren S. Grimes chose "grand jury" rather than "judge and jury."

CHAPTER FOUR
THE SENATE'S ROLE IN THE FEDERAL IMPEACHMENT PROCESS

1. U.S. Const. art. I, § 2, cl. 6.

2. Ibid., art. I, § 5, cl. 2.

3. See *Procedure and Guidelines for Impeachment Trials in the Senate* (rev. ed.), 99th Cong., 1st sess., August 15, 1986, S. Doc. 93–33, 2–8 (hereafter Senate Rules for Impeachment Trials).

4. Ibid.

5. For an even more detailed account of Senate impeachment trial procedures, see Gerhardt, "The Senate's Process for Removing Federal Judges," *Research Papers*, 139, 142–45.

6. National Commission on Judicial Discipline and Removal, *Hearings*, 50.

7. Rule XI, *Senate Rules for Impeachment Trials*, 4. See also U.S. Senate, *Report of the Hearings before the Senate Impeachment Trial Committee*, 99th Cong., 2d sess., 1986, pt. 1: 18 (hereafter *Claiborne Senate Hearings*) remarks of Committee Chairman, Senator Mathias, Organizational meeting of the trial committee.

8. U.S. Senate, *Proceedings of the U.S. Senate in the Trial of Impeachment of Halsted Ritter*, 74th Cong., 2d sess., 1936, S. Doc. 200, 47, 323–24, 534 (hereafter *Ritter Impeachment Trial*).

9. Rule XXIV, *Senate Rules for Impeachment Trials*, 6.

10. See generally, Williams, "Historical and Constitutional Bases," 512, 541–42.

11. *Cong. Rec.*, 74th Cong., 2d. sess., 1936, 80, pt. 3: 3423, 3425 (comments of Sen. Henry Ashurst).

12. *Cong. Rec.*, 74th Cong., 1st scss., 1935, 79, pt. 8: 8309, 8309–10.

13. See *Amending the Rules of Procedure and Practice in the Senate When Sitting on Impeachment Trials*, 99th Cong., 2d sess., 1986, S. Rep. 401, 5.

14. Rule XI, *Senate Rules for Impeachment Trials*, 4.

15. See *Claiborne Senate Hearings*, pt. 1: 18 (remarks of committee chairman, Senator Mathias, organizational meeting).

16. Rule XI, *Senate Rules for Impeachment Trials*, 4.

17. Ibid.

18. See Gerhardt, "Senate Process for Removing Federal Judges," App. A, 231–40, cataloging the survey results.

19. *Claiborne Senate Hearings*, pt. 1: 21. The longest impeachment trial lasted six weeks; the average trial lasts sixteen days. 95th Congress, 2d sess., 1978, S. Rep. 1035, 4 (comments from Senator Nunn).

20. See ibid., pts. 1–4.

21. The Senate report lists nine full-time staffers on the Hastings trial committee staff. In addition, another sixteen staffers are listed as assisting the twelve senators on the trial committee. *Hastings Senate Report*, pt. 1: ii.

22. Ibid., pt. 1: 281–94, 341–44, 483, 601–11, 737–40, 855–77.

23. *Cong. Rec.* 135, daily ed. (June 9, 1989): S6453.

24. *Hastings Senate Report* pts. 3–4.

25. *Hastings Impeachment*, 625–706.

26. U.S. Senate, *Report of the Senate Impeachment Trial Committee on the Articles Against Judge Walter L. Nixon, Jr., Hearings before the Senate Impeachment Trial Committee*, 101st Cong., 1st sess., 1989, pts: I–IV (hereinafter *Nixon Report*).

27. *Nixon Impeachment*.

28. See Williams, "Historical and Constitutional Bases," 514. "The impeachment mechanism, however, has many defects which have contributed to its declining use. It has been attacked as 'cumbersome,' 'unworkable,' and 'an utterly absurd task physically' (quoting Borkin, *The Corrupt Judge*, 193.

29. See, e.g., *Cong. Rec.* 80 1936, 3423, 3424 for the comments of Senator Thomas: "[T]he constant attention of a jury of 96 members . . . cannot be expected."

30. See, e.g., Williams, "Historical and Constitutional Bases," 516. "Given the enormous expansion of the congressional workload, it is clear that a removal mechanism which as a practical matter requires the complete suspension . . . of legislative responsibilities is of questionable utility."

31. Judge Louderback was tried and acquitted of five articles of impeachment in May 1933. See Staff of House Comm. on the Judiciary, *Impeachment: Selected Materials on Procedure*, 93d Cong., 2d sess., 1974, 850.

32. Judge Ritter was impeached and removed from office in 1936. *Cong. Rec.* 80 1936, 3066–92.

33. See U.S. Senate, *Calendar of Business*, final issue, 102d Cong., 2d sess., November 8, 1993, indicating that there were a total of 156 legislative working days for the 103d Congress, 1st Session; Ornstein, Mann, and Malbin, *Vital Statistics on Congress, 1991–1992*, 151–53, tables 6–1, 6–2 indicating that there were 158 legislative working days in 1991; *Congressional Quarterly Almanac*

147, 102d Cong., 1991, 11 indicating that there were 138 legislative working days in 1990.

34. See *Impeachment: Selected Materials*, 93d Cong., 1st sess., 1973, H.R. Doc. 7, 125–202.

35. See generally Luchsinger, Note, "Committee Impeachment Trials" 163, 168–69.

36. See notes 35, 36, and accompanying text in chap. 2.

37. National Commission on Judicial Discipline and Removal, *Hearings* 211, testimony of Sen. Charles Mathias on May 15, 1992. See also ibid., 172–73, testimony of Senator Levin: "I don't think too much of the Senate's time is taken up by impeachments. [E]ven if the average turns out to be one a year, that is not an excessive amount of time for something this serious"; *Cong. Rec.* 135, daily ed. (October 20, 1989): S13803, statement of Senator Specter: impeachments allow us "to see in a closeup and firsthand way how those th[e] laws [we have enacted] and the agencies they affect operate. That experience, difficult and time-consuming as it may be, makes us wiser in the discharge of our legislative responsibilities"; *Hearings*, 251, testimony of Judge Abner Mikva on May 15, 1992: "I recognize that sometimes [impeachment] has become very cumbersome. But I think it's necessary to preserve the independence of the judiciary as our framers intended."

38. See, e.g., *Cong. Rec.* 132, daily ed. (October 9, 15, 16 1986): S15760, S16571, S16821, S16823, 312–13, 355–58, 358–60, 361–66 (statements of Senators Exon, Evans, and Levin).

39. Heflin, "The Impeachment Process," 124.

40. Ibid., 124. *See also Cong. Rec.* 132, daily ed. (October 10, 1986): S15868, 336 (statement of Sen. Stevens admitting that he had attended no more than thirty-five minutes of the full Senate's proceedings on Judge Claiborne, had not read most of the trial committee's documents, and had found that most senators had not had "enough time to weigh independently the evidence"); ibid., *Cong. Rec.* 132, daily ed. (October 9, 1986): S15760-62 (Senator Stevens voting "present" on each of the articles of impeachment).

41. *Cong. Rec.* 135, daily ed. (October 20, 1989): S13803 (statement of Senator Specter).

42. *Cong. Rec.* 135, daily ed. (October 27, 1989): S14364 (statement of Senator Lieberman).

43. Williams, "Historical and Constitutional Bases," 541 (footnote omitted).

44. Ibid., 539–42.

45. *Time*, March 13, 1936, 18, quoted in Williams, "Historical and Constitutional Bases," 542n.160: "At one time only three senators were present and for ten days [Judge Louderback] presented evidence to what was practically an empty chamber").

46. Ibid., 541–42.

47. Stolz, "Disciplining Federal Judges," 659, 667.

48. Heflin, "Impeaching Federal Judges," 32. Senator Heflin counted thirty-seven absent senators during Judge Claiborne's presentation of his closing argument. *Claiborne Senate Hearing*, 318 (statement of Sen. Heflin). See also Heflin,

"The Impeachment Process," 124 complaining that "[d]uring Judge Claiborne's closing statement approximately 40 senators were not present in the chamber to hear any of his statement. Indeed, I would guess that at least 35 Senators were never present on the floor for any of the presentations by either the prosecution or the defense."

49. See Gerhardt, "The Senate's Process for Removing Federal Judges," 233–34, app. A.

50. There are four sources senators may consult for information about past impeachment trials. First, the *Senate Rules for Impeachment Trials* contains selected examples from precedents. Second, the Congressional Research Service has issued several documents, such as its *Compendium of Precedents Involving Evidentiary Rulings and Applications of Evidentiary Principles from Selected Impeachment Trials*, to familiarize senators with the removal process. Moreover, other collections exist, including, for example, the House's transcripts and records pertaining to its hearings on the impeachment of Harry Claiborne and the Senate impeachment trial committee's hearings on Judge Claiborne. Lastly, the Senate's Office of Legal Counsel provides legal advice to senators about past removal rulings and even compiles materials on past impeachment trials for senators to use in closed session. See, e.g., *Hastings Senate Report*, pt. 1: 74–75.

51. See Gerhardt, "The Senate's Process," 240, app. A, indicating that fifteen of the twenty-one respondents to the survey conducted by the National Commission on Judicial Discipline and Removal thought current materials were inadequate and the Senate should "commission [a] complete or comprehensive manual of precedents on impeachment trials."

52. The Fifth Amendment due process clause provides in pertinent part that "nor shall any person . . . be deprived of life, liberty, or property without due process of law . . ." U.S. Const., amend. V.

53. See *Hastings v. United States*, 802 F.Supp. 490 (D.D.C. 1992).

54. Ibid., 502.

55. Ibid., 988 F.2d 1280 (D.C. Cir. 1993).

56. 113 S.Ct. 732 (1992).

57. *Hastings v. United States*, 837 F.Supp. 3 (D.D.C. 1993).

58. *Hastings Impeachment*, 15–16.

59. See Hoffer and Hull, *Impeachment in America*, 213.

60. Cf. Black, *Impeachment*, 15, observing that the real question at issue here is what "things in the impeachment process . . . should be treated like the same things in a criminal trial, and what things need not be."

61. See ibid., 18.

62. Ibid.

63. See, e.g., *Claiborne Senate Hearings*, 21 (statement of then-Sen. Albert R. Gore, Jr.).

64. See generally Pierce, "Use of the Federal Rules of Evidence," 1.

65. See Gerhardt, *The Senate's Process*, 169.

66. *Hastings Senate Report*, 6.

67. See, e.g., *Hastings Senate Report*, 757–58 (statement of Senator Specter): "A uniform burden of proof would provide notice to the impeached official of "the standard by which he is being judged. . . . It is not sufficient to say that the

standard on burden of proof is left to the individual judgment of each Senator because that leaves the matter vague, indefinite, speculative, and subject even to individual whim or caprice. [T]he establishment of a standard on burden of proof would help the Senators themselves[, who have often said] that they were at a loss for the context in which to judge the complex case."

68. *Cong. Rec.* 132 daily ed. (October 7, 1986): S15507.

69. See *Hastings Senate Report*, pt. 1: 74–75 (statement of Senator Warren Rudman): "[The standard of proof] is what is in the mind of every Senator. If you want to use clear and convincing, preponderance, if you want to use beyond a reasonable doubt—I think it is what everybody decides themselves"; ibid. (statement of Senate legal counsel, Michael Davidson). Davidson agreed that "the Senate [in the Claiborne proceedings had] determined overwhelmingly [that] each member, as on any vote in the Senate, needs to establish his or her standards for that vote. The Senate has never presumed to instruct its members what quality of evidence, or what historical basis each member must have in order to determine that vote."; *Nixon Report*, pt. 1: 13 (statement of Michael Davidson).

70. *Cong. Rec.* 132, (Oct. 9, 1989): S15759 (statement of Senator Hatch).

71. Ibid., 791–92 (statement of Sen. Biden). See also ibid., 715–16 (statement of Senator Hatch).

72. See, e.g., *Cong. Rec.* 135, daily ed. (October 27, 1989): S14360 (statement of Senator Lieberman); *Hastings Impeachment*, 709, 711 (statement of Senator Bingamon).

73. See, e.g., *Claiborne Senate Hearings*, pt. 1: 98–99.

74. *Cong. Rec.* 132, daily ed. (July 22, 1986): H4712.

75. U.S. Senate, *Report of the Senate Impeachment Trial Committee: Hearings Before the Senate Impeachment Trial Committee*, 99th Cong., 2d sess., 1986, pt. I: 148–65.

76. Ibid., 169–87.

77. Ibid., 149, 165–67.

78. Ibid., 108–9.

79. *Claiborne Impeachment*, 289–97.

80. 113 S.Ct. 732 (1993).

81. See, e.g., Gerhardt, "The Senate's Process for Removing Federal Judges," 236, app. A, indicating that the respondents to the survey conducted by the National Commission on Judicial Discipline and Removal overwhelming supported the Senate's continued use of rule XI trial committees.

82. Stewart, "Commentary" 54.

83. *Accord Walter Nixon v. United States*, 938 F.2d 239, 265 (1991) (J. Edwards dissenting in part and concurring in the judgment), aff'd *Nixon v. United States*, 113 S. Ct. 732 (1993).

84. See generally, *Hearings*, 56.

85. See, e.g., *Claiborne Senate Hearings*, pt. 1: 19 (statement of Senator Rudman).

86. See *Hastings Senate Report*, pt. 1: 69 (statement of Senator Rudman); see also Gerhardt, "The Senate's Process," 185–88.

87. See *Hastings Senate Report*, pt. 1: 226–27 (statement of House Manager Jack Brooks).

88. Ibid., pt. 1: 479 (memorandum for the Hastings Record, May 17, 1989).

89. See generally, Gerhardt, "The Senate Process for Removing Federal Judges," 189–92.

90. See, e.g., *Hastings Senate Report*, pt. 1: 282, 287, 292 (Impeachment Trial Committee Disposition of Pretrial Issues [Order of April 14, 1989]).

91. See, e.g., ibid., 286, 287 (Impeachment Trial Committee Disposition of Pretrial Issues [Order of April 14, 1989]).

CHAPTER FIVE
IMPEACHMENT ISSUES INVOLVING CONGRESS AND
OTHER BRANCHES

1. See *Annals of Congress* 1 (1798 [1797–1798]): 948–51.

2. Ibid., 43–44.

3. *Annals of Congress* 2 (1798 [1798–1799]): 2247–48.

4. Ibid., 2271–72.

5. Ibid., 2270–72.

6. Ibid., 2318.

7. Ibid., 2319.

8. Interestingly, Republican Senator Henry Tazewell now seems precient for admonishing his colleagues in the midst of the Senate debate on Senator Blount's impeachment to seriously consider their reasons for voting one way or another, because their decision would serve as a "precedent for all future occasions." Melton, *The First Impeachment* (quoting Senator Tazewell).

9. National Commission on Judicial Discipline and Removal, *Hearings* (testimony of Senator Carl Levin on May 15, 1992).

10. *Claiborne Impeachment Trial*, 289–97.

11. *Hearings*, 161 (testimony of Senator Levin).

12. Burbank, "Alternative Career Resolution," 643, 683–84.

13. S. Res. 18, 74th Cong., 1st sess., *Cong. Rec.* 79, daily ed. (May 28, 1935): 8309–10.

14. *Ritter Impeachment Trial*, 47, 323–24.

15. See generally Miller, Comment, "The Justiciability of Legislative Rules," 1341, 1345.

16. Bushnell, *Crimes, Follies, and Misfortunes*.

17. Ibid., 29, 36.

18. See Hoffer and Hull, *Impeachment in America*, 162. "Blount's case was an object lesson to both Federalists and Republicans there was no hope for a sweeping politicization of impeachment law without a suitable revision or extension of the doctrine of impeachment."

19. Ibid., 26.

20. Hoffer and Hull, *Impeachment in America*, 202, 250–52.

21. Ibid., 153.

22. See *Annals of Congress* 2 (1804): 319–22.

23. Ibid., 328–30.

24. Hoffer and Hull, *Impeachment in America*, 217.

25. Ibid.

26. Ibid.

27. U.S. House Special Subcommitte on H.R. 920 of the House Committee on the Judiciary, *Legal Materials on Impeachment* 20, 91st Cong., 2d sess., 1970, Committee Print.

28. Morgan, Eastman, Gale, and Areen, "Impeachment," 689, 698.

29. Bushnell, *Crimes, Follies, and Misfortunes*, 51.

30. The five senators were Federalists Dayton and Samuel White (Delaware) and Republicans John Armstrong (New York), Stephen R. Bradley (Vermont), and David Stone (North Carolina). Ibid.

31. Ibid.

32. 1 John Quincy Adams, *Memoirs*, 1:309.

33. Hoffer and Hull, *Impeachment in America*, 217. In the Senate vote on removal, only one Federalist—William H. Wells from Delaware—moved sides, and, in doing so, joined the nineteen Republicans who had already voted to convict the judge. Ibid.

34. *Cong. Rec.* 4 (1876): 1433.

35. Ibid., 2081–82.

36. Ibid., 1429.

37. Ibid., 1433.

38. See ibid., 1429–32.

39. Ibid., 1430.

40. *Cong. Rec.*, 4 158 (1876) (Trial of William Belknap).

41. Hinds, *Hinds' Precedents*, 3, § 2459, 934.

42. *Trial of William Belknap*, *Cong. Rec.* 4, 357.

43. *Cong. Rec.* 4 (1876): 5082.

44. Ibid.

45. The four were Secretary of War William Belknap (charged with accepting bribes); Harry Claiborne (charged with wilfully making false tax statements); Alcee Hastings (charged with conspiring to solicit a bribe and perjury), and Walter Nixon (charged with perjury).

46. *Annals of Congress* 2 (1804): 319–22.

47. *Congressional Globe*, 37th Cong., 2d sess., (1862), 2949–50.

48. *Cong. Rec.* 48 (1912): 8910.

49. *Cong. Rec.* 80 (1936): 5606.

50. Ten Broeck, "Partisan Politics," 185, 198–99. See also Bushnell, *Crimes, Follies, and Misfortunes*, 286, suggesting that "because the House . . . had already investigated him in 1933, perhaps Judge Ritter's impeachment emerged as a ready-made and quick route for showing the judicial branch that Congress possessed, and would use, power to chasten it."

51. Ibid., 282.

52. See generally, U.S. House Special Subcommittee on H.R. Res. 920 of the House Committee on the Judiciary, *Final Report on Associate Justice William O. Douglas*, 91st Cong., 2d sess., 1970.

53. U.S. House, *Impeachment of Richard M. Nixon, President of the United States*, 93d Cong., 2d sess., 1974, H. Rep. 93–1305, 1–4 (hereafter *President Nixon Impeachment Report*).

54. Ibid., 499.

55. For a similar view, see Hoffer and Hull, *Impeachment in America*, 218–19, maintaining that "Pickering was removed because there was no other way to replace him. [His] was not a partisan case" in part because the Federalists underestimated the Republicans' ability to oppose impeaching judges on a partisan basis and "without strong cause. [Pickering] was not accused of misusing his office for political ends or of hectoring his political enemies in his court. . . . Out of the confusion over the liability of Pickering's conduct—whether a person incapable of crime (and incompetent to stand trial) could be impeached, tried, and removed—came the clear rule that incompetence was an impeachable offense."

56. See Rehnquist, *Grand Inquests*, Swindler, "High Court of Congress," 420, 423–24.

57. U.S. Const., art. I, § 5, cl. 1.

58. Ibid., art. I, § 3, cl. 7.

59. See Solomon, *History of the Seventh Circuit, 1891–1941*, 61–63.

60. For a thorough discussion of the relationship between Justice Department investigations and prosecutions and the removal, resignation, or impeachment of federal judges, see Van Tassel, "Resignations and Removals," 333, 379–93.

61. Ibid., 391–92.

62. For example, Judges John Warren Davis, Martin Manton, and Albert Johnson, were all indicted by the Justice Department, but each resigned before being prosecuted. See Borkin, *The Corrupt Judge*, 219–59.

63. See notes 35, 36, and accompanying text in chap. 2.

64. National Commission on Judicial Discipline and Removal, *Hearings*, 41–43.

65. Wallace Turner, "Impeachment May Focus on Intrigue," *New York Times*, August 11, 1986, A20.

66. Van Tassel, "Resignations and Removals," 370, 410–19, app., tbl. 1.

67. Ibid., 407.

68. Hinds *Hind's Precedents* 3, § 2397, 820 (Humpreys); Cannon, *Cannon's Precedents*, 6, § 512, 707 (Archbald).

69. *Ritter Impeachment Trial*, 628–37. After convicting Judge Ritter, the Senate voted not to bar Judge Ritter from future federal office. Ibid., 639–41.

70. *Claiborne Impeachment*, 291–97; *Hastings Impeachment*, 688–703; *Nixon Impeachment*, 432–35.

71. U.S. Const., amend. V.

72. See ibid., art. II, § 2, cl. 1.

73. National Commission on Judicial Discipline and Removal, *Hearings*.

74. *Nixon Report*, pt 1:117–19. (Motion of Judge Walter J. Nixon, Jr., for Defense Funds). See also *Hastings Senate Report*, pt. 1:259 (same arguments of Professor Terrance Anderson on behalf of Judge Hastings).

75. *Hastings Senate Report*, pt. 1:479 (Memorandum for the Record, May 17, 1989); *Nixon Report*, pt. 1:325 (Impeachment Trial Committee Disposition of Pre-Trial Motions First Order).

76. *Hastings v. United States*, 802 F. Supp. 490, 504–5 (D.D.C., citation omitted).

CHAPTER SIX
MAKING SENSE OF THE FEDERAL IMPEACHMENT PROCESS

1. U.S. Const. art. I, § 2, cl. 5.
2. Ibid., § 3, cl. 6.
3. Ibid., art. II, § 4.
4. Ibid., art. I, § 3, cl. 6.
5. Ibid.
6. Ibid.
7. Ibid., art. I, § 3, cl. 7.
8. Ibid., art. II, § 4.
9. Ibid.
10. Ibid., art. III, § 1.
11. Ibid., art. I, § 3, cl. 7.
12. Ibid.
13. Ibid., art. I, § 3, cl. 6.
14. Sunstein, "Constitutionalism After the New Deal," 421, 495.
15. Ibid., 495.
16. Shane, "Who May Discipline or Remove Federal Judges?" 209, 214.
17. 113 S. Ct. 732 (1993).
18. Carter, *The Confirmation Mess*, 151.
19. See Powell, "Rules for Originalists," 659, 669. "[T]he founders thought, argued, reached decisions, and wrote about the issues that mattered to them, not about our contemporary problems."
20. Shane, "Who May Discipline or Remove Federal Judges?" 211–12.
21. See, e.g., Ervin, "Separation of Powers," 108, 113–19; Shartel, "Federal Judges," 870, 893–94.
22. Koukoutchos, "Constitutional Kinetics," 635, 665.
23. Ibid., 666–67.
24. The fact that some governmental action or decision is plainly unconstitutional, however, does not necessarily mean that judicial review is available to provide a remedy. I discuss the justiciability of impeachments in chapter 11.
25. See, e.g., *Bowsher v. Synar*, 478 U.S. 714 (1986), which held that Congress could not hold the power of removal except by impeachment over an officer exercising purely executive functions; *INS v. Chadha*, 462 U.S. 919 (1983), which held that Congress violated the presentment and veto clauses of the Constitution in enacting a one-house veto over the decision of an executive officer; *Northern Pipeline Construction Co. v. Marathon Pipeline Co.*, 458 U.S. 50 (1982), which held that Congress could not assign Article III powers in the Bankruptcy Act to judges who did not have life tenure and protection against salary diminution); *Buckley v. Valeo*, 424 U.S. 1 (1976), which held that Congress violated the appointments clause when it retained the power to appoint members of the Federal Election Commission; *Myers v. United States*, 272 U.S. 57 (1926), which held that Congress could not condition the removal of a purely executive officer without violating the appointments clause.
26. See generally, Strauss, "Formal and Functional Approaches to Separation-

of-Powers Questions," 488, 489, 492, 499; Strauss, "The Place of Agencies in Government," 573.

27. See, e.g., *Morrison v. Olson*, 487 U.S. 654 (1988), which held that Congress could delegate appointment of an independent counsel to the judiciary since the counsel was a minor official and the removal power remained to a significant degree within the executive branch, thereby not seriously impringing upon the power of the president to carry out his constitutionally assigned functions; *Mistretta v. United States*, 488 U.S. 361 (1989), which upheld the constitutionality of the composition and lawmaking function of the United States Sentencing Commission, at least three of whose members are required to be judges and which is empowered to promulgate, review, and revise sentence-determinative guidelines.

28. U.S. Const. art. III, § 1.

29. 17 U.S. (4 Wheat.), 316 (1819).

30. *McCulloch*, 17 U.S. (4 Wheat), 406.

31. See U.S. Const. art. I, § 8, cl. 18 ("The Congress shall have Power[:] To make all laws which shall be necessary and proper for carrying into Execution the foregoing powers, and all other Powers vested by this Constitution in the Government of the United States, or in any Department or Officer thereof.").

32. *McCulloch*, 17 U.S. (4 Wheat), 406.

33. Ibid., 413.

34. See note 26.

35. Cf., e.g., *Walter Nixon v. United States*, 113 S.Ct. 732 (1993).

36. See, e.g., Ely, *Democracy and Distrust*, 76: ("interprevitism is incomplete: there are provisions in the Constitution that call for more . . ."); Shiffrin, "The First Amendment and Economic Regulation," 1212, 1251–53 defending balancing methodology in first-amendment cases. But see Tushnet, *Red, White, and Blue*," 182–83, 184–86, 186–87, criticizing balancing as failing to restrain judicial tyranny, as providing no criteria by which to evaluate judicial decisions, and as allowing the worst political decisions to be validated.

CHAPTER SEVEN
THE SCOPE OF IMPEACHABLE OFFICIALS AND APPLICABLE
PUNISHMENTS

1. U.S. Const. art. II, § 4.

2. *Records*, 2:66.

3. See, e.g., Hamilton, *The Federalist No. 79*, 474.

4. Shane, "Who May Discipline or Remove Federal Judges?" 209, 213. See also Gerhardt, "Constitutional Limits to Impeachment," 10n.29.

5. Berger, *Impeachment*, 214–23. See also Story, *Commentaries on the Constitution*, § 402: 285–86; Rotunda, "Essay," 707, 715–16.

6. Berger, *Impeachment*, 216.

7. See ibid., 218–19.

8. U.S. Const. art. II, § 3.

9. See Rotunda, "Essay," 715–16.

10. U.S. Const. art. I, § 6.

11. U.S. Const., art. II, § 2, cl. 2.

12. Ibid., art. I, § 5.

13. See notes 40–46 and accompanying text in chap. 2.

14. See generally, Tribe, *American Constitutional Law*, 244–46; Nowak and Rotunda, *Constitutional Law*, § 7.11: 256–57.

15. See notes 2–7, 15–20, and accompanying text in chap. 3.

16. U.S. Const. art. II, § 4.

17. Ibid., art. I, § 3, cl. 7.

18. Rotunda, "Essay," 718, citing Story, *Commentaries*, 289.

19. *Hearings*, 47.

20. The Senate disqualified Judges Humphreys and Archbald. Ibid., 30, 47.

21. The two attempted impeachments against officials who were no longer in office at the time the House or the Senate attempted to move against them were Secretary of War William Belknap; see Bestor; "Impeachment," 255, 280 (discussing Belknap), and Senator William Blount. See Rotunda, "Essay," 717.

22. See, e.g., Gerhardt, "Constitutional Limits to Impeachment," 94–97; Rotunda, "Essay," 716–18; Firmage and Mangrum, "Removal of the President," 1023, 1091–92; Bestor, "Impeachmnet," 277–81.

23. Bestor, "Impeachment," 277.

24. See ibid., 277.

25. Ibid., 278.

26. See Rotunda, "Essay," 716.

27. See Bestor, "Impeachment," 279.

28. *Records*, 2: 64–69.

29. Madison, *Federalist No. 39*, 242.

30. *Congressional Globe*, 29th Cong., 1st sess., 1846, 641 (statement of J. Q. Adams), quoted in Bestor, "Impeachment," 279.

31. Story, *Commentaries*, 283.

32. See Rotunda, "Essay," 717.

33. Ibid., 717.

34. See Franklin, "Romanist Infamy," 313.

CHAPTER EIGHT
IMPEACHMENT AS THE SOLE MEANS OF DISCIPLINING AND
REMOVING IMPEACHABLE OFFICIALS

1. U.S. Const. art. III, § 1. The phrase "during good Behavior" appeared in various state constitutions as well as the first draft of the federal Constitution. See generally Berger, *Impeachment*, 147–49, 159–65.

2. See ibid., 161.

3. See, e.g., Rotunda, "Essay" 707, 720n.67; Otis, *A Proposed Tribunal*, 37.

4. The clearest expression of this intention is the constitutional text itself. Although the Constitution provides that federal judges may serve "during good Behavior," the Constitution puts limits on the terms of the president and the vice-president and members of Congress. The president may serve no more than two terms of four years each and must be elected separately for each term he

serves. U.S. Const. art. II, § 1; ibid., amend. XXII. The vice-president serves for only four year terms at the pleasure of the president, who chooses him. Members of the House of Representatives must run for reelection every two years, and members of the Senate must run for reelection every six years. Ibid., art. I, § 2; ibid., amend. XVII. See also *Records*, 2:66 (statement of Mr. King contrasting presidential and judicial tenure).

5. See generally Wood, *The Creation of the American Republic*, 159–61; Feerick, "Impeaching Federal Judges," 1, 10–12.

6. See Hamilton, *Federalist No. 78*, 464–72.

7. Berger, *Impeachment*, 163 (citations omitted).

8. *Records*, 2:545.

9. Rotunda, "Essay," 720.

10. See *Nixon v. United States*, 113 S.Ct. 732, 738 (1993): "In our constitutional system, impeachment was designed to be the only check on the Judicial branch by the legislature."

11. I am indebted to Peter Shane for the distinction between *political* and *judiciary-dependent* mechanisms for judicial discipline and removal. See Shane, "Who May Discipline or Remove Federal Judges?" 209, 211.

12. See generally Shane, "Who May Discipline or Remove Federal Judges?" 7–12.

13. See G. Wood, *The Creation of the American Republic*, 160.

14. Smith, "An Independent Judiciary," 1104, 1113, describing the Pennsylvania assembly's attempt in the 1860s to insist that, at the request of the assembly, colonial judges be displaced for misbehavior; ibid., 1153–55, describing address under Massachusetts Constitution of 1780, the Delaware and Maryland Constitutions of 1776, and the South Carolina Constitution of 1778.

15. On the experiences of the states prior to the drafting of the Constitution, see Hoffer and Hull, *Impeachment in America*, 68–95.

16. See Smith, "An Independent Judiciary," 1105–10.

17. See The Declaration of Independence, para. 11, (U.S. 1776): "He has made Judges dependent on his Will alone, for the tenure of their offices, and the amount and payment of their salaries."

18. Berger, *Impeachment*, 150.

19. The four states providing for address were Maryland, Massachusetts, New Hampshire, and South Carolina. Georgia provided for a variant of address by requiring that every officer shall be liable to be called to account by the lower chamber (the house) of the Assembly. The six states that had impeachment mechanisms were Delaware, New York, New Jersey, Pennsylvania, Vermont, and Virginia. See Berger, *Impeachment*, 145 (categorizing state constitutional provisions on judicial removal).

20. *Records*, 2:428.

21. Ibid.

22. Hamilton, Federalist No. 79, 474.

23. Storing, *Essays of Brutus*, 163.

24. See Shane, "Who May Discipline or Remove Federal Judges?" 218.

25. See, e.g., *Myers v. United States*, 272 U.S. 52, 114–15, 170 (1926), quoting with approval President Coolidge's statement that "[t]he dismissal of an

officer of the Government . . . other than by impeachment, is exclusively an executive function; *Bowsher v. Synar*, 478 U.S. 714, 722–23 (1986), finding that officers of the United States can be removed "only upon impeachment by the House of Representatives and conviction by the Senate."

26. See Bowsher, 478 U.S., 722–23, concluding that such a role is not contemplated by the Constitution and is "inconsistent with separation of powers."

27. Shane, "Who May Discipline or Remove Federal Judges?" 219.

28. See, e.g., *Immigration and Naturalization Service v. Chadha*, 462 U.S. 919, 961–62 (1982) (Justice Powell, concurring); Wood, *The Creation of the American Republic*, 407.

29. Wood, *The Creation of the American Republic*, 160 (citation omitted).

30. Montesquieu, *Spirit of the Laws*, 1:152.

31. Shane, "Who May Discipline or Remove Federal Judges?" 222.

32. Ch. 9, § 21, 1 Stat. 117 (April 30, 1790).

33. See, e.g., Hamilton, *Federalist No. 65*, 398–99, arguing that the Supreme Court would be an improper forum for impeachment because of judicial involvement in any subsequent criminal prosecution of the impeached official; ibid., *No. 77*, 464, cataloguing the "requisites to safety, in a republican sense" imposed to insure presidential accountability to the people.

34. See, e.g., Berger, *Impeachment*, 127–31 Shartel, "Federal Judges," 870, 882–83.

35. See Ziskind, "Judicial Tenure in the American Constitution," 135, 138, suggesting that *scire facias* was, by 1787, not a "precedent," but a "fossil."

36. Ethics in Government Act, *U.S. Code*, vol. 28, §§ 591–99 (1988). The act was first enacted in 1978 and has been reenacted twice, most recently in 1987. See Independent Counsel Reauthorization Act of 1987, P.L. 100–191, 101 Stat. 1293 (1987).

37. See Grimes, "Hundred-Ton-Gun Control," 1209, 1218.

38. U.S. Const. art. I, § 3, cl. 7.

39. On numerous occasions, the Supreme Court has recognized that the actions of the First Congress illuminate the original understanding of the Constitution because twenty of its members had also been delegates at the constitutional convention. See, e.g., *Bowsher v. Synar*, 478 U.S. 714, 724n.3 (1986); *Marsh v. Chambers*, 463 U.S. 783, 790–91 (1983); *J.W. Hampton, Jr. & Co. v. United States*, 276 U.S. 394, 411–12 (1928); *McCulloch v. Maryland*, 17 U.S. (4 Wheat.) 316, 424 (1819).

40. Burbank, "Alternative Career Resolution," 643, 668–69.

41. See generally Shane, "Who May Discipline or Remove Federal Judges?" 15.

42. 493 F.2d 1124 (7th Cir.), *cert. denied*, 417 U.S. 976 (1974).

43. Ibid., 1142.

44. Ibid., 1144.

45. 765 F.2d 784 (9th Cir. 1985), *appeal denied*, 781 F.2d 1327 (9th Cir.), *stay of execution denied*, 790 F.2d 1355 (9th Cir. 1986).

46. *United States v. Claiborne*, 727 F.2d 842, 846 (9th Cir.), *cert. denied*, 469 U.S. 829 (1984).

47. See *Claiborne*, 727 F.2d, 845–46.

48. See ibid., 845–46.

49. See generally Baker, *Conflicting Loyalties*.

50. See, e.g., *United States v. Claiborne*, 727 F.2d 842, 847–48 (9th Cir.), *cert. denied*, 469 U.S. 829 (1984); *United States v. Hastings*, 681 F.2d 706, 710–11 (11th Cir. 1982), *cert. denied*, 459 U.S. 1203 (1983).

51. See generally Peterson, "The Role of the Executive Branch in the Discipline and Removal of Judges," 243, 277–318.

52. *See Claiborne*, 727 F.2d, 846.

53. *Claiborne*, 790 F.2d, 1360 (Justice Kozinski dissenting).

54. Catz, "Removal of Federal Judges by Imprisonment," 103, 109.

55. *See Claiborne*, 727 F.2d, 846–47.

56. Ibid., 846.

57. See, e.g., Maxman, Note, "In Defense of the Constitution's Judicial Impeachment Standard," 420, 457.

58. U.S. Const. art. I, § 6, cl. 1 provides in pertinent part that "The Senators and Representatives shall . . . in all cases, except treason, felony, and breach of peace, be privileged from arrest during their attendance at the session of their respective Houses, and in going to and returning from the same; and for any speech or debate in either House they shall not be questioned in any other place."

59. See *United States v. Lee*, 106 U.S. 196, 220 (1882), holding that "[a]ll officers of the government, from the highest to the lowest, are creatures of the law, and are bound to obey it"; *Claiborne*, 727 F.2d, 847, holding that "Article III protections, though deserving utmost fidelity, should not be expanded to insulate federal judges from punishment for their criminal wrongdoing."

60. *See Claiborne*, 765 F.2d, 788.

61. Burbank, "Alternative Career Resolution," 671. See also ibid., 671–72n.130 (citing authorities).

62. Ibid., 671–72.

63. 487 U.S. 654 (1988).

64. *U.S. Code*, vol. 28, §§591–98 (1988).

65. Brief of the United States as Amicus Curiae Supporting Appellees 47, quoted in Koukoutchos, "Constitutional Kinetics," 635, 710.

66. *Morrison*, 487 U.S., 714 (Justice Scalia dissenting).

67. The Judiciary Committee of the House or Senate, a majority of the majority party members of either House, or a majority of all party members of either such committee, may request, but not require, in writing that the attorney general apply for the appointment of an independent counsel. See *U.S. Code*, vol. 28, § 592 (g) (Supp. V 1987).

68. See ibid., § 592(b)(1).

69. See Koukoutchos, "Constitutional Kinetics," 711 and nn.430–31 noting prosecutions of two former attorneys general, federal judges, and the ABSCAM prosecutions of legislators); see also Logan, "Historical Uses of a Special Prosecution," discussing the St. Louis Whiskey Ring and Teapot Dome prosecutions and the scandal-induced prosecutions of various officers of the Reconstruction Finance Cooperation and the Internal Revenue Bureau.

70. Ervin, "Separation of Powers," 108, 118 and n.43.

71. The necessary and proper clause provides that the Congress shall have the

power "to make all laws which shall be necessary and proper for carrying into execution the foregoing powers, and all other powers vested by this Constitution in the Government of the United States, or any department or officer thereof." U.S. Const. art. I, § 8 (18).

72. See, e.g., U.S. Const. art. III, § 2, cl. 3.

73. For a more detailed discussion of the differences between the procedural protections available in impeachment and criminal trials, see chap. 10.

74. Constitutional Rountable Discussion before the National Commission on Judicial Discipline and Removal (December 18, 1992), Remarks of Professor Walter Dellinger, reprinted in *Hearings* 354–55.

75. See Hamilton, *Federalist No. 65*, 427–28.

76. U.S. Const. art. I, § 5, cl. 2: "Each House may determine the Rules of its Proceedings, punish its Members for disorderly Behavior, and, with the Concurrence of two thirds, expel a Member."

77. 272 U.S. 52 (1926).

78. 295 U.S. 602 (1935).

79. U.S. Const. art. II, § 2, cl. 2: "[The President] shall nominate, and by and with the Advice and Consent of the Senate, shall appoint Ambassadors, other public Ministers and Consuls, Judges of the supreme Court and all other officers of the United States, whose Appointments are not herein otherwise provided for, and which shall be established by Law. . . ."

80. *See Humphey's Executor*, 295 U.S., 629; *Reagan v. United States*, 182 U.S. 419, 425 (1901), *United States v. Perkins*, 116 U.S. 483, 485 (1886).

81. See *Myers v. United States*, 272 U.S. 52, 119 (1926).

82. See, e.g., S. 1506, 91st Cong., 1st sess., 1969, attempting to create a five-judge commission that would remove a federal judge after a formal hearing subject to Supreme Court review, noted in Kurland, "The Constitution and the Tenure of Federal Judges," 665; Act of February 13, 1801, ch. 4, 2 Stat. 89 (1850) (repealed by Act of March 8, 1802, Ch. 8, 2 Stat. 132 [1850]), creating an alternate means of removing a federal judge but raising questions of constitutionality that eventually led to repeal, noted in Kurland, "The Constitution and the Tenure of Federal Judges," 670.

83. 398 U.S. 74, 88 (1970), dismissing second appeal for lack of jurisdiction in light of the fact that Judge Chandler may have still had other avenues of relief available to him; see also *Chandler v. Judicial Council of the Tenth Circuit*, 382 U.S. 1003, 1003 (1966) (miscellaneous order), characterizing the Judicial Council's initial order to suspend Judge Chandler temporarily until a full hearing as interlocutory and a basis for dismissing his first appeal.

84. Act of June 25, 1948, c. 646, § 332, 62 Stat. 902 (1948) (codified at *U.S. Code*, vol. 28, § 332 [1988]).

85. *Chandler*, 382 U.S., 1004 (miscellaneous order; Justice Black dissenting).

86. Ibid., 1003.

87. See Chandler, 398 U.S., 86.

88. *Chandler*, 382 U.S., 1006 (miscellaneous order; Justice Black dissenting).

89. See Chandler, 398 U.S., 136, 140 (Justice Douglas dissenting).

90. See Berger, *Impeachment*, 174–80.

91. See generally Kaufman, "Chilling Judicial Independence," 681, 716.

92. Pub. L. No. 96–458, 94 Stat. 2035 (1980) (codified at *U.S. Code*, vol. 28, §§ 331, 332, 372, 604 [1988]).

93. See *U.S. Code*, vol. 28, § 372 (c)(1) (1988).

94. See ibid., § 372(c)(4)–(5).

95. See ibid., § 372 (c)(6).

96. See ibid., § 372(c)(7)–(c)(8).

97. See, e.g., *Mistretta v. United States*, 109 S.Ct. 647, 659 (1989); *Morrison*, 487 U.S., 694–97; *CFTC v. Schor*, 478 U.S. 833, 857 (1986); *Nixon v. Administrator of General Services*, 433 U.S. 425, 443 (1977); *United States v. Nixon*, 418 U.S. 683, 705–07 (1974).

98. U.S. House, Report No. 1313, 96th Cong., 2d sess., 1980, 17–18.

99. See generally Barr and Willging, "Decentralized Self-Regulation," 25, 183, suggesting that, thus far, the act's positive benefits have included "reinforcing the chief judge's traditional role as overseer of judicial conduct in the circuit; . . . reassuring that the public has an opportunity to complain about judicial conduct; and . . . assigning the process to judges familiar with local conditions. The negative effects reported were related exclusively to the lack of merit in most complaints and the burden the Act imposes on court resources."

CHAPTER NINE
THE SCOPE OF IMPEACHABLE OFFENSES

1. *Cong. Rec.* 116, daily ed. (April 15, 1970): 11,913. Ford catalogued various "offenses" Justice Douglas allegedly committed, including associating with publishers of obscene publications and members of the "new left." Ford also suggested that Justice Douglas had failed to recuse himself in several cases in which recusal would have been proper. Ibid., 11,912.

2. See, e.g., Berger, *Impeachment*, 123, discussing the extent of misbehavior historically required as grounds for impeachment; Thompson and Pollitt, "Impeachment of Federal Judges," 87, 107, criticizing Ford's statements and showing a series of unsuccessful attempts at politically motivated impeachments; Maxman, Note, "In Defense of the Constitution's Judicial Impeachment Standard," 420, 444n.135, noting that Ford called for Douglas's impeachment to retaliate for the Senate's rejection of two Nixon appointees to the Supreme Court.

3. See, e.g., Tribe, *American Constitutional Law*, 293–94; Berger, *Impeachment*, 56–57; Black, *Impeachment: A Handbook*, 33–35; Brant, *Impeachment: Trials and Errors*, 180–81. But see Thompson and Pollitt, "Impeachment of Federal Judges," 107, 108, 114–15 asserting that the House of Representatives is reluctant to impeach unless the targeted official is accused of a serious crime.

4. Cf. Berger, *Impeachment*, 70, discussing the eighteenth-century English political practice of impeaching the king's favorites for giving him bad advice; Kurland, "The Constitution and the Tenure of Federal Judges," 665, 697, asserting the unconstitutionality of legislation aimed at defining the limits of good behavior.

5. U.S. Const. art. II, § 4.

6. Ibid., art. III, § 3, cl. 1.

7. See ibid., art. II, § 4; *U.S. Code*, vol. 18, §§ 201–3 (1982 and Supp. V

1987); see also Act of April 30, 1790, ch. 9, § 21, 1 Stat. 112 (1845) establishing bribery for the first time as a federal criminal offense.

8. Berger, *Impeachment*, 61 (emphasis in original).

9. Ibid., 59–61.

10. Bestor, "Impeachment," 255, 264.

11. See Bestor, *Impeachment*, quoting Blackstone, *Commentaries on the Laws of England* 75. Blackstone commented that

> treason . . . in its very name (which is borrowed from the French) imports a betraying, treachery, or breach of faith. . . . [T]reason is . . . a general appellation, made use of by the law, to denote . . . that accumulation of guilt which arises whenever a superior reposes a confidence in a subject or inferior, . . . and the inferior . . . so forgets the obligations of duty, subjection, and allegiance, as to destroy the life of any such superior or lord. . . . [T]herefore for a wife to kill her lord or husband, a servant his lord or master, and an ecclesiastic his lord or ordinary; these, being breaches of the lower allegiance, of private and domestic faith, are denominated *petit* treasons. But when disloyalty so rears it's [*sic*] crest, as to attack even majesty itself, it is called by way of eminent distinction *high* treason, *alta proditio*; being equivalent to the *crimen laesae majestatis* of the Romans.

12. Bestor, "Impeachment," 263–64 (citation omitted).

13. Ibid., 265.

14. See ibid., 266.

15. See Berger, *Impeachment*, 88, observing that "James Iredell, later a Supreme Court Justice, told the North Carolina convention [during the ratification campaign] that the 'occasion for its exercise [impeachment] will arise from acts of great injury to the community'" (citation omitted).

16. Farrand, *Records*, 2:550.

17. Ibid.

18. Ibid.

19. Ibid.

20. Ibid. According to Blackstone, "high misdemeanors" in British usage included "mal-administration of such high officers, as are in public trust and employment." Rotunda, "Essay," 707, 723, quoting Blackstone, *Commentaries*, 4:121.

21. Rotunda, "Essay," 723, quoting Elliot, *Debates*, 4:47 quoting A. MacLaine of South Carolina.

22. Rotunda, "Essays," 723, quoting Elliot, *Debates*, 2:47 quoting S. Stillman of Massachusetts.

23. Hamilton, *Federalist No. 65*, 396.

24. Ibid.

25. 1 Wilson, *James Wilson Works*, 426.

26. Story, *Commentaries*, § 385, 272–73.

27. Ibid., 290.

28. Bestor, "Impeachment," 263, quoting Story, *Commentaries*, § 788, 256.

29. Story, *Commentaries*, § 405, 288.

30. Ibid., 287 (citations omitted).

31. *U.S. Code*, vol. 18, § 201 (1982).

32. Tribe, *American Constitutional Law*, 294.

33. Ibid.

34. See Bestor, "Impeachment," 263 citing Story, *Commentaries*, § 810, 278, § 788, 256, commenting that the penalties for impeachment were designed to " 'secure the public against political injuries.' And [Justice Story] defined the latter as 'such kind of misdeeds . . . as peculiarly injure the commonwealth by the abuse of high offices of trust.' "

35. See Abraham, *Justices and Presidents*, 47–48.

36. U.S. Const. art. 1, § 3, cl. 6.

37. See ibid.

38. See ibid.

39. Rotunda, "Essay," 726.

CHAPTER TEN
THE PROPER PROCEDURE FOR IMPEACHMENT PROCEEDINGS

1. See U.S. Const. art. I, § 3, cl. 7.

2. See ibid., art. I, § 2, cl. 5, committing impeachments to the "sole Power" of the House; ibid., art. I, § 3, cl. 6, committing impeachment trials to the "sole Power" of the Senate.

3. See ibid., art. II, § 2, cl. 1.

4. See U.S. Const. art. I, § 2, cl. 5, implying impeachments by the House require at least a majority vote; ibid., art. I, § 3, cl. 6, requiring a vote of at least "two thirds of the Members present" in the Senate to convict in an impeachment trial.

5. See ibid., art. II, § 4.

6. See ibid., art. I, § 3, cl. 7; ibid., art. II, § 2; ibid., art. III, § 2, cl. 3.

7. Black, *Impeachment: A Handbook*, 17.

8. See ibid., 17.

9. Ibid.

10. National Commission on Judicial Discipline and Removal, *Hearings*, 59, 60.

11. Black, *Impeachment: A Handbook*, 20.

12. Ibid., 20–21.

13. Tribe, *American Constitutional Law*, 288.

14. *Congressional Globe*, 27th Cong., 2d sess., 1842, 580.

15. The third article charged that "President Nixon's repeated refusal to comply with Judiciary Committee subpoenas issued in the course of the impeachment investigation was 'subversive of constitutional government,' since such refusal involved a presidential usurpation of 'functions and judgments necessary to the exercise of the sole power of impeachment vested by the Constitution in the House of Representatives.' " Tribe, *American Constitutional Law*, 289.

16. 418 U.S. 683 (1974).

17. Ibid., 713.

18. See Tribe, *American Constitutional Law*, 268–74.

19. See Black, *Impeachment: A Handbook*, 18.

20. Ibid.

21. Ibid.

22. 113 S.Ct. 732 (1993).

23. U.S. Const. art. I, § 3, cl. 6.

24. Brief of Petitioner in *Nixon v. United States*, No. 91–740, 25–28 (April 24, 1992).

25. Ibid., 28–31.

26. Ibid., 31.

27. Ibid., 33–40.

28. Ibid., 33.

29. See U.S. Const. art. I, § 3, cl. 6.

30. See ibid.

31. See ibid., art. I, § 3, cl. 7.

32. See ibid., art. I, § 3, cl. 6.

33. Ibid., art. I, § 5, cl. 2. But see *United States v. Ballin*, 144 U.S. 1, 5 (1892), observing that

> each house . . . may not by its rules ignore constitutional restraints or violate
> fundamental rights, and there should be a reasonable relation between the
> mode or method of proceeding established by the rule and the result which is
> sought to be attained. But within these limitations all matters of method are
> open to the determination of the house, and it is no impeachment of the rule to
> say that some other way would be better, more accurate or even more just. . . .
> [This rulemaking power is] within the limitations suggested, absolute and be-
> yond the challenge of any other body or tribunal.

34. See Jefferson, *Jefferson's Manual of Parliamentary Practice*, noting that the Senate's impeachment rules are in part derived from English parliamentary practice and that English practice permitted the use of evidentiary committees in conducting impeachment trials, noting, in fact, that "the practice is to swear the witnesses in open House, and then examine them there; or a committee may be named, who shall examine them in committee, either on interrogatories agreed on in the House, or such as the committee in their discretion shall demand."

35. See, e.g., Hamilton, *The Federalist No. 65*, 440, 442.

36. Prior to the constitutional convention, the states had on occasion used legislative committees to investigate whether to draw up articles of impeachment. See Hoffer and Hull, *Impeachment in America*, 29, 33. In addition, in colonial governments and state legislatures, the subjects of impeachment proceedings often appeared before committees to answer the charges against them. See *Walter Nixon v. United States*, 113 S.Ct. 732, 746 (1993) (Justice White concurring).

37. See generally Williams, "Historical and Constitutional Bases," 512, 523–32, reviewing English precedent relating to impeachment in detail and concluding that it "shows beyond doubt that the House of Lords used committees to hear evidence during impeachment trials in the early 17th century. . . . It is clear . . . that, unlike other practices which were outlawed by affirmative action of the House of Lords, the use of committees to take evidence and examine witnesses has never been banned or disavowed as precedent—as were other impeachment procedures considered to have been wrongly invoked" (footnotes omitted).

38. See ibid., 520, 537–39, 543–44. See also *Nixon v. United States*, F.2d 239, 259–65 (D.C. Cir. 1993; Justice Edwards dissenting in part and concurring in judgment).

39. See Wright, *The Law of Federal Courts*, § 109, 771.

40. *Ex Parte Peterson*, 253 U.S. 300, 312 (1920). See also ibid., recognizing this authority as part of a federal court's "inherent power." The power of federal courts to appoint special masters is now embodied in Rule 53 of the Federal Rules of Civil Procedure. That rule permits the master broad powers in receiving evidence and taking testimony for use by the court. Ibid., 53 (c).

41. U.S. Const. art. I, § 5.

42. *Barry v. United States* ex rel. *Cunningham*, 279 U.S. 597, 616 (1929).

CHAPTER ELEVEN
JUDICIAL REVIEW OF IMPEACHMENTS

1. *Walter Nixon v. United States*, 113 S.Ct. 732 (1993).

2. See generally Chemerinsky, *Federal Jurisdiction*, § 2.6, 124–30, 144–45.

3. Compare Black, *Impeachment: A Handbook* 53–64; Rotunda, "Essay," 707, 728, noting that impeachment raises issues that satisfy each of the elements of a political question as set forth by the Court in *Baker v. Carr*, 369 U.S. 186, 217 (1962); Gunther, "Judicial Hegemony and Legislative Autonomy," arguing that the Burger Court erred in not treating as a political question President Nixon's asserted claim of executive privilege in the Watergate tapes case; with Berger, *Impeachment*, 103–21; Brant, *Impeachment: Trials and Errors*, 183–87; Tushnet, "Principles, Politics, and Constitutional Law," 49, 57, agreeing that *Powell v. McCormack* compels the conclusion that such questions are justiciable; Feerick, "Impeaching Federal Judges," 1, 57.

4. For a more comprehensive examination of *Nixon*'s impact on the political question doctrine in general, see Gerhardt, "Rediscovering Nonjusticiability."

5. *Nixon*, 113 S.Ct., 736.

6. 369 U.S. 186, 217 (1962).

7. Ibid., 736.

8. U.S. Const. art. I, § 3, cl. 6.

9. *Nixon*, 113 S.Ct., 739.

10. 395 U.S. 486 (1969).

11. U.S. Const. art. I, § 5.

12. *Nixon*, 113 S.Ct., 739–40.

13. Ibid., 740 (emphasis in original).

14. Ibid.

15. Ibid., 741 (Justice White concurring in the judgment).

16. Ibid., 743.

17. Ibid., 744.

18. Ibid., 748 (Justice Souter concurring in the judgment).

19. Brown, "When Political Questions Affect Individual Rights," 125, 127.

20. Judge Raymond Randolph took this position in Nixon's case before the D.C. Circuit. He characterized the political question doctrine as " 'amorphous' " and as

ultimately . . . conferring on the courts a rather larger role in impeachments although the Framers intentionally excluded the judiciary. [I] view the controlling question as whether the judiciary can pass upon the validity of the Senate's procedural decisions. My conclusion that the courts have no such role to play in the impeachment process ultimately rests on my interpretation of the Constitution. (*Nixon v. United States*, 938 F.2d 239, 247–48 [D.C. Cir. 1991; Justice Randolph concurring; quotation omitted])

21. *Nixon*, 113 S. Ct., 735.
22. See ibid., 739–40.
23. *Nixon*, 113 S.Ct., 739. See also ibid., 739, expressing concerns that litigation over an impeachment could "expose the political life of the country to months, or perhaps years, of chaos" (quoting *Nixon v. United States*, 938 F.2d 239, 246 [D.C. Cir. 1991]).
24. *Nixon v. United States*, 938 F.2d, 255n.6 (Justice Edwards dissenting in part and concurring in the judgment; quoting Gerhardt, "The Constitutional Limits," 99–100).
25. *Nixon v. United States*, 939 F.2d, 255–59 (Justice Edwards dissenting in part and concurring in the judgment).
26. Cf. Powell, 395 U.S., 521 (citation omitted): " 'Deciding whether a matter has in any measure been committed by the Constitution to another branch of government, or whether the action of that branch exceeds whatever authority has been committed, is itself a delicate exercise in constitutional interpretation, and is a responsibility of this Court as ultimate interpreter of the Constitution.' "
27. In fact, Rebecca Brown suggests that, in determining whether a particular case actually involved a political question, the Court has relied on and is better off relying in the future instead on standing criteria, "including allegation[s] of injury, causation, and redressability by the courts." Ibid., 154. For a critique of her proposal, see Gerhardt, "Rediscovering Nonjusticiability," 244–45n.71.
28. 17 U.S. (4 Wheat.) 315, 404 (1819).
29. *Nixon*, 113 S.Ct., 737.
30. Ibid., 737.
31. Ibid., 738.
32. Ibid., 739 quoting from Cooke, *The Federalist*, 545.
33. *Nixon*, 113 S.Ct., 739.
34. Ibid.
35. Ibid., 740.
36. Ibid., 736, 739.
37. U.S. Const. art. I, § 3, cl. 7.
38. Ibid., art. II, § 4.
39. *Powell*, 395 U.S., 522.
40. *Nixon*, 113 S.Ct., 739–40.
41. Ibid., 739n.2.
42. See *Nixon*, 113 S.Ct., 738; ibid., 739; ibid., 739n.2.
43. Brown, "When Political Questions Affect Individual Rights," 129.
44. Ibid., 138–39.
45. Farrand, *Records*, 2:551.

46. Ibid.
47. Hamilton, *The Federalist No. 81*, 509.
48. See *Records*, 2:500, 551.
49. See generally Berger, *Impeachment*, 116–17.
50. Black, *Impeachment: A Handbook*, 57 (citations omitted).
51. *Records*, 2:430.
52. Ibid.
53. Ibid., 431.
54. Ibid., 431.
55. See *Nixon*, 113 S.Ct., 739.
56. U.S. Const. art. I, § 2, cl. 5.
57. Ibid., art. I, § 3, cl. 6.
58. See ibid., art. I, § 6, cl. 1, providing in pertinent part that "[t]he Senators and Representatives shall . . . in all Cases, except Treason, Felony, and Breach of the Peace, be privileged from Arrest during their Attendance at the Session of their respective Houses, and in going to and returning from the same; and for any Speech or Debate in either House, they shall not be questioned in any other Place."
59. See, e.g., *Eastland v. United States Serviceman's Fund*, 421 U.S. 491, 501–5 (1975); *Gravel v. United States*, 408 U.S. 606, 625 (1972); *United States v. Johnson*, 383 U.S. 169, 180 (1966). See also In re Request for Access to Grand Jury Materials, 833 F.2d 1438, 1446 (11th Cir. 1987).
60. U.S. Const. art. I, § 5, cl. 2.
61. *United States v. Ballin*, 144 U.S. 1, 5 (1892).
62. Ibid., § 396, 280.
63. Ibid., 290.
64. Ibid., 287.
65. 84 Ct. Cl. 293 (1936), cert. denied, 300 U.S. 668 (1937).
66. See ibid., 300, explaining that "the Senate was the sole tribunal that could take jurisdiction of the articles of impeachment presented to that body against the plaintiff and its decision is final."
67. See *Nixon*, 113 S. Ct., 739.
68. U.S. Const. art. I, § 5.
69. See *Powell*, 395 U.S., 508–12.
70. Ibid., 512.
71. Ibid., 507n.27.
72. Ibid., 553 (Justice Douglas concurrring).
73. Gerhardt, "The Constitutional Limits," 100.
74. *Powell*, 395 U.S., 540.
75. See DeCarli, Note, "The Constitutionality of State-Enacted Term Limits," 865.
76. 5 U.S. (1 Cranch) 137 (1803).
77. See *Coleman v. Miller*, 307 U.S. 433 (1939).
78. See *Pacific Telephone Co. v. Oregon*, 223 U.S. 118 (1912); *Luther v. Borden*, 7 How. 1 (1849).
79. See, e.g, *Japan Whaling Association v. Baldridge*, 478 U.S. 238 (1986), declining to hold nonjusticiable a question of statutory interpretation in a statute

passed to implement part of an agreement between Japan and the United States; *Dames & Moore v. Regan*, 453 U.S. 654 (1981), reaching merits of dispute over legality of President Carter's executive agreement for the release of U.S. hostages in Iran; *Youngstown Sheet & Tube Co. v. Sawyer*, 343 U.S. 579 (1952), invalidating President Truman's seizure of the nation's steel mills despite his claim that national emergency justified the seizure; *United States v. Curtiss-Wright Export Corp.*, 299 U.S. 304 (1936), adjudicating the merits of congressional delegation of power to the president to prohibit sale of arms to countries engaged in armed conflicts.

80. Cf. Ely, *Democracy and Distrust*, 183: "Constitutional law appropriately exists for those situations where representative government cannot be trusted, not those where we know it can." see also *United States v. Lee*, 106 U.S. 196, 217 (1882): "Hypothetical cases of great evils may be suggested by a particularly fruitful imagination in regard to almost every law upon which depend the rights of the individual and or of the government, and if the existence of laws is to depend upon their capacity to withstand such criticism, the whole fabric of the law must fail."

81. Ibid., 748 (Justice Souter concurring in the judgment).

82. Ibid., 741 (Justice White concurring in the judgment).

83. Bushnell, *Crimes, Follies, and Misdemeanors*.

84. Ibid.

85. Ibid., 739.

86. *Nixon*, 938 F.2d, 246.

87. I address the Senate's attitude regarding this potential claim in chap. 4, "The Senate's Role in the Federal Impeachment Process."

88. *Nixon*, 113 S.Ct., 739 (citation omitted).

89. See generally Nowak and Rotunda, *Constitutional Law*, § 13.2: 488–91.

90. See ibid., § 13.4:510, suggesting that "if in dismissing the employee, the government also forecloses the individual's possible employment in a wide range of activities in both the public and private sectors, this dismissal will constitute a deprivation of liberty sufficient to require that the individual be granted a fair hearing" (citations omitted).

91. *Hastings v. United States*, 802 F. Supp. 490 (D.D.C. 1992), re'vd and remanded Order No. 92–5327 (D.C. Cir. March 2, 1993).

92. *Hastings v. United States*, 837 F.Supp. 3 (D.D.C. 1993).

93. Nowak and Rotunda, *Constitutional Law*, § 13.5:513–16.

94. *Nixon*, 113 S.Ct., 736.

95. See chap. 4.

96. *Abbott Laboratories v. Gardner*, 387 U.S. 136, 140 (1967). The Court further stated that "only upon a showing of 'clear and convincing evidence' of a contrary legislative intent should the courts restrict access to judicial review." Ibid.

97. See generally Eskridge and Frickey, "Quasi-Constitutional Law," 593, 597.

98. Cf. *Webster v. Doe*, 108 S.Ct. 2047, 2053 (1988), holding that the decision of the Central Intelligence Agency to discharge an employee was so committed to agency discretion, unrestricted by any existing legislative or other judicially

cognizable legal standard, as to preclude judicial review, except for serious constitutional questions.

99. U.S. Const. art. I, § 3, cl. 6.

100. *Nixon*, 113 S.Ct., 739.

101. See above notes 48–52 and accompanying text.

102. See U.S. Const. art. III, § 2, cl. 2.

103. Ibid., art. III, § 2, cl. 1.

104. Bator et al., *The Federal Courts and the Federal System*, 960–62.

105. See U.S. Const. art. III, § 2, cl. 3.

106. See Black, *Impeachment: A Handbook*, 56.

107. U.S. Const. art. III, § 2, cl. 2.

PART IV
IMPEACHMENT REFORMS

1. See chap. 8.

2. See *Judicial Discipline and Tenure Proposals*, 96th Cong., 1st sess., 3 (American Enterprise Institute, 1979). See also National Commission on Judicial Discipline and Removal, *Hearings*, 31.

3. The standard form of the proposed amendments from this period provided for judicial removal by the president on the joint address of both Houses of Congress. See *Judicial Discipline and Tenure Proposals*, 3. Four of the proposed amendments simply provided for this basic mechanism, whereas three of them sought to amend the Constitution to provide for judicial removal by the president upon joint addresses by both Houses of Congress but specified the vote required in each House to do so. The other two proposed amendments combined judicial removal by address with a change in the term of office for Article III judges from life tenure to a term of years.

4. *Judicial Discipline and Tenure Proposals*, 3.

5. See ibid., 2–5.

6. See *Hearings*, 32.

CHAPTER TWELVE
PROPOSED PROCEDURAL REFORMS FOR JUDICIAL IMPEACHMENTS

1. U.S. Const. art. I, § 2, cl. 6.

2. *U.S. Code*, vol. 18, §§ 2517, 2518 (1988).

3. At present, section 372(c), created by the act, is unclear about the circumstances under which a circuit council should, despite the confidentiality restrictions of section 372(c)(14), release such materials to the Congress.

4. See, e.g., *Hearings*, 42–43, suggesting that changes could be made in the Federal Rules of Criminal Procedure, "providing under appropriate conditions for congressional access to both grand jury and electronic surveillance materials directly relevant to any House investigation involving a possible impeachment action," or Congress could enact a statute to permit the release of executive branch and grand jury materials to the appropriate House committee whenever requested by its chair and authorized by the attorney general or to permit the release of circuit court materials to the the relevant House committee when re-

quested by its chair and authorized by the circuit council or the Judicial Conference of the United States.

5. See chap. 8.

6. See *Morrison v. Olson*, 487 U.S. 654, 663–64 (1988); see also Gerhardt, "Constitutional Limits," 55–56, 64.

7. See chap. 4. See also *Hearings*, 165–67, testimony of Senator Carl Levin on May 15, 1992, proposing that issue preclusion should apply *only* in cases in which judges have been convicted and exhausted their appeals, at which point they should be removed solely on the basis of their convictions.

8. Burbank, "Alternative Career Resolution," 643, 691.

9. See chap. 4.

10. Burbank, "Alternative Career Resolution," 691.

11. *Claiborne Senate Hearings*, 52.

12. Burbank, "Alternative Career Resolution," 691.

13. See Statement of Senator Charles McC. Mathias, Jr. (Chairman of the Senate Rule XI Trial Committee), reprinted in *Claiborne Impeachment*, 342–43; see also Hamilton, *Federalist No. 65*, 399.

14. *Claiborne Senate Hearings*, pt. 1: 45. See also ibid., pt. 1:303–4, statement of Senator Hatch, arguing that "the separation of criminal and impeachment proceedings [precludes] this body from merely deferring to the existence of a criminal conviction. We have the duty to reach our own independent conclusion about the facts which give rise to these charges"; ibid., 312, statement of Senator Dixon, arguing that "the Senate has a responsibility to look behind the jury verdict and to make its own determination as to whether Judge Claiborne [willfully] and knowingly made a false statement on his tax returns"; ibid., 313, statement of Senator Specter, explaining that "the Senate has a duty to make an independent determination of the underlying facts. . . . The Senate should not merely accept the judgement of the U.S. District Court [convicting] Judge Claiborne. . . . I do not believe that Article III establishes in and of itself a basis of impeachment."

15. In fact, the Senate in the aftermath of the Claiborne impeachment trial revised rule XI to eliminate a set number of members for trial committees. See *Amending the Rules of Procedure and Practice in the Senate When Sitting on Impeachment Trials*, 99th Cong., 2d sess., 1986, S. Rep. 401, 5.

16. Burbank, "Alternative Career Resolution," 689.

17. See ibid., 690.

18. Ibid., 692.

19. Bushnell, *Crimes, Follies, and Misfortunes*, 284–85.

20. U.S. Const. art. I, § 3, cl. 6.

21. *Nixon v. United States*, 113 S. Ct. 732, 737 (1993).

22. See ibid., 737, quoting the petitioner's argument that the clause "means that 'the Senate—not the courts, not a lay jury, not a Senate Committee—shall try impeachments.' Brief for Petitioner 42."

23. Ibid., 737.

24. See ibid., 746–47 (Justice White concurring, joined by Justice Blackmun); and ibid., 748 (Justice Souter concurring).

25. See *Nixon v. United States*, 938, F.2d 239, 261–65 (D.C. Cir. 1991) (Justice Edwards dissenting in part and concurring in the judgment).

26. Williams, "Historical and Constitutional Bases," 512, 564 (citations omitted). See also ibid., 564n.265, citing Act of February 19, 1851, ch. 11, 9 Stat. 568 (codified as amended at *U.S. Code*, vol. 2, §§ 381–96 [1970]).

27. *Hearings*, 55.

28. See ibid., 62.

29. See ibid.

30. See, e.g., *Cong. Rec.* 135, daily ed. (Oct. 20, 1989): S13803 statement of Senator Specter, complaining at the end of the Hastings impeachment trial that the Claiborne, Hastings, and Nixon proceedings revealed disturbing prospects of prosecutorial misconduct. See also ibid.: "17 Senators had occasion to file floor statements discussing their reactions to the events in Claiborne. Of those 17, 8 (or nearly half)—Senators Bingaman, Hatch, Pryor, Heflin, McConnell, Bumpers, Levin, and Gore—had occasion to observe that the prosecutorial . . . misconduct that they observed in the Claiborne case ought to be the subject of further inquiry."

31. *State Bar of Nevada v. Harry Eugene Claiborne*, 104 Nev. 115, 756 P. 2d 464 (1988).

32. Ibid., 113.

33. U.S. Const. art. II, § 2, cl. 2.

CHAPTER THIRTEEN
PROPOSED STATUTORY CHANGES AND CONSTITUTIONAL AMENDMENTS TO THE IMPEACHMENT PROCESS

1. Act of April 30, 1790, ch. 9, § 21, 1 Stat. 112 (1845).

2. Statement by Senator Strom Thurmond, June 19, 1992, National Commission on Judicial Discipline and Removal, *Hearings*, 331.

3. Hamilton, *Federalist No. 65* 399.

4. Burbank, "Alternative Career Resolution," 643, 670–71.

5. See Hearings on H.R. 146 before a Subcommittee of the Senate Judiciary Committee, 77th Cong., 1st sess., 1941.

6. Ibid., 6.

7. Ibid.

8. Ibid., 3.

9. Ibid., 9.

10. Ibid., 13–14.

11. See ibid., 44 (statement of Congressman Sam Hobbs).

12. 113 S.Ct. 732 (1993).

13. Ibid., 736.

14. Hamilton, *Federalist No. 65*, 399.

15. Three of the five kinds of proposed amendments were discussed at length by their sponsors and others in a hearing before the Subcommittee on the Constitution of the Committee on the Judiciary, S. Hrg. 101–1275, 101st. Cong., 2d sess., March 21, 1990 (hereafter *Amendments Hearing*).

16. This is also the subject of many proposed statutes. It is beyond dispute that Article III grants life tenure to federal judges, so that any attempt to change that status is plainly unconstitutional. See chap. 8.

17. Bickel, *The Least Dangerous Branch*, 16.

18. See *Hearings*.

19. See, e.g., ibid., 23.

20. Ibid., 2–3.

21. See *Amendments Hearing*, 45, 50 (statement of Judge Warren Stapleton).

22. See *Hearings*, 24 citing S.J. Res. 232, 101st Cong., 1st sess., *Cong. Rec.* 135 (1989): S16816–8 (Joint Resolution proposed by Senator Howell Heflin).

23. See ibid.

24. *Amendment Hearings*, 4–7.

25. Ibid., 26.

26. Ibid., 26.

27. Ibid., 45.

28. Ibid., 50.

29. Ibid., 50.

30. Ibid., 19 (statement of Senator Heflin).

31. Ibid., 24.

32. See *Hearings*, 24, referring to S.J. Res. 233, 101st Cong., 1st sess., *Cong. Rec.* 135 (1989): S16816–8 (Joint Resolution Proposed by Senator Howell Heflin).

33. *Amendments Hearing*, 10–11.

34. Ibid., 52.

35. U.S. Const. art. I, § 5.

36. See *Hearings*, 25.

37. See *Hearings*, 323 (Testimony of Warren B. Rudman submitted on July 22, 1992).

38. Ibid., 325.

39. Ibid.

40. Ibid.

41. Senator DeConcini proposed a constitutional amendment that combines features from the Thurmond, Rudman, and Heflin amendments. See ibid., 320 (statement of Senator Dennis DeConcini submitted on May 15, 1992). The De-Concini amendment has

two parts. The first provided that an Article III judge who was convicted of a felony and has exhausted all the appeals would forfeit the office and all benefits thereof. [Part] two of the amendment was designed to put some teeth into the 1980 Act. It would give Congress the power to legislatively set some standards and guidelines by which the Supreme Court could discipline judges who have brought disrepute on the federal courts or the administration of justice[.] The constitutional amendment also makes clear that disciplining judges includes removal from office and reduction of compensation. (Ibid.)

Because the first part of the amendment is the same as Senator Thurmond's proposal, the former should be analyzed in the same way as the latter. Because the second part of the proposed amendment combines elements from the Heflin and Rudman proposals, the analyses of the relative merits of the latter two apply to the former.

POSTSCRIPT
THE FUTURE OF THE IMPEACHMENT PROCESS

1. The ninth circuit en banc reversed Judge Aguilar's convictions for obstruction of justice and disclosure of a wiretap after finding that the government had charged the judge under the wrong statute for making false statements to federal agents in a health care fraud investigation. The ninth circuit en banc also held that the statute under which Aguilar had been prosecuted for wiretap disclosure did not prohibit such disclosure if the authorization of the wiretap had expired at the time of the disclosure.

After this book went to press, the Supreme Court granted certiorari to consider and heard oral argument on whether Judge Aguilar had properly been prosecuted and convicted for violating the federal statute prohibiting obstruction of justice rather than a different statute barring witness tampering. The Supreme Court's resolution of the case poses a difficult issue for Congress on whether to proceed with impeachment proceedings against Judge Aguilar for his alleged misconduct regardless of the technical propriety or impropriety of his federal prosecution and conviction.

2. See, e.g., Burbank, "Alternative Career Resolution," 643, 671–73, arguing for adoption of congressional rules that accord substantial effect in an impeachment proceeding to factual findings necessary to a criminal conviction once that conviction is affirmed on appeal.

3. An impeachment tribunal could, for example, treat the fact-finding from a federal or state court conviction with the same deference as state court findings are given in a federal habeas corpus proceeding; see *U.S. Code*, vol. 28, § 2254(d) (1982), or findings by administrative law judges are given on appeals in federal court under *U.S. Code*, vol. 5, § 706(2)(A).

4. See, e.g., Stoltz, "Disciplining Federal Judges," arguing for an extensive revision of the impeachment process, including "(1) [c]reation of a bipartisan House Committee on Judicial Fitness; (2) creation of a permanent professional staff as an adjunct to the Committee; (3) use of a master or masters to conduct formal evidentiary hearings for the Senate and to prepare proposed findings of fact and conclusions of law which would be the basis for argument and decision in the Senate."

5. 113 S.Ct. 732 (1993).

6. 487 U.S. 654 (1988).

7. Ibid., 695–96.

8. Burbank, "Alternative Career Resolution," 670–71.

9. Speech by Winston S. Churchill to the House of Commons, Nov. 11, 1947, as quoted in *The Oxford Dictionary of Quotations*, 3d ed., s.v. "Churchill, Winston."

BIBLIOGRAPHY

PRIMARY SOURCES

Adams, John Quincy. *Memoirs*. Edited by Charles Francis Adams. 12 vols. Philadelphia: Lippincott, 1874–77.

Annals of the Congress of the United States, 1789–1824. 42 vols. Washington, D.C., 1789–1824.

Bingham, John A. *Argument of John A. Bingham before the Senate of the United States Sitting for the Trial of Andrew Johnson*. Washington, D.C.: F. & J. Rives and G. A. Bailey, 1868.

Congressional Globe. 46 vols. Washington, D.C., 1834–73.

Congressional Record. Vols. 4–135. Washington, D.C.

Congressional Research Service. *Compendium of Precedents Involving Evidentiary Rulings and Applications of Evidentiary Principles from Selected Impeachment Trials*. July 3, 1989.

Cooke, Jacob E., ed. *The Federalist*. Middletown, Conn.: Wesleyan University Press, 1961.

Dry, Murray. *The Anti-Federalist: An Abridgement by Murray Dry of the Complete Anti-Federalist*. Edited by Herbert J. Storing. Chicago: University of Chicago Press, 1985.

Elliot, Jonathan, ed. *The Debates in the Several State Conventions on the Adoption of the Federal Constitution*. Washington, D.C.: Printed by and for the editor, 1836–45. Reprint, Philadelphia: J. B. Lippincott, 1937, 1968.

Farrand, M., ed. *Records of the Federal Convention of 1787*. 1787. Reprint, New Haven: Yale University Press, 1966.

Federal Judicial History Office, Federal Judicial Center. *The History of Judicial Discipline and Removal in America: A Preliminary Working Bibliography*. Prepared for the National Commission on Judicial Discipline and Removal. Washington, D.C.: The National Commission on Judicial Discipline and Removal, 1992.

Hamilton, Alexander. *The Federalist Papers*. Edited by C. Rossiter. New York: New American Library, 1961.

Jefferson, Thomas. *Jefferson's Manual of Parliamentary Practice*. Reprinted in H. Doc. 277, 98th Cong., 2d sess., 1985, 109.

Jones, Thomas L. *Impeachment of the President, Speech of Hon. Thomas Lauren Jones of Kentucky*. Washington D.C.: F & J Rives and G. A. Bailey, 1868.

Judicial Discipline and Tenure Proposals. 96th Cong., 1st sess. Washington, D.C.: American Enterprise Institute for Public Policy Research, 1979.

National Commission on Judicial Discipline and Removal. *Report of the National Commission on Judicial Discipline and Removal*. Washington, D.C.: The National Commission on Judicial Discipline and Removal, 1993.

Reams, Bernard D., and Carol J. Gray. *The Congressional Impeachment Process and the Judiciary: Documents and Materials on the Removal of Federal District Judge Harry E. Claiborne*. Buffalo, N.Y.: W. S. Hein, 1987.

Staff of House Committee on the Judiciary. *Impeachment: Selected Materials on Procedure.* 93d Cong., 2d sess., 1974.

Tocqueville, Alexis de. *Democracy in America.* 1st rev. ed. Edited by F. Bowen and P. Bradley. New York: Vintage, 1945.

United States Constitution.

U.S. House. *Impeachment of Richard M. Nixon, President of the United States.* 93rd Cong., 2d sess., 1974. H. Rep. 93–1305.

U.S. House. Special Subcommittee on H.R. 920 of the House Committee on the Judiciary. *Final Report on Associate Justice William O. Douglas.* 91st Cong., 2d sess., 1970.

———.*Legal Materials on Impeachment.* 91st Cong., 2d sess., 1970. Committee Print.

U.S. Senate. *Amending the Rules of Procedure and Practice in the Senate When Sitting on Impeachment Trials.* 99th Cong., 2d sess, 1986. S. Rep. 401.

U.S. Senate. *Procedure and Guidelines for Impeachment Trials in the Senate.* Rev. Ed. 99th Cong., 1st sess., August 15, 1986. S. Doc. 93–33.

U.S. Senate. *Proceedings of the U.S. Senate in the Impeachment Trial of Alcee L. Hastings.* 101st Cong., 1st sess., 1989. S. Doc. 18.

U.S. Senate. *Proceedings of the U.S. Senate in the Impeachment Trial of Harry E. Claiborne.* 99th Cong., 2d sess., 1986, pt. 1:18.

U.S. Senate. *Proceedings of the U.S. Senate in the Impeachment Trial of Walter L. Nixon, Jr.* 101st Cong., 1st sess., 1989.

U.S. Senate. *Proceedings of the U.S. Senate in the Trial of Impeachment of Halsted Ritter.* 74th Cong., 2d sess., 1936. S. Doc. 200.

U.S. Senate. *Report of the Senate Impeachment Trial Committee on the Articles of Impeachment against Judge Alcee L. Hastings, Hearings Before the Senate Impeachment Trial Committee.* 101st Cong., 1st sess., 1989.

U.S. Senate. *Report of the Senate Impeachment Trial Committee on the Articles of Impeachment against Judge Harry E. Claiborne, Hearings Before the Senate Impeachment Trial Committee.* 99th Cong., 2d sess., 1986.

U.S. Senate. *Report of the Senate Impeachment Trial Committee on the Articles of Impeachment against Judge Walter L. Nixon, Jr., Hearings before the Senate Impeachment Trial Committee.* 101st Cong., 1st sess., 1989.

Wilson, James. *James Wilson Works.* Edited by Robert G. McCloskey. Cambridge: Harvard University Press, 1967.

Wilson, James. *The Works of James Wilson.* Edited by James D. Andrews. Chicago, 1896.

SECONDARY SOURCES

Books

Abraham, Henry. *Justices and Presidents: A Political History of Appointments to the Supreme Court.* 3d. ed. New York: Oxford University Press, 1993.

American Civil Liberties Union. *Why President Richard Nixon Should Be Impeached.* Washington, D.C.: Public Affairs Press, 1973.

Ashman, C. *The Finest Judges Money Can Buy.* Los Angeles, Calif.: Nash, 1973.

Baker, N. V. *Conflicting Loyalties: Law and Politics in the Attorney General's Office, 1789–1990.* Lawrence: University Press of Kansas, 1992.

Bator, Paul, Daniel Meltzer, and David Shapiro. *Hart & Weschsler's The Federal Courts and the Federal System*. Westbury, N.Y.: Foundation Press, 1988.

Berger, Raoul. *Impeachment: The Constitutional Problems*. Cambridge: Harvard University Press, 1973.

Berns, Walter. *The Writing of the Constitution of the United States*. Washington, D.C.: American Enterprise Institute, 1985.

Bickel, Alexander. *The Least Dangerous Branch: The Supreme Court at the Bar of Politics*. 2d ed. New Haven: Yale University Press, 1986.

Black, Charles. *Impeachment: A Handbook*. New Haven: Yale University Press, 1973.

Blackstone, W. *Commentaries on the Laws of England*. Edited by Stanley N. Katz. Chicago: University of Chicago Press, 1988.

Borkin, Joseph. *The Corrupt Judge: An Inquiry into Bribery and Other High Crimes and Misdemeanors in the Federal Courts*. New York: C.N. Potter, 1962.

Bowen, C.D. *Miracle at Philadelphia: The Story of the Constitutional Convention*. Boston: Little, Brown & Co., 1966.

Brant, Irving. *High Crimes and Misdemeanors*. New York: Funk and Wagnalls, 1973.

———. *Impeachment: Trials and Errors*. Cambridge: Harvard University Press, 1972.

Bryce, James. *American Commonwealth*. New York: Commonwealth Publishing, 1908.

Bushnell, Eleanore. *Crimes, Follies, and Misfortunes: The Federal Impeachment Trials*. Chicago: University of Illinois Press, 1992.

Cannon, Clarence. *Cannon's Precedents of the House of Representatives of the United States*. Washington, D.C.: Government Printing Office, 1935.

Carpenter, W. *Judicial Tenure in the United States*. New Haven: Yale University Press, 1918.

Carter, Stephen L. *The Confirmation Mess: Cleaning Up the Federal Appointments Process*. New York: Basic Books, 1994.

Chemerinsky, Erwin. *Federal Jurisdiction*. Boston: Little, Brown & Co., 1989.

Choper, Jesse H. *Judicial Review and the National Political Process*. Chicago: University of Chicago Press, 1980.

Corr, Kevin, and Larry Berkson. *Literature on Judicial Removal*. Chicago: American Judicature Society, 1992.

Davidson, Roger H. *The Role of the Congressman*. New York: Pegasas, 1969.

Dearing, Mary R. *Veterans in Politics: The Story of the G.A.R.* Baton Rouge: Louisiana State University Press, 1952.

Deschler, Lewis. *Deschler's Precedents of the United States House of Representatives*. Washington, D.C.: Superintendent of Documents, U.S. Government, 1977–.

Dewitt, David Miller. *The Impeachment and Trial of Andrew Johnson*. 1903. Reprint, New York: Russell & Russell, 1967.

Diamond, Robert A., ed. *Impeachment and the U.S. Congress*. Washington, D.C.: Congressional Quarterly, 1974.

Elsmere, Jane Shaffer. *Justice Samuel Chase*. Muncie, Ind.: Javenar Publishing Co., 1980.

Ely, John Hart. *Democracy and Distrust: A Theory of Judicial Review*. Cambridge: Harvard University Press, 1980.

Farrand, Max. *The Framing of the Constitution*. New Haven: Yale University Press, 1913.

Friedman, Leon, and Levantrosser, William F., eds. *Watergate and Afterward*. Westport, Conn.: Greenwood Press, 1992.

Gerson, Noel B. *The Trial of Andrew Johnson*. Nashville: T. Nelson, 1977.

Harding, Samuel. *The Contest over the Ratification of the Federal Constitution in the State of Massachusetts*. New York: Longman's Green, 1970.

Harris, Joseph P. *Congress and the Legislative Process*. New York: McGraw-Hill Book Co., 1963.

Hinds, Asher C. *Hinds' Precedents of the House of Representatives of the United States*. Washington, D.C.: Government Printing Office, 1907.

Hoffer, P., and N.E.H. Hull. *Impeachment in America, 1635–1805*. New Haven: Yale University Press, 1974.

Hrebenar, Ronald, and Ruth Scott. *Interest Group Politics in America*. Englewood Cliffs, N.J.: Prentice-Hall, 1990.

Jones, Charles O. *The United States Congress: People, Place and Policy*. Homewood, Il: Dorsey Press, 1982.

Kaminski, John, and Richard Leffler, eds. *Federalists and Antifederalists: The Debate over the Ratification of the Constitution*. Madison, Wis.: Madison House, 1989.

King, Anthony, ed. *The New Political System*. Washington, D.C.: AEI Press, 1990.

Kingdon, John W. *Congressmen's Voting Decisions*. Ann Arbor: The University of Michigan Press, 1989.

Kingsley, Thomas C. *The Federal Impeachment Process: A Bibliographic Guide to English and American Precedence* [sic]. Ithaca, N.Y.: Cornell Law Library, 1974.

Kutler, Stanley I. *The Wars of Watergate: The Last Crisis of Richard Nixon*. New York: Knopf, 1990.

Labovitz, John R. *Presidential Impeachment*. New Haven: Yale University Press, 1978.

Larue, L. H. *Political Discourse: A Case Study of the Watergate Affair*. Athens: University of Georgia Press, 1988.

Lasser, William. *The Limits of Judicial Power*. Chapel Hill: University of North Carolina Press, 1988.

Levy, Leonard W., and Dennis Mahoney, eds. *The Framing and Ratification of the Constitution*. New York: Macmillan, 1987.

Lunch, William M. *The Nationalization of American Politics*. Berkeley: University of California Press, 1987.

Marshall, P. *The Impeachment of Warren Hastings*. London: Oxford University Press, 1965.

Montesquieu, Baron de. *The Spirit of the Laws*. Translated by T. Nugent. New York: Hatner Publishing, 1949.

Murphy, Thomas P. *The New Politics Congress*. Lexington, Mass.: Lexington Books, 1974.

Nowak, John, and Ronald D. Rotunda. *Constitutional Law*. 5th ed. St. Paul, Minn.: West Publishing, 1992.

Ornstein, Norman J., Thomas Mann, and Michael J. Malbin. *Vital Statistics on Congress, 1991–1992*. Washington, D.C.: American Enterprise for Public Policy Research, 1992.

Perry, Michael J. *The Constitution in the Courts: Law or Politics*. New York: Oxford University Press, 1994.

Petracca, Mark P., ed. *The Politics of Interests: Interest Groups Transformed*. San Francisco: Westview Press, 1992.

Rehnquist, William. *Grand Inquests: The Historical Impeachments of Justice Samuel Chase and President Andrew Johnson*. New York: Morrow, 1992.

Rieselbach, Leroy N. *Congressional Politics*. New York: McGraw-Hill, 1973.

Ripley, Randall B. *Congress: Process and Policy*. New York: W.W. Norton & Co., 1975.

Rodell, Fred. *55 Men: The Story of the Constitution: Based on the Day-By-Day Notes of James Madison*. Harrisburg, Pa.: Stackpole Books, 1986.

Rossiter, Clinton. *1787: The Grand Convention*. New York: Macmillan, 1966.

Rutland, Robert A. *Ordeal of the Constitution; The Anti-Federalists and the Ratification Struggle of 1787–88*. Norman: University of Oklahoma Press, 1966.

Simpson, Alexander, Jr. *A Treatise on Federal Impeachments*. Philadelphia: Philadelphia Law Association, 1916.

Smith, Franklin B. *The Assassination of President Nixon*. Rutland, Vt.: Academy Books, 1976.

Smith, Gene. *High Crimes and Misdemeanors: The Impeachment and Trial of Andrew Johnson*. New York: Morrow, 1977.

Solomon, Rayman L. *History of the Seventh Circuit, 1891–1941*. Washington: Bicentennial Committee of the Judicial Conference of the United States, 1981.

Stern, Philip M. *The Best Congress Money Can Buy*. New York: Pantheon, 1988.

Story, Joseph. *Commentaries on the Constitution*. Edited by R. Rotunda and J. Nowak. Durham, N.C.: Carolina Academic Press, 1987.

Trefousse, Hans L. *Impeachment of a President: Andrew Johnson, the Blacks and Reconstruction*. Knoxville: University of Tennessee Press, 1975.

Trenholme, Louise Irby. *The Ratification of the Federal Constitution in North Carolina*. New York: Columbia University Press, 1932.

Tribe, Laurence. *American Constitutional Law*. 2d ed. New York: Foundation Press, 1988.

Tushnet, Mark V. *Red, White, and Blue: A Critical Analysis of Constitutional Law*. Cambridge, Mass.: Harvard University Press, 1988.

Vogler, David J., and Sidney R. Waldman. *Congress and Democracy*. Washington, D.C.: Congressional Quarterly, 1985.

Warren, Charles. *The Making of the Constitution*. Boston: Little, Brown & Co., 1928.

Wheeler, Russell. *The Writing and Ratification of the U.S. Constitution, a Bibliography*. Washington, D.C.: Federal Judicial Center, 1986.

White, Theodore H. *Breach of Faith: The Fall of Richard Nixon*. New York: Atheneum, 1975.

Wise, Charles R. *The Dynamics of Legislation: Leadership and Policy Change in the Congressional Process*. San Francisco: Jossey-Bass Publishers, 1991.

Wood, Gordon S. *The Creation of the American Republic, 1776–1787*. Chapel Hill: Published for the Institute of Early American History and Culture at Williamsburg, Virginia, by the University of North Carolina Press, 1969.

———. *The Making of the Constitution*. Waco, Tex.: Markham, 1987.

Wright, Charles Allen. *The Law of Federal Courts*. 4th ed. St. Paul, Minn.: West Publishing, 1983.

Articles

Allard, Robert E. "Judicial Discipline and Removal Plans." *Journal of the American Judicial Society* 48 (1965): 173.

Allen, Anita. Comment. "The Federalist's Plain Meaning: A Reply to Tushnet." *Southern California Law Review* 615 (1988): 1701.

Amar, Vikram D. Note. "The Senate and the Constitution." *Yale Law Journal* 97 (1988): 1111.

Auslander, Rose. Note. "Impeaching the Senate's Use of Trial Committees." *New York University Law Review* 67 (1992): 68.

Baker, Lynn. Note. "Unnecessary and Improper: The Judicial Councils Reform and Judicial Conduct and Disability Act of 1980." *Yale Law Journal* 94 (1985): 1117.

Barr, Jeffrey, and Thomas Willging. "Decentralized Self-Regulation, Accountability, and Judicial Independence under the Federal Judicial Conduct and Disability Act of 1980." *University of Pennsylvania Law Review* 142 (1993): 1.

Bestor, Arthur. "Impeachment." Review of *Impeachment: The Constitutional Problems*, by Raoul Berger. *Washington Law Review* 49 (1973): 255.

Block, Stewart A. Comment. "The Limitations of Article III on the Proposed Judicial Removal Machinery." *University of Pennsylvania Law Review* 118 (1970): 1064.

Broderick, Albert. "Citizen's Guide to Impeachment of a President: Problem Areas." *Catholic University Law Review* 23 (1973): 205.

Broeck, Jacobus ten. "Partisan Politics, and Federal Judgeship Impeachment since 1903." *Minnesota Law Review* 23 (1939): 185.

Brown, Rebecca L. "When Political Questions Affect Individual Rights, The Other *Nixon v. United States*." *1993 Supreme Court Review*, 1993, 125.

Brown, Wrisley. "The Impeachment of the Federal Judiciary." *Harvard Law Review* 26 (1913): 684.

Burbank, Stephen B. "Procedural Rule-making under the Judicial Councils Reform and Judicial Conduct and Disability Act of 1980." *University of Pennsylvania Law Review* 131 (1982): 283.

———. "Alternative Career Resolution: An Essay on the Removal of Federal Judges." *Kentucky Law Journal* 76 (1988): 643. Symposium on Judicial Discipline and Impeachment.

Burgess, Christine E. Note. "When May a President Refuse to Enforce the Law?" *Texas Law Review* 72 (1994): 471.

Bushnell, Eleanore. "The Impeachment and Trial and James H. Peck." *Missouri Historical Review* 74 (1980): 137.

———. "Judge Harry E. Claiborne and the Federal Impeachment Process." *Nevada Historical Society Quarterly* 32 (1989): 235.

———. "One of Twelve: The Nevada Impeachment Connection." *Nevada Historical Society Quarterly* 26 (1983): 2.

Catz, Robert. "Removal of Federal Judges by Imprisonment." *Rutgers Law Journal* 18 (1986): 103.

Clinton, Robert. "A Brief History of the Adoption of the U.S. Constitution." *Iowa Law Review* 75 (1990): 891.

DeCarli, Robert C. Note. "The Constitutionality of State-Enacted Term Limits under the Qualifications Clauses." *Texas Law Review* 71 (1993): 865.

Dougherty, J. Hampden. "Inherent Limitations upon Impeachment." *Yale Law Journal* 23 (1913): 60.

Easterbrook, Frank H. "Presidential Review." *Case Western Reserve Law Review* 90 (1990): 905.

Edwards, Drew. "Judicial Misconduct and Politics in the Federal System: A Proposal for Revising the Judicial Councils Act." *California Law Review* 75 (1987): 1071.

Edwards, Harry T. "Regulating Judicial Misconduct and Divining Good Behavior for Federal Judges." *Michigan Law Review* 87 (1989): 765.

Ervin, Samuel. "Separation of Powers: Judicial Independence." *Law and Contemporary Problems* 35 (1970): 108.

Eskridge, William N., Jr., and Philip P. Frickey. "Quasi-Constitutional Law: Clear Statement Rules as Constitutional Lawmaking." *Vanderbilt Law Journal* 45 (1992): 593.

Feerick, John. "Impeaching Federal Judges: A Study of the Constitutional Provisions." *Fordham Law Review* 39 (1970): 1.

Fenton, Paul. "The Scope of the Impeachment Power." *Northwestern University Law Review* 65 (1970) 719.

Firmage, Edwin B. "The Law of Presidential Impeachment." *1973 Utah Law Review*, winter 1973, 681.

Firmage, Edwin B., and Richard C. Mangrum. "Removal of the President: Resignation and the Procedural Law of Impeachment." *1974 Duke Law Journal*, 1974, 1023.

Fox, Brendan C. "Impeachment: The Justiciability of Challenges to the Senate Rules of Procedure for Impeachment Trials." *George Washington Law Review* 60 (1992): 1275.

Frankel, Jack E. "Judicial Discipline and Removal." *Texas Law Review* 44 (1966): 1117.

Franklin, Mitchell. "Romanist Infamy and the American Constitutional Conception of Impeachment." *Buffalo Law Review* 23 (1974): 313.

Futterman, Stanley N. "The Rules of Impeachment." *University of Kansas Law Review* 24 (1975): 105.

Garvey, Hohn. "Foreword: Judicial Discipline and Impeachment." *Kentucky Law Journal* 76 (1988): 633.

Gerhardt, Michael J. "The Constitutional Limits to Impeachment and Its Alternatives." *Texas Law Review* 68 (1989): 1.

———. "Rediscovering Nonjusticiability: Judicial Review of Impeachments after *Nixon*." *Duke Law Journal* 43 (1994): 231.

———. "The Senate's Process for Removing Federal Judges." *Research Papers of the National Commission on Judicial Discipline and Removal*. Washington, D.C.: U.S.G.P.O., 1993.

Geyh, Charles Gardner. "Informal Methods of Judicial Discipline." *University of Pennsylvania Law Review* 142 (1993): 243.

Gold, Steven W. Note. "Temporary Criminal Immunity for Federal Judges." *Brooklyn Law Review* 53 (1987): 699.

Goldberg, Ira M. "An Essay on Raoul Berger's Thesis for Judicial Interpretation in the Process of the Removal of the President of the United States." *1975 Wisconsin Law Review*, 1975, 414.

Grimes, Warren S. "Hundred-Ton-Gun Control: Preserving Impeachment as the Exclusive Removal Mechanism for Federal Judges." *UCLA Law Review* 38 (1991): 1209.

———. "The Role of the U.S. House of Representatives in Proceedings to Impeach and Remove Federal Judges." *Research Papers of the National Commission on Judicial Discipline and Removal*. Washington, D.C.: National Commission on Judicial Discipline and Removal, 1993.

Gunther, Gerald. "Judicial Hegemony and Legislative Autonomy: The Nixon Case and the Impeachment Process." *UCLA Law Review* 22 (1974): 30.

Hall, Kermit L. "West H. Humphreys and the Crisis of the Union." *Tennessee Historical Quarterly* (1975): 48.

Hamilton, William. Note. "Indictment of Federal Judges: Chilling Judicial Independence." *University of Florida Law Review* 35 (1983): 296.

Haley, Richard T. "The Impeachment of Federal Officers in United States History." *The Historian* 10 (1948): 135.

Havighurst, Harold C. "Doing Away with Presidential Impeachment: The Advantages of Parliamentary Government." *1974 Arizona State Law Journal* (1974): 223.

Heflin, Howell. "Impeaching Federal Judges: Making the Case for Change." *Trial* 71 (November 1990): 123.

———. "The Impeachment Process: Modernizing an Archaic System." *Judicature* 71 (August–September 1987): 124.

Holt, Wythe. " 'To Establish Justice': Politics, The Judicial Act of 1789, and Invention of the Federal Courts." *Duke Law Journal* 1189 (1989): 1421.

Hutson, James H.. "The Creation of the Constitution: The Integrity of the Documentary Record." *Texas Law Review* 65 (1968): 1.

Johnson, Herbert A. "Impeachment and Politics." *South Atlantic Quarterly* 63 (1964): 552.

Kainec, Lisa A. "Judicial Review of Senate Impeachment Proceedings: Is a Hands Off Approach Appropriate?" *Case Western Reserve Law Review* 43 (1993): 1499.

Kastenmier, Robert W., and Michael J. Remington. Symposium on Judicial Discipline and Impeachment: "Judicial Discipline: A Legal Perspective." *Kentucky Law Journal* 76 (1988): 763.

Kaufman, Irving. "Chilling Judicial Independence." *Yale Law Journal* 88 (1979): 681.

Koenig, Louis W. "'Consensus Politics,' 1800–1805." *American Heritage* (1967): 4.

Koukoutchos, Brian. "Constitutional Kinetics: The Independent Counsel Case and the Separation of Powers." *Wake Forest Law Review* 23 (1988): 635.

Kurland, Philip B. "The Constitution and the Tenure of Federal Judges: Some Notes from History." *University of Chicago Law Review* 36 (1969): 665.

———. "Watergate, Impeachment and the Constitution." *Mississippi Law Journal* 45 (1974): 531.

Logan, David. "Historical Uses of a Special Prosecution: The Administrations of Presidents Grant, Coolidge, and Truman." Prepared for the Government and General Research Division, Congressional Research Service, Library of Congress, November 23, 1973.

Luchsinger, Daniel. Note. "Committee Impeachment Trials: The Best Solution?" *Georgetown Law Journal* (1991): 163.

Marcus, Richard L. "Who Should Discipline Federal Judges and How?" *Federal Rules of Decision* 149 (1993): 375.

Maxman, Melissa. Note. "In Defense of the Constitution's Judicial Impeachment Standard." *Michigan Law Review* 86 (1987): 420.

McCalla, Patrick. Note. "Judicial Disciplining of Federal Judges is Constitutional." *Southern California Law Review* 62 (1989): 1263.

McConnel, Mitchell. "Reflections on the Senate's Role in the Judicial Impeachment Process and Proposals for Change." *Kentucky Law Journal* 76 (1988): 739.

McGinnis, Patrick J. "A Case of Judicial Misconduct: The Impeachment and Trial of Robert W. Archbald." *Pennsylvania Magazine of History and Biography* 101 (1977): 506.

Melton, Buckner F. "Federal Impeachment and Criminal Procedure: The Framers' Intent." *Maryland Law Review* 52 (1993):437.

———. "The First Impeachment: The Constitution's Framers and the Case of Senator William Blount." Ph.D. diss., Duke University, 1990.

Meltzer, Daniel J. "Article III and the Judiciary Act of 1789: The History and Structure of Article III." *University of Pennsylvania Law Review* 138 (1990): 1569.

Miller, Michael B. Comment. "The Justiciability of Legislative Rules and the 'Political' Political Question Doctrine." *California Law Review* 78 (1990): 1341.

Morgan, Charles, Jr., Hope Eastman, Mary Ellen Gale, and Judith Areen. "Impeachment: An Historical Overview." *Seton Hall Law Review* 5 (1974): 689.

Oliver, Philip. "Systematic Justice: A Proposed Constitutional Amendment to Establish Fixed, Staggered Terms for Members of the United States Supreme Court." *Ohio State Law Journal* 47 (1986): 799.

Otis, Merrill E. "A Proposed Tribunal: Is It Constitutional?" *University of Kansas City Law Review* 7 (1938): 3.

Peterson, Todd D. "The Role of the Executive Branch in the Discipline and Removal of Federal Judges." *University of Illinois Law Review* 1993: 809.

Pierce, Richard J. "Use of the Federal Rules of Evidence in Federal Agency Adjudications." *Administrative Law Review* 39 (1987): 1.

Powell, H. Jefferson. "The Original Understanding of the Original Intent." *Harvard Law Review* 98 (1985): 885.

———. "Rules for Originalists." *Virginia Law Review* 73 (1987): 659.

Quint, Peter E. "The Federalist Papers and the Constitution of the United States." *Kentucky Law Journal* 77 (1989): 369.

Ray, Laura Krugman. "Discipline through Delegation: Solving the Problem of Congressional House-Cleaning." *University of Pittsburgh Law Review* 55 (1994): 389.

Rehnquist, William. "The Impeachment Clause: A Wild Card in the Constitution." *Northwestern University Law Review* 85 (1991): 903.

Reinhardt, John. "The Impeachment Proceedings Against Judge James Hawkins Peck." *University of Kansas City Law Review* 12 (1944): 106.

Rezneck, Daniel. "Is Judicial Review of Impeachment Coming?" *American Bar Association Journal* 60 (1974): 681.

Rieger, Carol T. "The Judicial Council's Reform and Judicial Conduct and Disability Act: Will Judges Judge Judges." *Emory Law Journal* 37 (1988): 45.

Ross, G. W. C. " 'Good Behavior' of Federal Judges." *University of Kansas City Law Review* 12 (1944): 119.

Rotunda, Ronald D. "An Essay on the Constitutional Parameters of Federal Impeachment." *Kentucky Law Journal* 76 (1987): 707.

———. "Original Intent, the View of the Framers and the Role of the Ratifiers." *Vanderbilt Law Review* 41 (1988): 507.

Shane, Peter, M. "Who May Discipline or Remove Federal Judges? A Constitutional Analysis." *University of Pennsylvania Law Review* 142 (1993): 209.

Shartel, Burke. "Federal Judges—Appointment, Supervision and Removal—Some Possibilities under Constitution." *Michigan Law Review* 28 (1930): 870.

Shiffrin, Steven. "The First Amendment and Economic Regulation: Away from a General Theory of the First Amendment." *Northwestern University Law Review* 78 (1983): 1212.

Simon, Maria. Note. "Bribery and Other Not So 'Good Behavior': Criminal Prosecution as a Supplement to Impeachment of Federal Judges." *Columbia Law Review* 94 (1994): 1617.

Smith, David Todd. "A Claim that Senate Impeachment Rule XI Violates the Impeachment Trial Clause Is a Non Justiciable Political Question. *Nixon v. U.S.*" *St. Mary's Law Journal* 25 (1994): 855.

Smith, Joseph H. "An Independent Judiciary: The Colonial Background." *University of Pennsylvania Law Review* 124 (1976): 1104.

Stevens, John Paul. "Reflections on the Removal of Sitting Judges." *Stetson Law Review* 13 (1984): 215.

Stewart, David O. "Commentary: Impeachment by Ignorance." *American Bar Association Journal* 76 (June 1990): 52.

Stolz, Preble, "Disciplining Federal Judges: Is Impeachment Hopeless?" *California Law Review* 57 (1969): 659.

Strauss, Peter. "Formal and Functional Approaches to Separation-of-Powers Questions—A Foolish Inconsistency?" *Cornell Law Review* 72 (1987): 488.

————. "The Place of Agencies in Government, Separation of Powers and the Fourth Branch." *Columbia Law Review* 84 (1984): 573.

Sunstein, Cass R. "Constitutionalism after the New Deal." *Harvard Law Review* 101 (1987): 421.

Swain, Jonathan T. Comment. "The Procedures of Judicial Discipline." *Marquette Law Review* 59 (1976): 190.

Sweeney, J.P. Comment. "Presidential Impeachment and Judicial Review." *American University Law Review* 23 (1974): 959.

Swindler, William. "High Court of Congress: Impeachment and Trials, 1797–1936." *American Bar Association Journal* 60 (1974): 420.

Thompson, Frank, and Dan Pollitt. "Impeachment of Federal Judges: An Historical Overview." *North Carolina Law Review* 49 (1970): 87, 107.

Tushnet, Mark. "Constitutional Interpretation and Judicial Selection: A View from the Federalist Papers." *Southern California Law Review* 61 (1988): 1669.

————. "Principles, Politics, and Constitutional Law." *Michigan Law Review* 88 (1989): 49.

Tuttle, Elbert P., and Dean W. Russell. Symposium. "Separation of Powers: Preserving Judicial Integrity: Some Comments on the Role of the Judiciary under the 'Blending' of Powers." *Emory Law Journal* 37 (1988): 587.

Underwood, Richard H. "Comments on Professor Rotunda's Essay." *Kentucky Law Journal* 76 (1988): 733.

Van Tassel, Emily F. "Resignations and Removals: A History of Federal Judicial Service—1789–1992." *University of Pennsylvania Law Review* 142 (1993): 333.

Wallace, J. Clifford. "Judicial Administration in a System of Independents: A Tribe with Only Chiefs." *1978 Brigham Young University Law Review*, 1978, 39.

Weingarten, Reid H. "Judicial Misconduct: A View from the Department of Justice." *Kentucky Law Journal* 76 (1987–88): 799.

Williams, Napoleon B., Jr. "The Historical and Constitutional Bases for the Senate's Power to Use Masters or Committees to Receive Evidence in Impeachment Trials." *N.Y.U. Law Review* 50 (1975): 512.

Wilson, James G. "The Role of Public Opinion in Constitutional Interpretation." *1993 Brigham Young University Law Review*, 1993, 1037.

Yankwich, Leon R. "Impeachment of Civil Officers under the Federal Constitution." *Georgetown Law Review* 26 (1938): 849.

Ziskind, Martha Andres. "Judicial Tenure in the American Constitution: English and American Precedents." *Supreme Court Review*, 1969, 135.

INDEX

About the Author

MICHAEL J. GERHARDT is Professor of Constitutional Law at the
Marshall-Wythe School of Law and Lecturer in Government at The
College of William and Mary.